William —
What an honor!
You are an
inspiration!

Show Me
By Randall Kenneth Jones

Beware the Bunny!

SMART BUSINESS® BOOKS
An Imprint of Smart Business® Network Inc.

Published by Smart Business Books
An imprint of Smart Business Network Inc.
835 Sharon Drive, Suite 200
Westlake, OH 44145

Printed in the United States of America
Editor: Carole J Greene and Dustin S. Klein
Cover Design: Denise Wauters
Interior Design: April Grasso

ISBN: 978-1-945389-93-1 (hardcover)
ISBN: 978-1-945389-94-8 (e-book)
Library of Congress Control Number: 2016955908

Show Me is dedicated to my father, Kenneth Paul Jones.

One day you are going to arrive at the Pearly Gates
and God is going to look up and exclaim:
"Great! You're finally here. I need some time off,
you're in charge now."

After all, you show me how to be a better man every day.

TABLE OF CONTENTS

FOREWORD

I t is my pleasure to tell you about this extraordinary book, *Show Me*. And, if you haven't already met the author, Randall Kenneth Jones, I'm delighted to introduce him to you. My friend, Randy Jones, is one of the most creative—*and intuitive*—people I've ever met. His journalistic talents shine throughout the book's inspiring and witty chapters. These contain profiles and true-life stories of many of the individuals Randy personally interviewed in his role as a Naples, Florida-based business journalist. Who better to share—and show—readers the lessons and inspiration learned through these one-on-one interviews than Randy Jones, an energetic and gifted writer originally from the Show Me State of Missouri?

Randy and I first met a few years ago when he interviewed me for his "Business Class" column in the *Naples Daily News*. At that point, I was well into my nearly twenty-year career with The Emily Post Institute as spokesperson, author and director. I figured this would be like many of the hundreds of media interviews I'd experienced. It wasn't! And Randy was unlike any other writer I'd ever met.

That first meeting occurred at the coffee shop in a Naples bookstore. As his editorial platform grew from his strong desire to promote business courtesy, creative thinking and positive communication, he appeared to be excited about meeting "an etiquette expert." I recall a sincerely interested interviewer who listened to every word and who made our first meeting so very enjoyable. Randy exuded energy—a characteristic I have now learned is part of his everyday character.

I have since learned a lot about Randy Jones, the marketer, speaker and journalist, and how much hard work has gone into seeking out those he wanted to interview. What perseverance! As a special contributor to the *Naples Daily News*, he *personally* pursued his interviewees. From the beginning, Randy was on a quest to learn from the experiences and successes of the movers and shakers in the area. Talk about tenacity; often, it took several tries before he was able to line up an interview. In all, Randy interviewed eighty-five people for his "Business Class" column. He also connected with another thirty-eight people who provided further insight and commentary on those profiled.

Randy's experience as a husband, father, fifty-something-year-old marketer and creative writer has grown into an exciting quest for relevance and meaning in one's life's journey—as seen in his personal, often hysterical, coming-of-age stories juxtaposed against the wisdom of those he interviewed.

His subjects have candidly shared their thoughts, ideas, best practices and life stories, and Randy has been able to expertly find a balance between funny, human sadness and solid, timeless advice. The word *authentic* certainly fits as a "Randy adjective"—and he brings out the true essence of each of his interviewees.

He also found that those he interviewed shared a commonality of being passionate about *life*. So often, Randy heard that a person's work and personal worlds were closely interwoven. Another constant theme he encountered was the importance of establishing and maintaining positive relationships; and how being respectful and honest wins out every time. (Of course, this is music to *my* ears, a promoter of all things civil!)

Show Me is a fascinating read! The book is chock full of life lessons, presented in beautifully-written true stories amassed by Randy during more than ten years of journaling and four years of interviewing fascinating, accomplished people. The lives of these people have inspired Randy, and I'm confident they will inspire you, too.

Peggy Post
Director Emeritus
The Emily Post Institute
October 12, 2016

Kevin Randall Jones

INTRODUCTION

I t's all about the roles we play.

And now, I am trying to walk a mile in Randall Kenneth Jones' writer/journalist shoes. Though he has written about *me*, it's my turn to write about *him*.

I am certainly not a writer or journalist; then again, my mother was both. This feels oddly familiar. It reminds me of the role reversal in the film *Erin Brockovich,* where Julia Roberts portrayed, oh yes, me! Oh heavens, this just got stranger. Erin, Randy, Julia, my mom? *Who is who*, and how does it all make sense? Though my motto is to "right wrong," today it's "try to write right!"

Hmm…as Randy is theatrical, should I approach this introduction as a script? *When Erin Met Randy? Brockovich Jones and the Temple of Doom? Erin Jones's Diary?* Of course, there's Randy's dream of starring in *Erin Brockovich, The Musical.* His performance of "They're Called Boobs, Ed" would definitely bring down the house!

Whatever the title, it would be *fun* because Randy is fun and has a BIG personality, which is why we hit it off instantaneously. When we first met, it felt like finding my long-lost brother—one who immediately understood my thoughts. We were instant kindred spirits.

But my role today is to tell you about my friend. And when I think about it, *Show Me* is actually an investigation of our various roles—at work, at home and everywhere in between. Investigation seems to be *our* thing.

The day we met, I immediately felt at ease. Randy was—*and is*—so happy, fearless and open. He is quick-witted and downright funny. Time spent with him is guaranteed to make you laugh. He is not only engaged in each conversation, he is caring, compassionate and thoughtful as to *what* he writes and *how* he shares a person's story. Humor aside, Randy is focused and a deep thinker. Yes, he is all of this *and more*.

Part of our connection likely comes from our very similar upbringings. We are both from college towns in the Midwest; however, I must clarify: I am from Kansas and he is from Missouri. While my values and Randy's do not rival each other, we are sports rivals. He is an (ugh) University of Missouri Tiger and I am a loud-and-proud Kansas Jayhawker.

Now, I don't want to date myself—or Randy, for that matter—but we are only two years apart in age. We share the same historic news events and pop culture influencers. We are from a generation born of Midwest values: respect, honesty, and something that I talk about all the time—a characteristic taught to me by my mother—stick-to-itiveness. Don't try telling me or Randy "no." Just give in and say "yes" immediately 'cause we're not giving up until we get you there!

Despite our similarities, I find Randy to be so *unique*. He is like no other journalist I have encountered. He loves people, and he LISTENS—key word here, LISTENS.

Randy takes "our" Midwest upbringing and applies it to his writing. He sees the positive in people—he focuses intently on his interviewees *and* their stories. And here come his investigative skills: *he tells it like it is,* but does so with RESPECT and GRACE.

Show Me is a direct result of Randy's obsession to bring a positive voice to journalism alongside a renewed focus on common sense. And no one knows better than me how obsessed you can get when your goal is simply to do the right thing and help other people.

After all, he is from Missouri and, for those of you who don't know, Missouri is the Show Me State. Need I say more?

As Randy recently said: "Though I left the Midwest in 1984, it took me more than thirty years, 100-plus interviews and *writing a book* to discover that I never really left. When all is said and done, I'm still just Nellie Pearl and Kenny's somewhat awkward, overexcited and, thankfully, idealistic son."

Show Me is the written proof of Randy's journey, his character, his inspired-yet-traditional ideals, and his Midwestern roots.

Then again, as a famous *Kansan* once said, "There's no place like home."

Erin Brockovich
September 27, 2016

HAPPY DAYS

AUTHOR'S NOTE

Andy Warhol famously prophesized that during their lifetime, everyone would experience fifteen minutes of fame. I can't really complain because I technically already got my time—plus a couple of other people's minutes as well.

I must confess that *younger me* was always willing to grab (seize, snatch, steal, pilfer, devour) additional fame minutes should they come my way—such minutes defined as special moments of vast achievement followed by handshakes, backslapping, cheek kisses, media coverage and money, but also laughter, tears, and yes, even applause.

For example, I am 100 percent confident that I am the only person on the planet who has sung Barry Manilow's "I Made It Through the Rain" to an adoring crowd in Bulgaria accompanied on piano by fellow Missouri-native Sheryl Crow. If anyone else can make this claim, I'd like to meet them.

However, a few decades later, somewhat like the fictitious musical town of Lerner and Loewe's *Brigadoon*, I found my youthful sense of wonder dissipating into my middle-aged mist.

As is the case for so many of us "of a certain age," we begin to wonder: What am I supposed to do now? Is it too late to make a difference in the world? Do I have value? Are all the happy days behind me?

Am I old?

ON JANUARY 1, 2010, I WAS FORTY-SEVEN YEARS OLD and, not only had I *seen* it all, I *knew* it all too. Or so I kept telling myself.

Like so many in my age demographic, I was also in a quandary—weary from the hands on my grandfather clock revolving so quickly that I constantly found myself in an almost perpetual state of developmental dizziness. Had I done everything I wanted to do professionally? *No.* Was I too "war fatigued" to keep trying? *Perhaps.* Was growth, breakthrough success, innovation and even fame reserved for those whose age begins with a "two" or a "three"? Kinda sorta. (Thank you, youth-obsessed culture.)

On the positive side, I had managed to raise two college-aged children who, to the best of my knowledge, had not ended up on drugs or in jail. Both were reasonably responsible and neither had allowed their hormones to go too terribly haywire, so I had also avoided membership in the elite "young grandparents" club. (Once again, as far as I know.)

So when Florida's sun and surf beckoned, my similarly middle-aged husband Derek and I proudly offered a *been-there-done-that* salute to the rut that was our lives in Washington, DC's congested Northern Virginia suburbs and moved to Naples, Florida.

It has often been said that Naples is home to 350 retired CEOs. All any Neapolitan has to do is poll his or her fellow Walgreens shoppers on any given day to find a collective curricula vitae of business expertise more impressive than can be found in practically any other community in the country.

Whatever "C" branch these men and women represent(ed), "EO," "OO," "FO," or "MO," the combined accomplishments of these full- and part-time residents and guests have much to teach area business professionals—me included. Add in an equally impressive collection of Ps, VPs, and business-savvy celebrities, and the local learning list seemingly goes on and on. Think: influence, power, money.

Naples is an affluent town where, as Derek so cleverly explains: "a Mercedes is essentially viewed as the equivalent of a Chevy anywhere else." Think: Bentley, Jag, Rolls.

However, unlike many of my Neapolitan neighbors, when I arrived I was *not* wealthy. I still had to work. I still needed to plan for retirement. And battle-scarred or not, a part of me knew I still had something to prove—if not to others, then definitely to myself.

I was proud of my résumé, having achieved moderate success as a creative thinker and marketing business owner—one blessed with the opportunity to represent some of our nation's most formidable brands in the publishing, retail and consumer products and services industries.

Sure, there's more sophisticated business men and women out there. I can even think of several creative thinkers who could give me a run for my money. But my secret weapon: I *cared deeply* about the quality of my work—I took it *very personally*. It's often been said that no one lies on his or her deathbed thinking: "I wish I had spent more time at work." But if I'm being totally honest, I just might.

Feeling confident of my own professional abilities, I was ready to meet some of my new Naples neighbors. What I was actually looking for was access to their brains, guidance and influence—and if I played my cards right, perhaps even earn their respect. As someone whose dream job was—and still is—to be a *teacher*, I ached to be a *student*. The problem: I already knew everything I needed to know, didn't I?

I quickly discovered that the powerful company I wished to keep kept company elsewhere, frequently surrounded by similarly financed folks at $500-a-plate fundraisers. Alas, my simple tastes—and simpler budget—favored IHOP.

What happened next upended my views of my education and expertise, my potential—and most important—my life.

With my IHOP co-diners more focused on pancakes than profitability, I had to find a clever way to fill the mentor gap. So I turned to my one true love. My passion. I applied the very tools that made it possible for me to be long-winded in the first place: words! Next, I set my sights on publishing interviews with those I *wanted* to meet. And it worked!

Hey, Naples—GOTCHA!

MY VERY FIRST Neapolitan interview...

Myra Janco Daniels is a very familiar name to those in my new hometown. Just Google her and witness your browser window fill up with pages of content. In fact, her late husband, legendary ad exec and Marlboro Man creator Draper Daniels, was the inspiration for Jon Hamm's Don Draper character on TV's *Mad Men*.

Myra was the first woman to head up a national advertising agency and the youngest woman to win the National Advertising Federation "Advertising Woman of the Year" award. The year was 1965. After "retirement," she spearheaded a public relations and fundraising movement to create the world-renowned Philharmonic Center for the Arts in Naples. (Later renamed Artis—Naples.)

With an overwhelming sense of both excitement and apprehension—my photographer sidekick, Peter Berec, and I entered Mrs. Daniels' office. As a "mad man" myself, I was extremely excited to meet Mrs. Daniels, the icon. Mrs. Daniels, the overachiever. Mrs. Daniels, the force of nature. But the woman sitting before me was Myra, the person, the philanthropist, the teacher, and yes, thankfully, the force of nature.

Widely recognized for her inestimable contribution to the local arts community, Myra Daniels spoke and I listened.

"In my house, the arts were more important than food. Which is good because my mother couldn't cook," Myra recalled with a playful smile. As the arts had provided the very backbone of my education, I quickly fell under her spell.

When she spoke in passionate detail of the various arts programs her organization offered to students, I couldn't help but detect a warm glow in her eyes. However, it was her unexpected segue into the importance of stimulating adult brainpower that provided the greatest surprise: "No matter what I have done, I have always considered myself to be a teacher—and a student."

Feeling just a tad out of my league at this point, I was about to *attempt* to gain credibility with the (not terribly remarkable) fact that *Mad Men* star Jon Hamm and I were both graduates of the University of Missouri-Columbia when Myra saved me from my inane instinctual idiocy with the question: "Have you read my book?"

"Uh…no…I just discovered you had a book yesterday," I responded. My unfortunate lack of preparation forced me to sink a bit further into my chair.

Myra produced a copy, autographed it, and handed to me. The title: *Secrets of a Rutbuster, Breaking Rules and Selling Dreams.*

(Sound EFX: A ton of bricks hitting me.)

Did I move to Florida to break out of my own personal and professional rut? *Yes.* Nevertheless, had I done much of anything to positively transform my life? *No.* Did I still have much to learn? *Actually, yes.* Was meeting Myra Daniels the single most perfectly timed "education" I could ask for? *Absolutely.*

Here I was, writing a Greater Naples Chamber of Commerce article on (arguably) the Queen of Naples only to slowly realize that the sum total of my accomplishments wouldn't fill the pencil holder on Myra's desk. To make matters worse, despite eventually becoming my "friend" on Facebook, Jon Hamm did not have a clue who I was.

Nevertheless, with the discovery of a shared belief regarding the respect owed our senior population, I innocently commented, "I recall attending

Peter Berec

my great-grandmother's 100th birthday party. My relatives tend to live very long lives."

With the knowledge that I sat before her as a forty-seven-year-old man with a somewhat eternal gene pool, Myra nonchalantly observed: "Well then, you've got a long way to go—you better get busy."

Though many have credited Oprah for any number of "aha" moments, Myra Daniels, the one-time queen of the advertising world, provided a wake-up call that proved more thought-provoking and inspirational than any in recent memory.

As our eyes met again, I found myself speechless. (Trust me—that's rare.) Here was a woman—a perpetual powerhouse—whose age allegedly began with an "eight"—yet she was still climbing mountains. Intentional or not, Myra forced me to look at my "four" status through a wildly different lens, practically a different camera. I wasn't old—and youth does not have to be wasted on the young. To Myra, I was a *young* man who could still pursue his dreams *with the benefit* of age and experience on his side.

What's more, I still had potential.

With her final confident smile, Myra metaphorically blessed me, sprinkled a handful of fairy dust atop my head and sent me out into the world to *do good*.

As photographer Peter and I walked out of the building, I stopped, paused for a moment and declared: "I want to go back inside, hug her, sneak her

> ## SHOWMEJONES.COM
>
> "No matter what I have done, I have always considered myself to be a teacher—and a student."
>
> —Myra Janco Daniels

Like this quote? Take a picture and post it! #ShowMeJones

out to Anderson Mini Cooper (my car—the Naples version of the Ford Pinto), take her to my house and keep her."

After returning home—alas, without Myra—I tore through every page of her book, whereupon I was pummeled by the final brick: the source of that special light I saw radiate so often in Myra's eyes. Shining through Myra were her parents, her joyful exposure to the arts as a child and, most important, the spirit of her beloved and influential grandmother, Sophie Jancowitz, whose legacy has lived on in Myra's every word, action and deed.

Nothing beats family.

THROUGH MYRA DANIELS' lifelong commitment to arts education, she had actually accomplished so much more: Heart Education. That day, my *heart* would forever be changed—and prepared or not, my *education* was beginning all over again.

Meeting Myra launched me into a frenzy of activity. Just a few months later, another University of Missouri grad, (then) editor of the *Naples Daily News* Phil Lewis, greenlit my "Business Class" newspaper column concept. By the following summer, the Myra-inspired "Business Class" column hit newsstands with a very simple goal: to explore best practices in business based on conversations with Naples' impressive list of business leaders, high-profile executives, newsmakers and business-savvy celebrities.

As a newbie columnist, I had the enviable opportunity to have some of the best and brightest minds in the country influence my future and, of course, *show me* the ropes. My desired outcome? That I wouldn't inadvertently hang myself along the way.

As for my interview process: my subject and I would just chat. I listened. I learned. I subsequently shared both the expected and the *unexpected* "lessons" with my reader. Before each meeting, I would literally pinch myself. After each meeting, I'd do it again. I was *finally* a teacher—in print at least.

From its launch in July 2012, "Business Class" (consciously) did not offer tips on how to best choose airline seating. Nevertheless, one central lesson quickly began to emerge: "success" seemed to be equal parts business, class, education and edification. From "listen" and "communicate clearly" to "don't pretend you are the smartest one in the room," the majority of those I profiled credited the skill sets of others as instrumental in their achievements.

Just look at the emphasis former Kohl's President Jay Baker places on teaming up with the right business partners, as well as the way his eyes light up when wife/partner Patty enters the room. In this case, Baker's "actions" and "words" seem to speak with equal volume. For Baker, the secret to success doesn't seem to be all that furtive: "Have a true passion for what you do…. I never had a day I didn't want to go to work."

If Myra Janco Daniels is the column's unofficial Godmother—having debunked any possible connection between one's age and one's value—then former *Good Morning America* President Phil Beuth is its Godfather. Phil is the man/mentor who arranged meetings with Charles "the importance of gaining trust" Gibson and Jack "I operate by The Golden Rule" Hanna. Phil's candid feedback became instrumental in the column's growth and development. Always a gentleman, Phil was—and still is—that enviable guy everyone wants to please.

Some lessons were unexpected, such as when Regis Philbin treated a twenty-minute, fact-finding phone call as if it was the single most important item on his to-do list. (Lesson No. 1: focus; Lesson No. 2: pay attention or you'll miss Lesson No. 1.)

As business professionals, we can be very forgiving. We forgive *ourselves* for ignoring emails and dismissing phone messages. We pardon ourselves for broadcasting emails and leaving messages no one wants to receive. We also excuse ourselves for failing to provide timely updates on current projects. Instead, we traipse off to Happy Hour where we post our post-workday antics on Facebook for those we just blew off to see.

With time at a premium, we sometimes get frustrated and—intentional or not—we pay it forward and cause even more frustration. We can even give ourselves a pass for using electronic messaging to communicate less-than-positive remarks—comments we would likely never say in person.

When these challenging situations arise and four-letter words (i.e. dork, fool, stop and OMG!) ache to exit our fingertips and strike our keyboards, consider asking: "What would Peggy Post do?" The result: civility, common sense, and even tranquility will likely prevail. In so many ways, Peggy

Post, Director Emeritus of The Emily Post Institute, inspired much of the *heart* of "Business Class" and, in turn, *Show Me*.

This process also taught me about *compassion*: "What you contribute forms the basis of who you are as a person. The key is respect. Let the personal satisfaction be the engine, not the personal glory," a sentiment shared by Mimi Chapin Gregory, longtime Naples resident and Commander, France's National Order of Merit.

NFL Hall of Fame Quarterback Sonny Jurgensen teaches us to "play to our strengths" while voice-over icon Peter Thomas shares the profoundly simple—yet often overlooked—lesson to "think before you speak." *Laverne and Shirley's* Eddie Mekka advises to "be comfortable in your own shoes" just as author Janet Evanovich spent years walking in a mother's shoes before spinning those experiences into a wildly successful career as a "mother working." In a few easy steps, Janet dramatically changed the life of a member of my family, too.

SHOWMEJONES.COM

"What you contribute forms the basis of who you are as a person. The key is respect. Let the personal satisfaction be the engine, not the personal glory."

—Mimi Chapin Gregory

In some cases, business services and business ethics blend effortlessly. HGTV's Candice Olson mixes modern elements with classic style in the great room and in the boardroom. Daytime Television's Kassie DePaiva fearlessly takes on workplace drama by applying her own on-set experiences. And renowned nature photographer Clyde Butcher shines a special light on business practices: a little extra thought, as well as an attention to—and respect for—detail, goes a very long way.

Even the column resulting from my chat with conservative talk show host Sean Hannity left the majority of readers on both sides of the political fence nodding their heads in agreement.

As you weave your way through this book, it would be a huge mistake to apply any preconceived notions about a specific individual and prejudge the lesson. Why? Predictability is NOT my thing. Plus, it's so important we don't play it safe and simply interact with those with whom we agree. It's essential to look for common ground with those who have alternate points of view. Trust me, areas of agreement are much easier to find than you think.

Though not everyone I interviewed was entrenched in their "Golden Years," many were—and doing it with more skill and panache than I ever thought possible. In many ways, my heart belongs to the "seniors"—the sevens, eights and nines—those who have earned the right to be heard and respected. In the end, what is "seniority" if not a tip of the hat to longevity? It has often been joked that Florida is God's waiting room. Well, if that's true, God has *a lot* to look forward to.

We all have something to learn from those in our social and business circles. Plus, we all have something to teach the aforementioned band of influencers. Sure Naples, Florida, is blessed with an impressive list of full- and part-time residents and visitors, but great minds and great stories can be found in *every community* in the country.

This book is the "Best of." In some cases, the original columns have been reproduced exactly as written. Other times, I highlight specific quotes, stories and/or anecdotes for those situations where a specific aspect of the interaction intensified over time. Though an attempt has been made to update the biographical data on each subject, I can't tell someone to *stop achieving,* so that information will naturally change. What will NOT change are the *timeless* lessons learned from each extraordinary individual.

Perhaps most important, *I will not apologize* for my decision to focus on the positive attributes of those I interviewed. Are they all perfect? No, certainly not. Nor am I. But if it is lessons on "bad behavior" you're after, America's foibles are constantly on public display. That thingamajig called the World Wide Web is chock-full of the stuff.

Show Me is a result of more than fifty years of research: fifty-plus years of living a life, ten years of journaling about that life, and four years as a columnist writing about people who—at one time—I assumed lived a better life than I did.

Now, with the help of my treasured gallery of informants—starting with the influencers from my days as a as a showy-yet-sensitive, bunny-fearing Mid-Missouri youngster to today's "Business Class" elite—I hope to SHOW YOU what all of these extraordinary people so graciously SHOWED ME: how to learn from your past, embrace your present, grow personally and professionally, laugh at yourself and banish mediocrity—by listening, learning and respecting the never-ending balance between ambition and tradition.

ALL IN THE FAMILY

My hometown sits smack dab in the middle of the Show Me State of Missouri. In fact, I have always considered Columbia to be the center of the United States because I was raised to believe that Kansas didn't really exist and was merely an urban legend. Most important, Columbia, Missouri, is a place where a term like "smack dab" is both understood and expected.

"CoMo" is also home to the main campus of the University of Missouri—or "Mizzou." I have always maintained I was registered at birth to attend my hometown institute of higher education, that a representative from the Mizzou Admissions Office tackled unsuspecting parents as they exited the hospital with their newborns and forced them to sign away their child to the University system. After my arrival on September 13, 1962, at Boone County Hospital—though there is no actual proof—Nellie and Ken Jones dutifully signed me over to a Mizzou admissions officer, effective August 1980.

Despite twenty-five post-college years in the Washington, DC, suburbs and a few more in Southwest Florida, I still demonstrate—for better or for worse—a healthy amount of "Show Me" behavioral traits. For those who have spent any time with a diehard Missouri native, you'll understand the almost perverse power of the "Show Me" thinker:

🐾 Don't ask me to read the textbook. SHOW ME what you want me to learn.

🐇 Don't just rattle off directions. SHOW ME how to get there.
🐇 Don't just tell me to figure it out. SHOW ME what to do.

Though some may feel the "Show Me" method is the ultimate example of lazy, those of us from the Show Me State simply view it as a critical time management skill. Oh—and we're not going to change, either.

On the other hand, as a Show Me State resident gets older, though we continue to exasperate the masses, we ultimately discover we have been seeking something much more important all long: clarity.

When I was less than a week old, my parents moved me into the house on Columbia's Braemore Road where I would live for the next twenty-one years. My colorful roommates included my mother, Nellie Pearl, my father, Kenneth Paul, and my two older sisters, Janice Lynn (six) and Paula Gail (three).

As we grew up, the "Braemorons": teenage Janice, Paula, Kevin and Lisa Thompson, Christy and Keith Cramer, Marsha and Maurice Duff, Hank and Hugh Emerson, Ruth Eubanks, Rilla Snodgrass, Mark Golden and more, depending on the day, would gather under the street light at the corner of Braemore Road and Skye Wynd Court. The older kids played kickball and Capture the Flag and, no doubt, engaged in other mature activities I was too young to understand.

I suspect that while a '70s-era Mark Rice (Braemore's David Cassidy, a.k.a. Keith Partridge) serenaded the teen set with his fancy-schmancy twelve-string guitar, Shelley Caldwell gave Christy Cramer her first kiss. And yes, Shelley was a boy. As far as I know there was no girl-on-girl action on Braemore.

In the late '60s and early '70s, most teen-girl Braemorons wanted to be one-part Laurie Partridge, one-part Marcia Brady and one-part Ginger from *Gilligan's Island*. In truth, they were all about 80 percent Mary Ann—and 20 percent Morticia Addams.

Aww, it's baby Randy!

Paula

Janice

Me

Understandably, the younger Braemorons were often the neighborhood castaways. Scott and Suzi Steinman were my closest friends, but Carrie Cramer, who was only a week older than me, always bucked the system and got included in the older-kid activities. Carrie was not exactly a child who took "no" for an answer. She was essentially Danny Partridge with boobs.

Neurotic, eccentric and/or uppity Reuben Kincaid wannabes seemed to occupy one-half of the homes on the street. My particular residence had shining examples of offbeat Reubens living on each side: a curmudgeon and an intimidator. Oddball Kincaid, played by actor Dave Madden on TV's *The Partridge Family*, had nothing on the inimitable men of Braemore Road.

Perhaps the most exciting part of being a child is the unadulterated use of one's imagination. Fueled by network television and AM radio, my mind was constantly in overdrive. For example, when brunette Jeremy Gelbwaks was inexplicably replaced by blond Brian Forster as Chris Partridge in 1971, I went wild. If there was to be a revolving door of young actors appearing in the coveted role of Chris Partridge on *The Partridge Family*, I wanted in on the action.

Television families quickly became our fantasy families. They often represented a life we thought we wanted, could not really understand and, in most cases, would never have. TV stars were people we admired, imitated and, in my case, irritated with excessive fan mail.

However, as a preteen with a budding interest in acting, music and musical theatre, I worshipped at the prime-time throne of the one and only Shirley Jones. Even at a young age, I knew her résumé.

Shirley Jones was the star of stage and screen. Shirley Jones was uber-cool Mama Partridge. Shirley Jones could out sing God! And though Nellie Jones did a fine job as a mother, she couldn't carry a tune. To make matters worse, she drove a boring, monochromatic Plymouth. I used to fantasize that Shirley Jones was my long-lost relative—one who would eventually emerge from the wings of my life and whisk me off to Hollywood.

Many years, many cars, and many moves later—without the benefit of a shared family tree—Shirley Jones would come into my life....

Kevin Randall Jones

SHIRLEY JONES

A young Robert Morse did not "text" his way to the top in the 1967 film *How to Succeed in Business Without Really Trying.* Oz's Wicked Witch didn't "tweet" her messages of gloom and doom: i.e. #SurrenderDorothy.

Shirley Jones did not surf the web for outstanding arrest warrants against Robert Preston's Harold Hill in 1962's *The Music Man.* Her "Marian the Librarian" was forced to conduct research using an antique—a book.

In fact, 1970s single-working-mom Shirley Jones managed to keep her five (often hormonally charged) rock-star Partridge kids out of harm's way without tethering them to cellphones with GPS tracking. She just corralled them in a multicolored bus.

It's not that Shirley dismisses technology but, as a woman who "loves to watch Turner Classic Movies all day long," she pines for a bygone era—a feeling stemming from fond memories of beloved colleagues ("Jimmy Stewart was the most wonderful man in the world.") and respect for a pre-smartphone age when people actually sat down and talked to each other. Shirley simply believes that movies, and people in general, used to place a greater emphasis on "heart" as well as its first cousins: compassion, concentration, compromise, understanding and forgiveness.

For those who talk about the differences in how people worked in, for example, 1990 and now, imagine having your professional coming of age in the '50s, '60s and '70s. Yet, without an endless series of programmer-fed zeros and ones to usurp the human voice or the handwritten memo, worker bees like Shirley Jones managed to persevere.

Plucked from obscurity by fate—with the help of Richard Rodgers and Oscar Hammerstein II—the Smithton, Pennsylvania, teenager found herself and her "God-given" vocal talent on a mind-numbing career fast track. With the theatrical release of the glorious *Oklahoma!* in 1955, Shirley Jones' star status was established in record time.

In the nearly seven decades that followed, she has enjoyed enviable career longevity without succumbing to today's common practice of reinventing oneself. Shirley maintained her priorities and remained objective. Career-wise, "If it didn't happen, it didn't happen," she says. "I could spend more time with my family."

Her primary focus: "I just worked at being the very best 'Shirley Jones' I could be."

SHOWMEJONES.COM

"Have something people want. As long as people still want it, they'll be there for you."

—Shirley Jones

Feeling inspired? Take a pic & post NOW! #ShowMeJones

Shirley is living proof that age and experience provide the wisdom to recognize that our "at work" and "at home" personalities eventually merge into a single, multifaceted persona—one capable of simultaneously embracing the skills necessary to navigate home, hearth, progress and success.

Her outcome: Laurey in *Oklahoma!*, Julie in *Carousel*, her Oscar-winning turn as prostitute Lulu Baines in 1960's *Elmer Gantry* as well as the aforementioned Marian Paroo, sitcom-mom Shirley Partridge and an ostensibly endless IMDB.com listing.

That said, she unapologetically places "wife," "mother" and "grandmother" at the top of her list of accomplishments. It doesn't take long to understand that she would gladly trade in her Oscar statuette should that trade benefit any member of her family.

At times, Shirley appears cautious to share personal advice. Instead, she advocates an individual's responsibility to take the time to understand herself. For example, Shirley on quality: "Everyone has their own feeling of what perfection is." On fixing the unfixable: "You have to know how much you can give and how much you can take."

Though her durable career can arguably be attributed to how much she is loved by the public, Shirley is dubious about the relationship between professional adoration and career duration. "There are dynamos in business who are certainly *not* loved," she observes.

Moments later, she suggests a more plausible explanation for enduring success: "Have something people want. As long as people still want it, they'll be there for you"—a profound insight based on equal parts heart, experience and yet another skill that has become markedly uncommon: common sense.

True, some may have been surprised by the candid nature of her 2013 book, *Shirley Jones: A Memoir*. However, it could be said it's merely "Know Thyself," Shirley Jones style—an honest update on self-awareness and her goal "to be the best 'Shirley Jones' [she] could be."

Because, succeed or fail, everything matters—"as long as you laugh a lot along the way."

When asked for her final thoughts on the ever-elusive secret to success, she paused briefly, and—in a superlative salute to our shared surname— whimsically responded: "Your last name has to be Jones."

So yes, it appears that Shirley, approximately 2,004,500 other Joneses in the U.S. and I have a working advantage. As for the rest of you, it also sounds like a clever hint to start keeping up with the Joneses.

KEN JONES

Though many would argue that you *can* create your own family, '70s Shirley and kids didn't seem to show much interest in my goals or musical abilities. My geographic location—1,745 miles away from Los Angeles—didn't help matters. So I forged ahead with those I refer to as "the biologicals."

My sister Janice is almost seven years my senior. My memories of young Jan seem almost inextricably linked to her onetime obsession with Carole King's *Tapestry*—an album I am now convinced she inspired. The day I got home from the hospital Janice managed to *feel the earth move* with love and affection toward her *beautiful* new baby brother. She even cried at the thought of going to school and being *so far away*. Once *home again*, she sweetly assured me: *You've got a friend.* Alas, the novelty wore off pretty quickly—i.e. the following day.

Though no one else supports this claim, in an effort to restore her kingdom to a sister-led sovereignty, I swear Janice once hid me *up on a roof*, hoping no one would find me.

In other words, had newborn me asked six-year-old Janice, "*Will you still love me tomorrow?*" the answer would have been—uh—no. Janice viewed me as the same annoying baby until I was about thirty-five years old.

Second-child Paula made an absolute art form out of being the middle child. In fact, she could have easily taught TV's Jan Brady a thing or two about assimilation. Paula was smart enough to play her cards pretty close to her (somewhat limited) chest and managed to go unnoticed her entire life. She was the type of teen who would sneak the younger girls down to the boys' cabins at 4-H Camp, lead them in the front door for a "raid" and slip out the back door leaving her young charges to take the blame.

In short, Paula turned anonymity into power—hence the nickname: "Paula Perfect." It's not that she was a faultless child—she just never got caught. For all practical purposes, Paula Perfect disappeared from the day I was born until just a few days before her high school graduation. Once the Rock Bridge High School Commencement invitations had gone out, we sort of had to notice her again. To this day, no matter what the situation, Paula Gail Jones blissfully flies under the radar.

A product of the 1950s, my mother obviously thought she was supposed to be June Clever but got there by way of Beatrice Arthur's *Maude* and Irene Ryan's Granny Clampett. Frankly, like most *real* mothers of the era, any signs of a Shirley Jones coolness seemed woefully out of my mother's wheelhouse.

When my mother would get really mad, her face turned completely red, almost crimson in color, and her normally beautiful brown eyes became pinched and pea-sized. She also chain smoked, so it wasn't unusual to enjoy the added special effect of smoke pouring from her nose and mouth during any and all maternal outbursts.

Nellie Pearl Kyger Jones not only marched to the beat of her own drum, she was the drum, the drumsticks, the drummer and the band. There will never be another human being like her.

As for me: with the endless questions, the borderline psychotic imagination, the awkward sensitivity and the unyielding need to be noticed, I essentially sucked the life out of the room. Many would say I still do.

Then there's my dad.

Not long ago, I was faced with the fast-approaching Father's Day holiday and an expected patriarchal emphasis for my newspaper column. Though "Business Class" typically covered individuals with some sort of Florida affiliation, my editor quickly approved my Show Me State-based father as my focus.

As I would like to believe my dad considers me to be among his "best work," I would like to think I gave him some of mine too.

AFTER TWO YEARS IN THE U.S. AIR FORCE, Ken Jones began his career at MFA Insurance Cos. on March 1, 1956. Ken would then go on to essentially make the same 0.9 mile trek from his Columbia, Missouri, ranch home to the same office building for the next forty years.

Though kids may not always know what their parents actually *do* for a living, Ken Jones clearly impacted at least two of his three children. His daughters, Janice Jones Nelson and Paula Jones Brown, followed in his footsteps to spend the majority of their careers at their father's professional home.

Nevertheless, as youngsters, whenever Janice or Paula asked what the elder Jones actually did at MFA, his trademark wit quickly emerged: "Well, MFA stands for 'Mostly Fooling Around.'"

In 1981, MFA would be rechristened Shelter Insurance Co.

Upon his retirement in 1996, Ken held the title of Director of Product Development. Basically, his final professional responsibility was to convert legal insurance jargon into "easy-to-read" consumer language.

The secret to Jones' success, at home and at work, may also be found in this job description. "It was actually my dad who was 'easy to read' and everyone, everywhere, loved him for it," says daughter Paula Brown.

According to Jones' former colleague Jerald Mason, "Ken's knowledge was respected by all, and he was often a go-to guy for his ideas. Ken never met a stranger, and a good-natured joke was always at hand." Former associate Martha Traxler adds, "He always supported me as a working mother. Ken was like a brother to me—we were like a family."

Essentially a product of the *Mad Men* "do as I say, not as I do" business world of the 1960s, Ken Jones proved to be ahead of his time as a leader who promoted collaboration, shared goals, open communication, empathy and family life balance to motivate those around him.

Living in Naples, Florida, I find it easy to gain access to titans of industry— those who have achieved extraordinary success as members of the corporate C-suite or as visionary entrepreneurs. However, the vast majority of Americans make their living essentially helping other people make money.

Ken Jones is one of countless unsung industry heroes who helped said others achieve their "titan" status—an accomplishment equally deserving of our admiration and respect.

Though Shelter Insurance Co. was his workplace, Ken's greatest achievement was his ability to provide shelter at home. According to daughter Janice Nelson, "Dad was the same down-to-earth man at home or at work. He is truly one of the good guys."

Ken himself quips, "I am the last of a dying breed—I've had only one job and one wife."

As for his black-sheep third child who rejected the family business, he wrote and published a Father's Day-inspired business column honoring the considerable accomplishments of his incomparable dad. That column grew to become the tome you now hold in your hands—a book dedicated to all the "good" that epitomizes the life and times of Mr. Kenneth Paul Jones.

For every father who has attempted to be a role model to his children, may you one day see definitive proof of the impact of your actions. Because even in his eighties, my dad—humorous, honest, humble and easy-to-read Ken Jones—can be summed up in two words: He's perfect.

ONE PROBLEM. THANKS TO MY FATHER'S decision to avoid all-things-computer, he would not see the *Naples Daily News* until well after Father's Day. Not to be defeated, I contacted my hometown newspaper, the *Columbia Daily Tribune*. Without hesitation, Team Tribune became my Operation Father's Day co-conspirators and a top-secret plan was hatched.

On Father's Day, my dad opened his *Tribune* to find his face looking back at him. Next to his photo was my Father's Day column for all to see.

Surprise!

Here was a man who never craved the spotlight—who never expected anything from anyone. One of the good guys who silently yet resolutely stood by his family regardless of the situation. My dad was now a local media star. His phone began to ring; the clippings began to arrive tucked neatly inside cards and letters. He was suddenly being stopped on the street and in Wal-Mart. He suffered spirited abuse at the hands of his early morning McDonald's coffee klatch. For perhaps the first time in his life, Ken Jones was forced into the limelight as the single most important member of the Jones family—and he was.

Yes, it took me more than fifty years to do Father's Day right, and short of eventually getting my dad declared *Time* magazine's "Person of the Year," I'll probably never top it.

Hey Time, *have you met my dad?*

What we learn from our family—those we are born with and those we appoint—requires a lifetime of listening, loving, confrontation, communication, cooperation, patience and support. Take just one small moment for granted and you're likely to miss something extraordinary.

As I have grown older, my appreciation for my father has increased exponentially. Though many suggest I'm my mother with a penis, thankfully, I inherited my dad's sense of humor, work ethic and Y chromosome. As a matter of fact, Dad's commonsensical concept of "easy-to-read" is something I advocate in business to this day.

It seems the son/apple didn't fall far from that father/tree after all.

Dad, as "cousin" Shirley Jones famously sang: "I think I love you."

Nope, think = KNOW.

CHEERS

PETER & STELLA THOMAS

When I first met voiceover wizard Peter Thomas in early 2014, he not only became the subject of a "Business Class" column, he assumed the role of trusted ally. As was the case with my father, Peter represented the type of professional—the type of man—I aspire to be: honest, kind, compassionate, giving, and above all, authentic. In a world where we are so often judged solely on our short-term value, it's easy to question if anyone is still willing to invest in the potential of long-term benefit.

Peter Thomas' impact on my personal and professional development didn't end with our first interview. That's when it began. For example, it was Peter who responded to my claim: "I'm not right for voiceover work" with a private coaching and recording session at his home studio.

After his passing on Saturday, April 30, 2016, at age ninety-one, the *Naples Daily News* published a revised version of my original "Business Class" column—an adaptation that better represented the unexpected joy that Peter continued to bring into my life.

We often hear that a person who has enjoyed a long and prolific career has "seen it all." For Peter Thomas, a more appropriate observation could be that he has "said it all." In many ways, Peter's work served as the narration for my childhood.

"Wouldn't you really rather have a Buick?" (General Motors)

"The taste people hate twice a day." (Listerine)

"Helping people find the answers." (IBM)

"Don't leave home without it." (American Express)

Whether Peter was an American Express cardholder, I will never know. However, I do know he never left home without his considerable heart.

With a career that spanned seven decades, Peter and his highly recognizable voice helped to build the integrity of consumer brands and add authenticity to films, television programs and documentaries—all with the goal of boosting the emotional impact of scripted words and screen images.

If a writer's words are the paint, Peter's voice was the brush that enhances the metaphorical canvas: the broad strokes of descriptive adjectives, the thin strokes of whimsy, a long stroke for special emphasis and a short stroke to bring the point home.

Without question, Peter Thomas was an artist. In fact, the International Television and Radio Association Lifetime Achievement Award winner continued to work regularly into his late eighties.

A Pensacola native, Peter was the son of a Welsh minister—an earnest man who taught his children the importance of both recitation and memorization. Dr. John D. Thomas encouraged young Peter to "see the picture" rather than just "read the words." His father's advice ultimately served as the foundation for his dynamic career.

Throughout the years, Peter's talent, work ethic and integrity earned him the respect of countless industry professionals. According to former New York casting director Karen Kayser Benson, "Peter was a product of the early days of the 'big voice'; however, he is widely credited with ushering in a more respected era of believability and honesty."

Though Peter's first meeting with a promising "up and comer" named Johnny Carson occurred years before Carson's ascent to "broadcast legend" status, Peter Thomas—and his inimitable voice—were later chosen by Carson to lead a wedding ceremony for one of Carson's own children.

Despite numerous awards, Peter, a proud World War II veteran, would light up when discussing one specific project: the Oscar-winning HBO documentary *One Survivor Remembers*. The celebrated movie tells the story of Nazi survivor Gerda Weissmann Klein, who, as a teen, was tragically interred in various labor camps. This was a topic close to his heart, because Peter was part of a military unit that participated in the liberation of Nordhausen Concentration Camp.

Though countless "Business Class" subjects have shared the advice to "be passionate about what you do," Peter Thomas didn't have to—at least, not in a traditional fashion. His passion was automatically on display every time he spoke.

Regardless of your method of—or reason for—communicating, Peter advised: "You have to believe in what you say. It has to be a part of you." His creative process always tracked back to his father's early influence: "See the picture in your mind—pause—see the next picture and *then* speak."

SHOWMEJONES.COM

"See the picture in your mind—pause—see the next picture and *then* speak."

—Peter Thomas

For those who struggle with finding the right words, Peter suggested: "Stop and think about it. Go to sleep, wake up and think about it again." What's more, Peter intuitively knew exactly when to stop talking. Now, stop and ask yourself: How many people do you know who carefully consider the impact of their words? Or, equally important, who understand exactly when it's time to be quiet?

Peter's advice for broadcasters: *"Think before you speak."*

Peter's advice for the rest of us: *"Think before you speak."*

A lesson as profound in its simplicity as it is in its significance.

Peter's undeniable muse was his wife of almost seventy years, Stella Barrineau Thomas.

The last time I saw Peter, I held his hand and asked permission to write about what I learned from my time with Stella. His answer came in the form of a warm smile, a slight moistening of the eyes, and a simple nod of the head: "Yes, I think Stella would like that."

I met Stella Thomas in 2014, six months before she passed away. Though she was in poor health, her generosity of spirit was less easily erased. When I subsequently shared my admiration for Stella in public, I was sometimes greeted with the comment: "I wish you had known Stella 'when.'" When what? When Stella was younger and healthier? Had aging, ailing Stella suddenly become less of a person?

The Stella Thomas I spent time with was perfect. I never felt limited by meeting her so close to the end of her life. The true tragedy would have been in not meeting her at all. Stella's inadvertent lesson: We can have a positive impact on all those who cross our paths—every single day of our lives. None of us is defined by whether or not our heart is beating, but by who—and what—it beats for. Influence is timeless.

You see, Stella Thomas was a lady and Peter Thomas was a gentleman. What's more, how many people can any of us describe as either a "lady" or a "gentleman"?

Peter and Stella Thomas will be with me for the rest of my life. And as long as this book continues to circulate, their innate goodness has the ability to inspire others.

True, much has been written about creating a legacy. I don't know if Peter and Stella ever seriously considered theirs—I somehow doubt it. Then again, shouldn't our legacies be defined by a history of authentic actions as opposed to a deliberate plan of action?

ShowMeJones.com

"We can have a positive impact on all those who cross our paths—every single day of our lives. None of us is defined by whether or not our heart is beating, but by who—and what—it beats for. Influence is timeless."

—Randall Kenneth Jones

That said, the Thomases ultimately left the most potent legacy of all: they truly made the world a better place.

Nothing more need be said…

…*or so I thought.* I still had to manage to make it through Peter and Stella's Memorial Service. As Pastor Kirt Anderson of Naples Community Church began, he commented that *a recent newspaper article* had inspired his opening remarks.

I stopped breathing.

He then proceeded to quote advice from Peter—wisdom attained during our very precious time together: "See the picture in your mind—pause—see the next picture and *then* speak." Pastor Anderson's subsequent vision of Peter and Stella's heavenly reunion was—*it must be said*—picture perfect.

If there was ever an argument for the importance of capturing an individual's legacy wisdom, this was certainly it.

Though I respect each person's views on religion, mine are nonnegotiable. On a day set aside to celebrate Peter and Stella's life—and their ascent to God's Kingdom—I felt as though I was being sent a message: **It's time.**

It's time to abandon my fear of literary failure.

It's time to share these lessons with a larger audience.

It's time to put all this work to work.

I took my first serious steps toward the publication of this book the very next day.

Though I'm not typically one to share compliments directed toward me, my friend Cynthia Rhodes responded to this story with an observation I will never forget—*and one so many can apply and learn from:* "God talks to us all the time, but you, sweet Randy, have a heart that listens."

WIDE WORLD OF SPORTS

I am not a terribly athletic guy. If I were being chased by a chainsaw-wielding madman, I'd probably try to talk him out of severing my limbs before I would trust my athleticism and resort to actual running. My guess is that most six-year-olds would best me in a race. My only real hope is that the weight and movement of the chainsaw would slow down my assailant in time for me to find safety inside—for example—the nearest IHOP.

I have avoided most physical endeavors throughout my life out of *fear*. For example, I have never gone skiing. Why? I am convinced that some merciless millennial with a smartphone will be lurking nearby to film my inevitable crash at the bottom of the Bunny Hill—a spectacle that, back in the day, would have made its way to ABC Sports executives, therefore branding me the next "agony of defeat" poster child in the opening credits of *ABC's Wide World of Sports*.

However, to deny the obvious allegorical correlations between the business world and sports is as ridiculous as saying that Waffle House is as good as IHOP.

Flashback, 1972: Paula Perfect's true passion was softball and, despite possessing virtually no athletic prowess whatsoever, I was naturally drawn to the sport as well. As a teen, Paula played on the "Cogents" girls' softball team. Evidently, when forming the team, the players found the name by randomly opening a dictionary and pointing to the first word they saw: cogent.

co·gent · *adjective* · having power to compel or constrain

I always loved that word. To this day, I *believe* in that word—I love nothing more than making cogent remarks and observations whenever possible.

It was at a Cogents' game that I got my first taste of management—or, at least, of possessing something resembling authority. On this ultimately inauspicious day, my beloved Cogents were, once again, playing their arch rivals, the Purple Martins. I despised the Purple Martins as I knew, as all hardcore Cogents fans knew, that they were evil and were coached by Satan himself. Well, I also knew the Purple Martins kicked Cogent ass fairly regularly, too.

At this day's game, management was missing a first base umpire and no volunteers were rushing forward to fill the position. I'm sure I had to get in everyone's face and beg for the job but, whatever the sequence of events, I eventually took my place of honor at the first base line, ready to do my duty. I thought I was King Shit on Turd Island, but I was also aching to prove myself in the adult world of professional athletics.

So there I stood, my characteristic wide stance presenting an appearance of both confidence and ability. Though melting from the unbearable Missouri humidity, with lines of sweat cascading down my somewhat robust preteen body, I could barely hide the ecstasy of standing in my new place of honor. Finally—I had POWER!

Not much happened for the first several batters—at least nothing that concerned the newly anointed first base ump. Other than the bases now being loaded, the lack of important first-base activity rendered those plays as not worthy of my attention. I stood and waited for the action to come my way.

Cogents' pitcher Jani Hoft cast a formidable stare as the next batter, Teri Samuels of the Purple Martins, sauntered confidently up to the plate.

Strike One.

Wow, it's hot out here.

Ball One.

I may be the youngest of three but look at me now, world!

Ball Two.

How long before we get to go to Dairy Queen? A dipped cone would be great right now...

Strike Two.

...or maybe pancakes...

As Jani skillfully let go of another pitch, Teri grunted, as Purple Martins were prone to do, swung hard and smacked a powerful grounder to Marla Opie at third base.

If you have ever seen teens play ball, you also know that when the bases are loaded, chaos can prevail. Before I knew it, Purple Martins appeared to be running *everywhere*—a force play here, a run scored there. *Every single Cogent* seemed to have possession of the ball at some point during the play.

It all came down to Marla Opie, catching the ball as it returned to third and forcing an approaching Teri Samuels back to Galen Sights at second. My head was spinning from all the commotion, but it didn't matter because, once again, the action had moved well past my first base perch so I was in the clear.

Yes, breakfast for dinner. I want breakfast for dinner.

Unfortunately, NO ONE TOLD ME what happened if the play was at second base. Imagine my shock when Coach Duke started screaming for me to run to second base to make the call. *I froze.* It was one of those terrifying situations where your head is telling you that you are moving but your body decides otherwise and remains cemented to the ground.

As Teri just missed mowing down skinny little shortstop Mary Hill on her way back from third to second base, third base's Marla lobbed the ball to second base's Galen, who managed to tag Teri as she steamrolled to the base.

There I stood, planted beside first base, not having moved. I then noticed that all eyes were fixated on me—players, spectators, coaches and, worst of all, Teri Samuels. Everyone was perfectly silent as the almighty first base ump—me—had both teams' undivided attention. With the most powerful voice I could muster, I instinctively called the play:

"Out?"

Despite what has ever been said about me, I'm a rule follower and have always believed in playing fair. I hated the Purple Martins, but consciously cheating was not an option.

Amateur sports fans can be mean but, in this case, I'm lucky that the KOMU-TV ten o'clock news didn't lead with the story: "Chubby Preteen First Base Ump Massacred by Outraged Purple Martin Fans." Based on the less-than-positive reaction from the crowd, it was clear that I had just made my first *and last* call of the game.

Yes, I completely failed in my first attempt at being an authority figure and I knew it. But I took the risk and made the, albeit brief, change from spectator to the most infamous (and distracted) first base ump in Cogents softball history.

Nonetheless, at a minimum, I *briefly* felt as though I were part of the TEAM—and I *liked* it.

Confession: Teri Samuels was probably safe. On some unconscious level, Paula, Marla, Mary, Jani and Galen won out and my loyalty to the Cogents kicked in. It's not like I had exactly kept my head in the game. Yes, my mind had wandered briefly to eggs, bacon and toast for dinner only to be rudely forced back to the present with those very same eggs metaphorically taking up residence on my face.

Flash forward a few decades: During a recent visit to my hometown, Paula Perfect, eldest sister Janice and I spent the day together. For some reason, during the requisite "childhood memories" part of our day, Paula mentioned something about once filling in on the field as a Purple Martin. Even as a middle-aged man, I was shocked and somewhat appalled at this news. I had always been loyal to my beloved Cogents and my hatred for the Purple Martins never completely went away. Despite my preteen public ridicule, and a lifelong fear of Teri Samuels' inevitable retaliation, here was Paula essentially confessing to sleeping with the enemy.

As much as I have always wanted to believe in the concept of "loyalty," especially between family and close friends, a long-feared hypothesis was confirmed that very day: one man's loyalty is another woman's chance to expand her résumé.

Bitch.

As fate would have it, I eventually crossed paths again with the lovely Teri Samuels. *Fair, kind, wise, forgiving* Teri Samuels.

Without hesitation, Teri began: "Well, well, well—after all this time I have finally found that skinny little chicken-shit, blind-moron Jones kid slash umpire who made that ridiculous call. The only thing that saved your Cogent-fan hide from a total flogging by this Purple Martin was that you disappeared while we had our team meeting after the game."

Though I had already lost my ability to breathe and was well on my way to self-induced asphyxiation, Teri continued: "Of course, we're older and more mature now—but I'm still going to rip you apart, use your head for batting practice and your limbs for bats."

The exchange actually went better than I expected: she called me "skinny!"

THERE'S NO QUESTION that the majority of my role models have been female: my mother, sisters, bosses, clients and yes, even (the actually quite lovely) Teri Samuels. I have always attributed this fact to two things: 1) women have had to work harder for many of the opportunities automatically afforded to men; and 2) due to their naturally more caring and compassionate nature, women are more likely to nurture those around them—*and I loved attention.*

For anyone who has a daughter as I do, enough cannot be said about the importance of female role models—both personally and professionally—inside the family unit and celebrated in the public.

As for those women who find (or seek) success in what is traditionally regarded as a "man's world," they often end up having to work even harder. Former professional tennis player and celebrated sports analyst Mary Carillo answered my question: "Why are you successful?" with one of the most uplifting comments I have ever heard. It seems that, regardless of the athletic or journalistic opportunity presented, according to Carillo: "I always said YES!"

When we think of professional athletes, many characteristics come to mind: discipline, drive, determination and, of course, an unparalleled desire to win. In other words, a whole lotta YES.

These same words can also be used to describe successful people; characteristics that have no bias based on one's sex. Nevertheless, a lucky few—male and female—possess a little something extra that sets them apart.

Brian Boitano

I t's been said that you haven't truly "arrived" until you are the focus of a joke on one of pop culture's satirical media platforms. Just look at 1988's Olympic Gold Medal figure skating champion, Brian Boitano. His journey has taken him from Mountain View, California, to the gold medal podium at the Olympics to the Food Network. If that's not enough, Boitano has allegedly spent time in a small, animated town known to TV audiences as South Park, Colorado.

In 1995, Brian Boitano was surprised to find his image depicted in Trey Parker and Matt Stone's animated short, *The Spirit of Christmas*. "I broke up a fight between Jesus and Santa Claus," he joked. The film ultimately led to the 1997 *South Park* series launch on Comedy Central, with "Brian Boitano" as a recurring character. Ask any fan of the show—or the subsequent movie, *South Park: Bigger, Longer & Uncut*—and he will likely tell you exactly how to withstand any crisis.

Simply ask yourself: *What Would Brian Boitano Do?*

The catchphrase ultimately became widely recognized—in South Park and beyond. Brian's reaction? "Initially, I ignored it. But I saw the movie and was pleasantly surprised."

Written by *South Park* co-creator Trey Parker and composer Marc Shaiman, "What Would Brian Boitano Do?" is also a song in the 1999 film. Whether cartoon Brian fought grizzly bears using his magical fire breath or traveled through time to fight evil robot kings, he always managed to save the human race from one catastrophic death spiral after another.

Though cast as the hero of markedly absurd situations, Brian thought: "Okay, this will blow over in a couple of months. I didn't really worry about it and how it would affect me. It worked out the opposite way. The more time went on, *everybody* knew what it was. Then I started embracing it."

Ah, accept what you cannot change and make it work for you.

Brian's first benefit: "I think it definitely expanded my demographic. I skew younger than most figure skaters my age." Brian's *South Park* connection has kept the public eye aimed in his seemingly omniscient direction for years. Nevertheless, many *South Park* fans know little about him other than he skates—and presumably has "magical fire breath." Time to change that.

An alternate for the 1980 U.S. Olympic figure skating team, Brian finished fifth in the 1984 Winter Games in Sarajevo. The next year, he won the first of four consecutive U.S. National Championships. In the 1988 Winter Games in Calgary, he performed his signature tano lutz—as well as eight successful triple jumps—to win Olympic Gold.

An injured Brian Boitano fearlessly returned to the 1994 Olympic Games in Lillehammer and finished in sixth place. In 1996, Brian was inducted into both the World and the United States Figure Skating Hall of Fame. More recently, he capitalized on his culinary savvy, Olympic fame and *South Park* notoriety as the host of *What Would Brian Boitano Make?* on the Food Channel.

However, one can't help but wonder: what would Brian Boitano actually *do?* So I asked him:

Because we all face competition: *"A competitor is behaving in a disrespectful manner toward you. What do you do?"*
Brian: *"I would ignore him and let it strengthen my focus."*

For those who never settle for anything less than their best: *"You're guaranteed the Silver Medal, but the Gold is within reach. What do you do?"*
Brian: *"What I do doesn't change. My goal—as a person and as an athlete—is to do my best. Usually, you can kill two birds with one stone: if you do your best you're going to win."*

Because crisis management is a given: *"You're preparing a large meal, but you're missing one key ingredient. What do you do?"*
Brian: *"I'd figure out the best substitute. Usually the substitution doesn't change the dynamic that much."*

Since we all make important decisions: *"There's a difference in how we react—or what we DO—in different situations. What impacts your decision-making?"*

Brian: *"My decisions are gut reactions. No matter what else comes to mind, it usually comes back to what my gut reaction was."*

And now, the flip side: *"What would Brian Boitano NOT do? What irritates you?"*

Brian: *"Chaos. I don't like chaos at all. I like control. I like people doing the best job around me to help support my focus."*

Of course, that answer does not bode well for his chaos-imbued *South Park* doppelganger.

For those who feel they have read similar advice before, consider this: the journey from "reading" to "doing" comes with a level of difficulty higher than most poor souls can achieve. As a champion of the rink and the kitchen, no one does "do" better than Brian Boitano. Though he certainly skates (i.e. move on ice in a gliding fashion), he absolutely never skates (i.e. pass over or refer only fleetingly to a subject or problem).

In short, Brian is a doer *and* a thinker.

In their own mischievous ways, *South Park's* Stan, Cartman, Kyle, Kenny—and Brian—have reinforced the notion: No single person has all the answers. We must carefully consider the gifts and advice of those around us as part of our daily decision-making routine.

But more important, how does Brian Boitano do it? "Preparation is everything," he confirms. "Preparation gives you confidence. Whether it's confidence on the ice or in the kitchen."

And if appropriate preparation is not part of the mix, skater Brian and/or baker Brian can—simply put—fall flat on his face. As can we all.

"If I was prepared, I knew in my gut that I could do it," he says. "No matter what I'm doing, if I'm completely prepared, I feel like I'm on my game."

But think about it—did *South Park* get it wrong? Check out the lyrics from the first verse of "What Would Brian Boitano Do?":

What would Brian Boitano do
If he was here right now,
He'd make a plan
And he'd follow through,
That's what Brian Boitano'd do.

Sounds *exactly* like what Brian Boitano would do—and has done—with his enviable energy, skill and finesse.

Plus, let's face it, it never hurts to be animated.

Peter Berec

Jack McKinney

Though few would follow my lead if given the chance to chat with basketball great Earvin "Magic" Johnson, when it happened to me, I chose to deliberately throw myself under my own athletically-challenged bus:

"Well Mr. Johnson, at one time I thought I was pretty good at basketball. But in seventh grade, I was placed on the 'C' team—and I don't mean *third string* either." Obviously confused by the unexpected confession of my embarrassing lack of athletic prowess, Johnson clearly did not know how to respond.

Note to self: Uh oh, Magic Johnson thinks I'm a fool.

Undaunted, I continued, "So I'd like to thank you for picking up the mantle, having the career I *thought* I was meant to have, and allowing me to live vicariously through you." Magic chuckled—and it must be said, no one chuckles with more warmth than Magic Johnson.

Such was a day in the life of a tenderfoot business columnist—one intent on sharing lessons on success and professional development even if that requires the occasional personally awkward under-the-bus scenario to elicit more compelling responses.

The Magic Johnson interview was intended to support a column celebrating the career of Jack McKinney, former head coach of the Los Angeles Lakers and the Indiana Pacers. Jack also holds the honor of being Magic's first coach in the NBA.

Through the same affiliation, I also received a late-night return phone call from basketball great and Pacific-time-zone resident, Bill Walton. A pervasive hoops hero during my teen years, the dynamic and articulate basketball great did not disappoint. Not because he took a personal interest in my extremely limited free throw skills, but because he, like Magic, enthusiastically embraced the opportunity to celebrate the great work of his former leader.

Like so many of us, I have been subject to countless managerial claims of the importance of teamwork. Therefore, it seemed appropriate to speak to those who have experienced teamwork in its *original* athletic-team configuration.

A recent Google search of the words "business teamwork" returned more than 55,700,000 results.

It's one thing for business professionals to advocate working as a *team*— it's another to gain perspective from someone who has led a team in its more traditional format.

Inspired by his lifelong mentor, legendary coach Jack Ramsay, Jack McKinney would ultimately come to symbolize leadership *and* teamwork. In addition to being named NBA Coach of the Year in 1981, he is the recipient of two NBA Championship rings as a member of the coaching staffs of the Portland Trail Blazers (1977) and the Lakers (1980).

Compare the hardwood to the boardroom and you will discover an element of immediacy in sports that the business world typically can't emulate. After all, basketball is a face-to-face endeavor. However, with technology actively chipping away at one-to-one communication, a business email haphazardly forwarded without clear instruction is the basketball equivalent of a careless pass landing out of bounds.

No team can exist without decisive leadership, clear communication, defined expectations, respect and shared goals. Plus, according to Jack, "Teamwork has to have mental focus."

As a leader, Jack often proactively met with new team members on their home turf—a process enabling him to make his expectations clear while beginning to understand each player's unique needs. "I wanted to start in the right vein—'you are important to me and I am important to you,'" he explains.

Furthermore, he suggests his subsequent "open door" coaching style helped build players' confidence in his ability to lead.

Jack also endorses a positive environment enabling leaders to emerge from *within* his teams. According to Magic, "He was a master at practice— great leaders prepare their staffs to lead."

For his part, Bill Walton uses words such as "upbeat," "brilliant" and "genius" when describing his former coach. "He has all the qualities of the greatest of leaders in the world. Jack McKinney was kind and compassionate in an often unkind and brutal world."

In addition, Jack's proclivity for clear, measured speech tracks back to Jack Ramsay's early influence. In Magic's words, "He spoke slow—but firm and gentle at the same time. He had a feel for how to talk to everyone as an individual."

Jack McKinney's time-honored belief system is also a strong indication that successful teamwork produces great loyalty. More than thirty years later, Magic is living proof. "He was an amazing man and an amazing coach—and notice I said 'amazing man' first."

Walton adds, "Jack McKinney made me. How lucky am I that I got to play for Jack. I'm a better man for that. We are so privileged to have him in our world."

Above all, as a team leader and coach, Jack was present when it mattered the most. For all you managers keeping score, being "present" isn't the same as a text message.

As a Floridian, I have encountered countless retirees who understandably wonder if their work still mattered. Those who ask themselves: Does anybody remember me? Am I still relevant? What now?

As his work focused on the success of a *team*, Jack is not one of those people. Even his wife, Claire, recently told me: "We appreciate what we have rather than dwelling on what we lost."

That said, after this story ran, Jack seemed to have a little extra spring in his step. Whether he desired the recognition or not, he was reminded of his professional and personal impact. Jack McKinney mattered then; Jack McKinney matters now.

For the first time, I truly understood the importance of this process—the power of my published words. I experienced a sense of euphoria unlike any I had previously known. Yes, I may have authored the column, but Jack and Claire McKinney—and those who love and respect them—were the benefactors. Jack knew, without question, that his work was still valued. The winning spirit—the fire that defined his career—could never, and would never be extinguished.

What else could I possibly ask for than the opportunity to validate and celebrate another human being's life's work?

Nothing.

Margo Jurgensen

SONNY JURGENSEN

My father waited more than fifty years to have a meaningful conversation with his arts-obsessed son about football. Thanks to the time he spent preparing me for my interview with Hall of Fame Washington Redskins quarterback Jurgensen, he *finally* got it, too.

According to Merriam-Webster.com, a quarterback is defined as follows:

1. an offensive back in football who usually lines up behind the center, calls the signals, and directs the offensive play of the team
2. one who directs and leads

Allegedly, countless Americans perform this function from their "armchair" and/or on a "Monday morning." Still another subset claims to "quarterback" their business teams. Yes, the world has also attempted to apply gridiron lingo to the games people play in Corporate America. References to "game plan," "run with the ball" and "tackle a problem" run wild in the boardroom.

With respect to Merriam-Webster, corporate leaders and armchair quarterbacks everywhere, to understand how to "quarterback" a team, go to the source: *an actual quarterback.*

Hall of Famer Sonny Jurgensen ruled the National Football League for eighteen seasons as a member of the Philadelphia Eagles and Washington Redskins. A five-time Pro Bowl selection, Sonny enjoyed a remarkable career that included 2,433 pass completions for 32,224 yards and 255 touchdowns.

However, to set the quarterback-as-leader record straight, Sonny states: "When it's your job, quarterback is the toughest position. When it isn't your job, it's the easiest position to play." A comment that also gives new meaning to the importance of "walking a mile in another man's...cleats."

From a leadership perspective, Sonny explains: "The entire game goes through the quarterback. You have to do more work, as everything goes through you."

"Quarterbacking" = accepting unparalleled responsibility.

In 1969, Sonny Jurgensen found himself working under new Redskins head coach, the legendary Vince Lombardi. Their connection was established early due to Lombardi's ability to "lead by example" as well as his support: "Be yourself and we can make this work."

Later, when asked if he planned to (micromanage) Sonny's on-the-field decision-making, Lombardi responded: "If I haven't been able to convey to him what I want him to call by now, you should fire me."

For anyone wondering if the role of lifelong mentor requires a lifetime of interaction, Sonny would likely say no. Though Lombardi died from cancer in 1970, Sonny still speaks of him with absolute reverence and appreciation.

Then there's the infamous '70s-era "feud" between Sonny and "rival" Redskins quarterback Billy Kilmer—one that played out in the media and not on the field. "Billy and I knew it was going to take both of us to get the job done, and the team would benefit from our contrasting styles on the field." As proven by Jurgensen, Lombardi and Kilmer: in the game of life, respect, support and trust simply cannot be beat.

Again, some argue that Corporate America can never achieve the same level of teamwork as professional sports—the innate focus on human interaction and immediacy cannot be simulated in our technology-driven business world. This sense of immediacy also impacts accountability. Sonny explains, "You can't hide. It's all out there on the field for everyone to see."

On his success, Sonny once said: "I beat people by throwing, not running. I won't let them intimidate me into doing something that is not the best thing I can do."

When asked for advice for future quarterbacks as well as leaders, Jurgensen scores a highly philosophical touchdown: "Make sure everyone on your team is given the chance to play to their strengths."

Sounds like a (game) plan.

IN TRUTH, MY ROAD TO the Sonnyville was not a smooth one.

From 1984 to 2009, I lived just outside Sonny's adopted hometown of Washington, DC. Not only was he a highly celebrated local hero, but after his 1974 NFL retirement, he maintained a strong media presence as a football commentator on local and national television. Part of my goal for meeting Sonny was based on my *lack* of knowledge about his sport. If I wanted to learn, I had to force myself out of my editorial comfort zone and into the end zone of Sonny's somewhat unfamiliar career.

After all, for *any* of us to learn, we must aggressively pursue new interests and ideals.

However, our interview took place three months after originally scheduled. As is often the case with aging, bodies don't seem to always cooperate—even for those of us whose bodies literally provided the backbone of our careers.

Sonny's wife Margo called quite unexpectedly the night before the original interview date to inform me that Sonny had experienced some sort of health-related episode. No, I didn't ask for details, as I didn't need to know. This interview—*any interview*—would never be as important as caring *for* and caring *about* someone whose health had been compromised.

As the months passed, Margo—herself, effortlessly appealing—would update me via email with details about Sonny's ongoing improvement. Although I never asked to reschedule the interview, Margo wrote one day to ask if I was interested. My answer was a resounding YES.

Less than a week later, Sonny greeted me at the door of his Naples home. He had the same genuine smile I had seen countless times on TV, the same laid-back charm that had always served him so well. Did he move a bit slower? Yes. Did he carefully ponder each question before answering? Yes again. However, did he *attempt* to show me how to correctly hold a football and then smile politely as I fumbled from a sitting position? Yes, he did. Regardless of any previous health issues, Sonny Jurgensen was every bit the gridiron hero I ached to meet—I *needed* to meet.

> SHOWMEJONES.COM
>
> "Make sure everyone on your team is given the chance to play to their strengths."
>
> —Sonny Jurgensen

As we chatted, I respected his unrivalled expertise on his sport; he respected my sincere interest as an acceptable substitute for actual hands-on experience. In short, Sonny quickly became a member of my own personal Pro Bowl of interviewees.

Upon returning home, I found this unexpected email from Margo in my inbox:

Randy,

I am so appreciative of your gentleness with Sonny. He was not entirely his old self, but this experience was good enough to boost his self-confidence and let him know he could make himself understood and not stumble over his words. You don't know what a good thing you did today.

Margo

I sobbed. Not tears of sadness, but the emotional-surge-related blubbering that always manages to sneak up on you at the end of *It's a Wonderful Life*. You know, the waterworks that accompany the lump in your throat as Harry Bailey declares: "Here's to my big brother George, the richest man in town." Yes, *that* kind of cry.

Although part of the "power of the pen" *should be* to help others, I didn't feel as if I had done anything special. I was never a football fan per se, but Sonny was an idol to so many and deserved nothing less than my admiration—if not my "gentleness." Whatever he needed, I had an obligation to provide. In my mind, I was simply playing to my strengths, too.

But here I was, a self-described "artsy" kid from the Show Me State, a man who had never stepped foot on a football field, arguably a "nobody," yet I was somehow being credited with having a positive impact on the life of a Hall of Fame quarterback.

Touchdown!

My friend and new hero—the indomitable Sonny Jurgensen—returned to his TV gig on the Washington, DC-based *Redskins Report* the following season. Though entirely unexpected, meeting Sonny was a wildly profound example of the best possible outcome: *a win-win situation.*

EIGHT IS ENOUGH

Jo Ann Ward

I t was the business lunch from hell.

There I was, at a Naples Press Club luncheon, seated next to none other than Charles Gibson, the deeply admired former king of *Good Morning America*. I was speechless to the point of being borderline catatonic.

I had arguably logged in more Charlie Gibson-TV-viewing hours than his wife, Arlene, whom I have to believe occasionally felt as though she saw enough of her husband at home and may have secretly opted out of a hubby-hosted broadcast in favor of, for example, an *I Love Lucy* rerun, *Jeopardy!* or *Wheel of Fortune*.

If, by chance, you do not know who Charlie Gibson is, take whatever device you are using to read this and hit yourself on the head. Then Google him and afterwards, hit yourself again. Even if you are reading this on your precious new iPad, do it. Yes, the metals and sharp edges may hurt, but I'm fine with that because you should have known who he was without any help from me or from Google.

Charles deWolf "Charlie" Gibson is the former host of *Good Morning America* from 1987 to 1998, and 1999 to 2006, and anchor of *World News with Charles Gibson* from 2006 to 2009. During all of these time periods, ABC and Charles Gibson owned me as well as my potential consumer purchasing power if directed toward their commercial sponsors.

As I took my place at the packed head table at the aforementioned NPC luncheon, I found myself wedged between retired CBS News journalist Phil Jones (no relation) on my left and Gibson, my former journalistic addiction, on my right.

Okay, we've all been there. You're at a dining table in a public venue and you look down only to find *way too many* utensils, plates and glasses staring back at you. (Think Julia Roberts in *Pretty Woman*.) Yes, *it's terrifying*. Most of us wisely tend to limit our kitchenware usage at home. Even IHOP keeps cutlery to a minimum out of respect for befuddled patrons and dishwashing staff.

To exacerbate this situation, due to the popularity of both Gibson and Jones, our table, like any number of commercial airlines, was "oversold." If Gibson and I were any closer, I would have had to take up residence on his lap. Not to say that Phil Jones' opinion of me did not matter, but he already knew me. Call me naïve, but I had also convinced myself that Phil, approximately 2,004,500 other Joneses in the U.S. and I lived inside a figurative "Jones Zone" of unconditional support.

Business lunches are tricky at best. In what ultimately becomes a culinary ping pong game of attention vs. nutrition, you have to somehow balance "conversation" with "food consumption." You have to *ping* a witty question across the table, grab a quick bite and prepare to receive a conversational *pong* and start all over again. At best, you're likely to enjoy only the banter *or* the food. As I was far too nervous to say much to Gibson—and I was not the table's preferred "Jones"—I decided to focus my attention on enjoying the feast. At least I would *appear* to be functional.

Let me draw you a clearer picture: add the pressure of high-profile dinner companions to an already complicated scenario and even the most robust Emily Post etiquette training becomes a disjointed jumble in your head. To make matters worse, I was staring at *two* teas and *two* water glasses—each practically performing a mating ritual due to their overlapping juxtaposition. Finally, I thought to myself: "Fine. I *think* this is *my* tea and that is *his* water. I'm going for it."

Then it suddenly occurred to me: "What if Charlie Gibson is confused too?" After all, it's tough to tell where one place setting ends and another one begins. Plus, he's Charlie Gibson, he can pretty much eat *anything* on the table and NO ONE is going to stop him. If Charlie Gibson wants to nosh on butter pats, salad dressing and Sweet'N Low, he is certainly free to do so.

At this point, my head imploded:

What if I claim Charlie Gibson's coffee cup as my own?

What if I actually drink from Charlie Gibson's water glass?

What if I get salad residue stuck in my teeth or Thousand Island dressing on my face?

Wait! What if someone had the brilliant idea to serve an entrée with red sauce? (Food tends to enjoy my outsides as much as my insides. I think it's genetic.)

And the worst: Please God, don't let a meatball roll off my plate and onto Charlie Gibson's lap. What would I do? It's not like I can discreetly try to retrieve it.

Sadly, I finally realized that no one was going to come around and (quite literally) spoon feed me any cutting-edge solutions.

When all was said, done—*and eaten*—I am happy to report that, although I was not much of a conversationalist that day, I *survived* without a single meal malfunction, including a wayward meatball. How? I sat there, somewhat motionless, until Gibson and Jones staked a claim on their preferred tableware and beverages. Had I ultimately made a lunchtime faux pas, I'm pretty sure Charlie would have been a gentleman and resisted the urge to point out my bad behavior. I mean, isn't Charlie Gibson basically perfect?

As much of his discussion that day taught me about the importance of gaining trust, I ultimately *trusted* Charlie to forgive me if I made a distasteful banqueting boo boo. Yes, regardless of your companions, business lunches can be fraught with peril. However, by keeping a cool head, you can survive.

Eating a bit less is always better than eating crow.

FOOD IS MY ENEMY. I eat too much of it, I eat the wrong varieties of it and, perhaps more tragic, I am clueless in the kitchen—a fact that makes throwing a dinner party close to impossible.

Throughout their childhood, I candidly told my children: "*What* and *how* I have chosen to feed the two of you is just wrong. Please do not do this to your kids." You see, in my rather unique view, one moves from "food preparation" to "cooking" as soon as Mrs. Dash becomes part of the equation. So yes, if you choose to put Mrs. Dash Garlic & Herb salt-free seasoning on your Rice Krispies®, *you are cooking!*

But what if I could assemble a group of my interviewees for an intimate dinner party? What's the recipe for success at entertaining? Good food, good friends, good conversation? And in more ways than one: Snap, Crackle and Pop?

So I challenged myself to choose eight people for my *fantasy dining* experience. Thankfully, as this is an imaginary soiree, I don't have to actually FEED them. But a gathering of any sort is guaranteed to be more successful the more we know about those in attendance….

Judy Berman

JEFFREY HAYZLETT
THOUGHT LEADER

W hat is thought?
Ideas? Opinions? Instincts? A series of mental impulses that can morph, quite literally, into "headstrong" words? Scientists have been trying to define "thought" for as long as inquisitive brains have been around to explore it.

Although the actual thought *process* is up for debate, just look at the hodgepodge of individuals and groups whose singular mission is to tell us exactly what to think. In this grown-up, often detrimental version of Follow the Leader, many seem willing to accept the thoughts of others without the benefit of first thinking for themselves. Ironic, considering thought is such a highly personal process.

And the common elements between Follow the Leader/Kids and Follow the Leader/Adults? Immaturity, blind faith, a loss of individuality and the risk of being led headfirst into a wall. In truth, "taught thought" will never be as powerful as a personal, fact-based belief system. Of course, that takes (*gasp!*) time. Whatever will we do?

Thankfully, there is a much shorter list of folks whose goal is to lead us to think for ourselves, and Jeffrey Hayzlett is one of the nation's most distinguished thought leaders. A global business celebrity, speaker and bestselling author, Hayzlett is chairman of C-Suite Network, the world's most trusted group of C-suite leaders.

In addition to being an inspiration-filled, member-based think-tank for corporate executives, the C-Suite Network showcases on-demand business programming, inspirational written content, conferences, networking and business books for executives and highly motivated worker bees of all shapes and sizes.

Hayzlett has been cited in *Forbes, SUCCESS,* Mashable, *Marketing Week* and *Chief Executive.* He also shares his executive insight and commentary on Bloomberg, MSNBC, Fox Business and C-Suite TV, and has appeared as a guest celebrity judge on NBC's *Celebrity Apprentice.*

Jeffrey Hayzlett is "thought provoking" in its purest, most literal form.

If thought reveals our inner desires, then thought-leader Hayzlett introduces us to our inner selves: our character, potential, inspirations and aspirations. Nonetheless, much of his success tracks back to his willingness to be led by—and subsequently celebrate—a variety of great minds.

"I don't know what I don't know. I want to walk around in a constant state of awareness," explains Hayzlett. "The best people in business are the most inquisitive."

From my experience, most interviewees reveal their primary platforms early in a discussion; however, Jeffrey Hayzlett takes you into his world, layer by layer, thought by thought. In person, he strikes an impressive balance between speaking and listening. Regardless of the platform, Hayzlett initiates thought based on his discovery of the intellectual holes that need to be filled.

One issue: "I think a lot of people in leadership roles don't always ask introspective questions."

In other words, you can't truly understand what's happening around you unless you first evaluate what's happening within you. Through his C-Suite Network, Hayzlett wants to change our collective lack of self-awareness— just as he warns of the pitfalls associated with change itself: "You have to adapt to change or you die."

As for specific advantages to thought, Hayzlett adds: "It's amazing the number of executives I know who are dyslexic." In fact, their condition forces them to pay stricter attention and think with greater veracity—a successful dyslexic person never takes the receipt of information for granted.

When it comes to human nature, Hayzlett is a realist: "A 'thought leader' is someone who has haters; a thought leader is someone who has people who are inspired. You can't be a thought leader without having haters—you have to cause tension."

Though sometimes used to avoid inner turmoil, the old standby, "things happen for a reason," must never be allowed to evolve into an impetuous excuse for inactivity. Hayzlett's spin: "Yes, things always happen for a reason, but they may not always be the reason you want. We don't always see the reason forthright. What's good about having things happen to you—or *for* you—is it forces you to take action."

He also suggests: "In business, things happen, and we either have to positively or negatively respond to them. That's a good thing." And our most important decision-making tool in this scenario? You guessed it: thought. Better yet: informed thought.

Jeffrey Hayzlett is also a business maverick, a loud and proud nonconformist: "I hate anyone telling me we can't do things. They tell me 'these are the rules.' There are no rules. It always comes down to what should be your own driving conditions of satisfaction: What you want to drive out of life and out of business."

SHOWMEJONES.COM

"I don't know what I don't know. I want to walk around in a constant state of awareness. The best people in business are the most inquisitive."

—Jeffrey Hayzlett

If, like me, you've never really thought much about "thought" before, that's fine. And just because you claim to have an open mind doesn't necessarily mean your cerebral cortex isn't running on empty. If someone yells in your ear and hears an echo, that's not a good sign.

Perhaps today's biggest mistake would be to take this Hayzlett/Jones mash-up for granted—to quickly sift through with only a single, frivolous takeaway: Well, this Randall Kenneth Jones certainly likes this Jeffrey Hayzlett. True, but not our point.

Simply stated, Jeffrey Hayzlett wants to give you the tools necessary to think for yourself and—in turn—lead others in both thought and action.

Bearing in mind that our jobs provide our income and our livelihood: Prior to right now, when was the last time you invested in yourself and, for example, read a book on professional development? Now, when was the last time you shared a "funny cat video" or some such fodder on social media? I follow Hayzlett religiously on social media, and though he is quite entertaining, I have yet to see an amusing feline take center stage.

Jeffrey Hayzlett invites you to his platform with the sole purpose of helping you define—or redefine—your own manifesto. The good news: It's impossible to explore Hayzlettland and not become immersed in thought.

In truth, you don't have to think very hard to figure out what Jeffrey Hayzlett is selling: he's selling *you* to *you*. Nevertheless, your willingness to buy into his rhetoric—or the thoughts of the C-Suite Network's impressive list of influencers—likely has a direct correlation to your ability to buy into yourself. And if you can't uphold your own unique belief system, you're going to be hard pressed to sell yourself to anyone else.

Let's give that some thought now, shall we?

Reason for dinner invitation: *If you have to ask, then you've not really taken any time to* think *about it.*

SUZI WEINERT
MYSTERY WRITER

Just a few years ago, former "military brat," current military wife, mother, grandmother, and great-grandmother Suzi Weinert found herself rebranded—yet again. Suzi was no longer known just as "the general's wife." In fact, retired Brigadier General Don Weinert has increasingly become known as "the author's husband."

With the publication of her first three books: *Garage Sale Stalker, Garage Sale Diamonds* and *Garage Sale Riddle*, Suzi Weinert put an end to the *mystery* of success after seventy.

Born in Detroit in 1935, Suzi made the first of ten childhood moves just three weeks later. Her father, Wilford Maschmeyer, a colonel in the U.S. Air Force, fought in World War II and died in 1953 while on active duty. In 1957, Suzi Maschmeyer married West Point graduate Don Weinert. Over the course of his career, she successfully navigated her husband and five children through eleven military moves—eventually landing in McLean, Virginia, for a record twenty-five-year stint.

"Moving so many times creates a daunting drag to some, but an opportunity for stimulation and growth to others," she says. Suzi's resultant skills: curiosity, fortitude and a careful balance of flexibility and stability.

Due to the "unload and reload" reality for our nomadic military families,

Suzi Weinert often turned to military thrift shops, a practice that matched her infatuation with another bastion of American consumerism: garage sales. However, having so often seen her personal memories sell for between fifty cents and $5, she understood something many of us have overlooked: "Every garage sale has a story. People die but their things continue to circulate."

Garage sales also tell a story about the people involved: the books read, the items collected, the music enjoyed. To Suzi: "It's really quite revealing."

In fact, her literary heroine—thrifty, crime-solving sleuth Jennifer Shannon—is no different from any number of moms. "Logic and intuition are an important part of the problem-solving tool kit," she says. The same should be said of all successful business people. Not surprising, like Suzi's, Jennifer Shannon's skills include: curiosity, fortitude and a careful balance of flexibility and stability.

> ## SHOWMEJONES.COM
> "Every garage sale has a story. People die but their things continue to circulate."
>
> —Suzi Weinert

Thanks to Hallmark Movies and Mysteries Channel, Suzi Weinert's cunning characters jumped effortlessly from page to screen in 2013. The first film adaptation, *Garage Sale Mystery*, starred Lori Loughlin (*Full House*) and attracted millions of viewers. The movie was so popular that Hallmark launched an ongoing series of Garage Sale Mystery movies based on Weinert's original concept.

Though Producer Jonathan Axelrod describes the original manuscripts as "too violent for Hallmark," he found Weinert's premise enormously engaging and the subsequent burst of Garage Sale moviemaking reflects her well-crafted characters. As Axelrod puts it: "The books are the foundation and we're the builders."

Peter DeLuise, who has directed every film installment thus far, recalls the excitement and responsibility of the author's first visit to the set: "I really wanted her to see that we respected her original characters."

DeLuise, the son of legendary actor Dom DeLuise, has his own scavenger-hunt back story. The proud son of a "trash man," Dom DeLuise would regularly load his young family into the car to comb through the neighborhood's curbed refuse—albeit, a very nontraditional family activity in tony Pacific Palisades, California. Even Young DeLuise's catcher's mitt was purchased at a garage sale for fifty cents. "Had we found a first-baseman's mitt, I guess I would have played first base," quips DeLuise.

DeLuise's experience represents more proof to the widespread theory: "One man's trash is another man's treasure." A concept that works in any number of professional settings—and one that Weinert has literally taken to the bank.

Though DeLuise cleverly asserts: "When Jennifer Shannon shows up, people are going to die," Suzi's Jennifer Shannon is alive and well and flourishing at Hallmark. As for Producer Alexrod's spin on the series creator: "I just wish Suzi had started writing earlier—she has a God-given talent."

So what's the secret to Suzi Weinert's Second Act unexpected success? Though not consciously trying to be the guardian of geriatric achievement, she simply keeps moving. It's second nature to her. Just like her intuitive heroine Jennifer Shannon, Suzi has also learned the following important lesson: regardless of your age, *it won't kill you* to just follow your instincts.

Reason for dinner invitation: *As Suzi is very attentive, she makes a great addition to any guest list. Then again, if she gets bored, she can just lose herself in her mystery-writer mind and quietly concoct clever ways to knock off everyone in attendance—likely starting with me because I served Rice Krispies Treats® as an appetizer.*

VICKI GUNVALSON
REAL HOUSEWIFE

Just look at the hodgepodge of viewpoints expressed on social media and you quickly realize that opinions rule the world. Then, ask around and you'll likely discover that most people understand the perverse power of perception; that is, until their own belief systems are called into question.

What starts as *perception* can whiz down a path to *reality* and *fact* faster than a two-armed and dangerous Real Housewife can flip a table on her dinner guests. And few understand the nuances separating perception and reality better than *The Real Housewives of Orange County's* Vicki Gunvalson.

Gunvalson joined the first incarnation of Bravo TV's (then) new reality show in 2005. Since then, she has survived more woebegone weekend getaways and doomed dinner parties than any other woman in the (now) massive franchise. To producers, nothing seems to be off-limits. For example, her much disparaged former boyfriend's alleged cancer diagnosis and her beloved mother's passing have generated major plot lines. Her primary business has not always fared so well.

For those who maintain reality TV is scripted, Vicki says: "We don't have a script. However, in real life if you told me you had cancer am I going to say 'prove it to me'? That's not reality. Nobody would say that if there weren't cameras on." Then again, don't most of us behave differently when we know we're being watched?

In person, Vicki is a realist—a mother, grandmother, successful business owner and reality TV star who proved to be more willing than most to throw herself in front of an oncoming Jimmy Choo-Choo train. She candidly admits she sometimes makes an "ass" out of herself in front of the camera. "I'm a lot of things but I'm not a liar," she explains. "Do I fabricate the truth sometimes because I want people to feel sorry for me? Yes—*we all do.*"

She then addresses the topic at hand: "The reality is I'm typically very calm and quiet and reserved—the perception is I'm screaming and yelling at people; I'm in their face. I'm not that person. However, you push the wrong button too many times and 'she' is going to come out." And "she" has—much to the delight and/or dismay of the millions of viewers of the highly lucrative franchise.

Born in 1962 just outside Chicago, Vicki is one of five children. Her father owned a large construction company and her mother was the epitome of the original definition of a real "housewife"—and deserving of all the respect that word should generate. Vicki learned her work ethic at home: "My father really took me under his wing. I was twelve years old and I was in his office balancing ledgers and doing accounts payable and receivable. I'm Middle America. I'm not from a doctor/lawyer family. I don't know that life. I know: 'work hard and you'll reap the rewards.'"

Vicki Gunvalson began her career in the insurance industry in Chicago and opened a home-based agency when she moved to California in 2001. Since then, Coto Insurance and Financial Services has experienced exceptional growth with Gunvalson regularly acknowledged as an industry Top Producer. "My typical client is over age fifty-five and getting ready to retire," she explains. "We have three phases of life: accumulation, preservation and distribution. I work in those last two phases. I make sure they preserve what they worked so hard for and distribute it over their lifetime."

The question is: How do perception and reality co-exist when crossing workplace platforms?

"The disadvantage of doing a reality show is my clients sometimes say: 'Are you serious about this business—being my adviser, my insurance agent—or are you more serious about TV drama?' Of course, my family and my business are my core." On the flip side: "A lot of clients come to me knowing I am the businesswoman in the group."

Then there's editing. Much of Vicki's assumed "reality" lands in the hands of Bravo's producers and editors. That's their business model.

"We are asked to give our opinions on the show," she says. "If you're not opinionated, you're *off* the show." And isn't reality TV the ultimate commercial beneficiary of perception vs. reality? A pop-culture phenomenon driven by the ability of executives and consumers to pick and choose?

In reality, *don't we all edit?*

For example, those who only *read* my work will mentally "edit" my character based solely on the written word. Hopefully, this edit outlines me as a slightly whacky, fair-minded essayist who mourns the disintegration of common sense yet celebrates positive communication and creative thinking.

My business associates in the marketing, PR, editorial and public speaking worlds are left with an enhanced "edit" based on sound bites, experiences and memories of our interactions. My millennial children have assembled a much more complicated love/hate "edit" of life with father. And perhaps it is best we simply not discuss the observations running amok in the mysterious mind of my ex-wife—bless her heart.

> ## SHOWMEJONES.COM
> "In the battle of perception vs. reality the winner is always choice—the opportunity to form opinions based on reality, a factual response, or perception, an emotional response."
>
> —Randall Kenneth Jones

Likewise, don't business leaders invest heavily in crafting marketing and PR messages to showcase the storylines that provide the most benefit? No matter what the format—media, workplace, politics, reality TV or everyday life—each individual sees what he chooses and "edits" accordingly. The result: Our cerebral cutting-room floors are littered with lost insight, forgotten facts and shocking revelations—about ourselves and those who cross our paths.

Vicki adds: "When I die, my children and my friends will say 'she had a wild ride. She knew how to have fun. She knew how to work hard. She never had to depend on anyone else.' That's my legacy: I'm a self-made woman. I don't need a man to take care of me."

Yes, Vicki Gunvalson and I believe we can learn from *everyone* we meet—a philosophy you can accept or reject, but that's our story and we're sticking to it. However, in the battle of perception vs. reality the winner is always *choice*—the opportunity to form opinions based on reality, a factual response, or perception, an emotional response.

Gunvalson's truth: "I balance life and work as best as I can. I'm not 100 percent successful at it. I'm stressed out all the time, but I don't know anything different."

When I watch any edition of *Real Housewives*, I am prepared to applaud the positives—of which there are many—and roll my eyes at the behavioral faux pas of an often silver-spoon-fed collection of cast mates. Essentially, I understand I'm watching *television*.

After this column was published, Vicki tweeted it to her 600,000-plus followers. As my Twitter handle was *included* in her tweet, I also received feedback from her followers—in theory, her *supporters*. Ah, but the *haters* came out in full force, too. And it seemed like some of them had a *personal* vendetta. Though I'm not sure if there are official stages for acceptance of *hate*, I quickly moved through periods of shock, anger and dismay. I even briefly considered tweeting this oxymoronically-laced response: Thank you for placing your feedback in a public forum. I can now publish it and offer the world a peek into your true character.

True, the hot-blooded hater population helps fuel reality TV's financial fire, but in this case, hater after hater *proved my point*—a fact I suspect left the more intellectually enlightened followers giggling behind the scenes. The *edit*-loving hater population's *perception* did indeed whizz down a path to *reality* and *fact* without even the slightest sign of remorse. Plus, to a hater, reading actual attached content is apparently optional.

The emotion I ultimately landed on was pity. Yes, I have most certainly judged others unfairly and, no doubt, will do it again; however, when any of us deflects our personal boredom and self-loathing onto total strangers—whether they are in the public eye or not—it's a clear indication of the *real* target of the hate: ourselves.

Kinda gives "Get a Life" a brand new meaning, huh?

Reason for dinner invitation: *There's no such thing as a dinner party involving members of Bravo's* Real Housewives *franchise that doesn't include unexpected twists and turns. Vicki will keep things interesting!*

SHOWMEJONES.COM

"If you don't ask, you don't get."

—Michael Feuer

MICHAEL FEUER
SERIAL ENTREPRENEUR

Michael Feuer wants to look you in the eye. A man who demands accountability, Feuer eschews the concept of using texts and email as technological hiding places. If you have something important to tell him, look him in the eye and say it. Whether the goal is to brainstorm or to confess, to Feuer, nothing will ever replace the revealing benefits of one-to-one communication.

Feuer is a passionate combination of confidence, focus, and candor juxtaposed against equally potent character traits spotlighting his wit and self-deprecating manner—a man who takes himself very seriously yet not too seriously. But mostly, Michael Feuer elevates the concept of "what you see is what you get" to genius level.

These combined qualities enabled the OfficeMax co-founder and its sixteen-year CEO to take a single store and a personal investment of only $20,000—plus unimaginable tenacity—and transform the retailer into 1,000 stores worldwide with annual sales of approximately $5 billion.

Though few can argue the benefits of openness and honesty, in his books, *The Benevolent Dictator* and *Tips from the Top,* Michael Feuer provides much more than just a peek under the hood. His accounts are ultimately a time-honored how-to guide: how to build and grow a business; how to negotiate your way through Corporate America; and for those who want an inside track, how to deal effectively with Michael Feuer—who, himself, is an open book.

According to Fred Koury, president and CEO of Smart Business Network and publisher of Feuer's national magazine column, "He doesn't expect anything from you he doesn't expect from himself." Fearless Feuer adds: "If you are guarded, you can't tell people what they need to hear and I always insist on a free flow of information."

With his heightened understanding of the importance of personal *and* business branding, Michael suggests, "Build your own brand and credibility, because you've got to get people to follow you. Position yourself *or* your competitors will do it for you."

Without question, the way we view ourselves directly influences the way we are viewed by others—the same "others" who ultimately affect our success or failure. Chief among Feuer's principles: "If I tell you I'm going to do something, I do it." Koury interjects: "He is not 'theoretical.' Everything he says and does is based on experience."

SHOWMEJONES.COM

"Sadly, it often seems that, if you can't put out someone's fire today—and address an immediate need—they won't give you time to get them fired up about tomorrow."

—Randall Kenneth Jones

In the oft-described "dog-eat-dog" business world—one suffused with competition, intense negotiations, and veiled deception—Michael offers simple yet optimistic advice for those who wish to celebrate at the end of a hard-fought battle: "Success is the greatest revenge."

Lucky for me, my Michael-Feuer-inspired *takeaways* didn't end with our first meeting, *or* the publication of my initial column.

Tip: That's why we call them takeaways, *we are actually supposed to* **take** *inspired ideas* **away** *and* **think** *about them, not dismiss them as we race to our* **smart***phones to check on the latest infusion of alleged intelligence from the Twittersphere.*

Though Michael is not the first to make the following observation, he was the first to *emotionally* position its potential in a way that forced me to take serious note: "If you don't ask, you don't get." This phrase subsequently became my newfound mantra, in part because there was a time when many of us didn't always *need* to ask. Especially those like me whose careers were defined by building personal relationships.

Just try to build a personal relationship today with a voicemail, a text message, a tweet or a string of thought-crushing emails.

True, most of us work *faster* now than in bygone decades; however, we sometimes lose sight of *work fast's* required companion: *work smart*. Yet there was a time when *time* allowed for a greater exploration of mutual benefit. For example, let's look at old-school networking: You meet, you find common ground, you discover a connection, and *you take the time to consider one another's full potential*—not just what Person X or Y can offer the here and now.

Sadly, it often seems that, if you can't put out someone's *fire* today—and address an immediate need—they won't give you time to get them *fired up* about tomorrow.

Almost immediately following our first meeting, Michael Feuer adopted a more active role as one of my most-trusted mentors. Ironically, I didn't *ask* for help, he graciously *offered* to advise me on building my platform. It's safe to say, this book would likely not be in your hands today without his generous advice.

Though Michael is aware of his reputation as a tough businessman, with a corporate landscape sometimes characterized by *thoughtless* thinkers, half-truths and hidden agendas, he has bamboozled the competition through his unbridled passion for active, ongoing, truth-seeking, inspirational, no-holds-barred thought.

Yep, that's what we in the industry call: *something to think about.*

Reason for dinner invitation: *As far as food, it will be fun to see what he ASKS for because chances are good he won't get it. If he were a "cereal" entrepreneur, not a serial entrepreneur, he'd likely end up happier.*

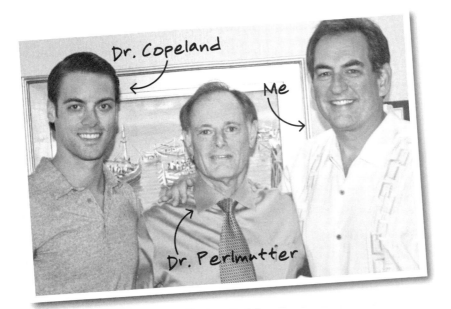

Dr. David Perlmutter
Gut Truster

The "gut" has gotten a lot of attention over the years. For example, we know it's possible to "spill our guts" and "bust a gut." We have also learned to embrace our "gut feelings" and/or "gut reactions." Plus, for some of the more juvenile thinkers among us, we have even been known to "hate someone's guts."

However, after I met with acclaimed neurologist, No. 1 *New York Times* bestselling author Dr. David Perlmutter, I came to another possible conclusion: failing to care for our gut could result in our gut metaphorically hating us right back.

Perlmutter is the celebrated author of *Grain Brain: The Surprising Truth About Wheat, Carbs, and Sugar—Your Brain's Silent Killers.* Having spent dozens of weeks on the *New York Times* Bestseller list, *Grain Brain* has enjoyed multiple printings and is published in more than twenty countries. His revolutionary *Grain Brain* assessment: "Carbs are destroying our brain—not just unhealthy carbs but even healthy ones such as whole grains can cause dementia, ADHD, anxiety, chronic headaches, depression, and much more."

A board-certified neurologist and Fellow of the American College of Nutrition, Perlmutter has been a frequent lecturer at such prestigious medical institutions as Columbia University, Scripps Institute, New York University and Harvard University. His high-profile work has led to appearances on *20/20, Larry King Live,* CNN, Fox News, *Fox and Friends, The Today Show, Oprah, The CBS Early Show* and *The Dr. Oz Show.*

To Dr. David Perlmutter, "gut" matters—in more ways than one. After all, countless medical professionals and business people have credited the careful balance of skill, experience, vision and "gut" with their ability to succeed.

"The gut has now been called the body's 'second brain' as it has such a profound effect on mood and cognition as was recently revealed in *Scientific American,*" says Perlmutter, "When it comes to decision-making, there's a lot of science behind the idea of following your gut feelings."

SHOWMEJONES.COM

"If success is truly a combination of data and instinct, then learning when and how to 'trust your gut' is critically important. Nevertheless, none of this matters if your gut can't trust you back."

—Randall Kenneth Jones

In his work as a neurologist and his actions as a business professional, Perlmutter has no problem *going against the grain* and challenging traditional beliefs: "Clearly, I had a sense to move on to other things. I have never been satisfied with status quo."

It could be said his gut reaction to a profession seemingly focused on *treating symptoms* resulted in the science explored in *Grain Brain* and Perlmutter's subsequent similarly themed titles. According to Perlmutter: "Medicine is reactive and puts out the fire. I say bring in the fire marshal ahead of time to make sure the outlets aren't going to explode."

Grain Brain is simply one example of Perlmutter's gutsy "fire marshal" attitude at work.

Clearly, gut trusting and "what if" thinking enjoy a mutually beneficial relationship. Consider the business columnist who proactively engaged a medical expert, Perlmutter-aficionado Dr. Cade Copeland, as a credibility-enhancing interview companion. Why? It wasn't a "what if," it was a foregone conclusion that Perlmutter would speak about bodily functions I did not understand, so I wisely chose to take along knowledgeable backup.

And Copeland's reaction: "I've always said we should pay more attention to our health future than our history. Dr. Perlmutter's pioneering voice—connecting cutting-edge research and real-life results—is ultimately changing lives and the system we know today."

If success is truly a combination of data and instinct, then learning when and how to "trust your gut" is critically important. Nevertheless, none of this matters if your gut can't trust you back.

Reason for dinner invitation: *This is my interpretation of living dangerously. When I first met Dr. Perlmutter I candidly explained: "If your book was made into a movie, it would be a horror film in my house." In theory, his inclusion on this guest list should force me to up my culinary game—or die trying.*

GARY ROSEN *PUBLICIST &*
CRISIS MANAGEMENT PROFESSIONAL

When twelve-year-old Gary Rosen approached the front door of 1000 North Roxbury Drive in Beverly Hills, despite the lack of a formal invitation from its residents, he was exhilarated at the prospect of meeting his TV idol. Though the door was never opened, a voice from inside shared the unfortunate news: Lucille Ball was not at home.

Disappointment aside, young Gary managed to recognize the milestone reached that day: he had the courage to try.

Gary Rosen's determination—coupled with his learned ability to topple closed doors—ultimately took him from Rockland County, New York, to president of his own public relations firm, Gary Rosen Communications.

A youngster with an unrelenting focus on a career in television, Rosen graduated from Fordham University. By age twenty-four, the self-described "walking *TV Guide*" of television trivia was living his dream as a writer for *TV Guide* itself. A handful of editorial and agency doors later, Rosen embraced the risk and opened his own PR firm.

As a publicist for more than twenty television programs throughout his career, Gary specializes in nationally syndicated talk, court and magazine shows. Additionally, his expertise in crisis management has proved to be highly beneficial to several major corporations. His industry cred is also responsible for landing him commentator spots on national media outlets such as Fox News, CNN, E! and HLN. Noteworthy clients include the iconic Judge Judith Sheindlin and the Sheindlin-created *Hot Bench*.

"I don't think of myself as just a publicist. I'm a strategist with the mentality of a reporter and a clear understanding of what a reporter wants to hear," he says. Essentially, as Rosen has walked the walk, he knows exactly how to talk the talk.

Just as his once benign attempt to ambush Lucille Ball prophesied, Gary remains an advocate for a "no risk, no reward" professional lifestyle. "Most successful people in the world are risk takers. They understand they have to set themselves apart."

On the importance of originality, Gary points to the legendary Joan Rivers—whom he first met backstage when he was fifteen years old. "Joan invented the concept of reinventing yourself. Her passing was so impactful because she was in a league of her own. She was a true survivor."

"Survivor" is also a word Gary attributes to his mother, Bess. He credits her with instilling the qualities that guided his professional footsteps. "She raised three children alone, worked seven days a week, and taught me her work ethic and the value of a dollar. She was like the 'Martin' to my 'Lewis' and vice versa."

In fact, peek at his professional dance card and you'll quickly see that Rosen is professionally attracted to "women who don't embrace the status quo." Think: Judge Judy Sheindlin, Joan Rivers, Lucille Ball and, of course, his mother, Bess Rosenstock. He also celebrates the importance of diversity and passion: "I have friends ranging from servers to celebrities, from retail employees to multimillionaires, from twenty-one to eighty-five years old. I don't care what you do—just be passionate and you'll never be bored and you'll always be interesting."

Nevertheless, for Gary Rosen, it's not just about taking risks but enjoying the risk taking. Once again, he salutes his mother: "There was nothing in my childhood that was 'cookie cutter'—professionally, I took that concept and ran with it."

Celebrate passion. Seize the risk. Set yourself apart and—no matter what it takes—get the doors opened.

As for you C-suiters who keep your tangible and technological doors shut tight, be careful. One day, a creative-thinking Gary-Rosen type is going to knock on your door. Listen up—and open it.

Reason for invitation: *Do I really have to explain the benefit to having a crisis management expert on this guest list?*

Peggy Post

HELOISE
COLUMNIST & CLEAN FREAK

Dear Me:

I recently accepted the daunting task of writing a column on one of the most famous columnists of all time: the ever-helpful, hygienic and habitually hands-on Heloise.

"Hints from Heloise" runs seven days a week in more than 500 newspapers in the United States and internationally. Additionally, Heloise is a longtime contributing editor and monthly columnist for Good Housekeeping *and has appeared on countless radio and television programs.*

As Heloise has reached the pinnacle of success in our field, I'm feeling a bit intimidated. Plus, she stands for cleanliness and I'm not exactly a tidy guy.

My dilemma: How do I pull off this column without Heloise wanting to clean my clock?

Sincerely,
Immaculate Exception

Dear ImEx:

Well, you sound a lot like me. In fact, we could be one and the same. *Okay, we are the same person; however, once I literally adopted Heloise's literary format and* **wrote to me for help***, I gained a new level of clarity I didn't anticipate—and I responded in kind.*

To begin, Heloise is never going to clean anyone's clock—she'd never resort to fisticuffs. That said, she knows how to get blood stains out of practically anything.

Simply follow Heloise's lead. As her "hints" are often the result of readers' queries, just anticipate the questions that your audience would want to have answered. Come to think of it, this advice applies to virtually any type of effective written or verbal communication.

Having recently spent several hours with Her Royal Spotlessness—both on the phone and at a book signing at Jennifer's Boutique in Fort Myers—I suggest the following "hints" to maximize your column's impact.

1. **Include her full name.**

    Ponce Kiah Marchelle Heloise Cruse Evans. At a minimum, your reader will better understand why a single moniker makes more sense.

2. **Explain the difference between Heloise—the mother—and Heloise—the daughter.**

    When Heloise Bowles Cruse, the original "Heloise," had the idea to write a newspaper column for "housewives," she approached her local newspaper in Honolulu and offered to work for free for thirty days if they would take a chance on the concept. "The Readers' Exchange" subsequently launched in 1959.

    In 1961, King Features Syndicate convinced Heloise to syndicate her column with a new title, "Hints from Heloise." By 1962, the column was running in 158 newspapers. By 1964, it appeared in 593 newspapers in America and abroad. The irony? By appealing to women, Heloise, now a publishing giant, became a dominant force in the "man's world" of the '60s and '70s.

    Daughter Heloise began working for her mother three years before the elder Heloise passed away in 1977. Though daughter Heloise lightheartedly describes her boss/mother as "straight out of the movie, *The Devil Wears Prada*," she eventually understood her mother's seemingly Machiavellian motivations. When daughter Heloise officially took over her mother's column, she was prepared.

    "I was raised in a 'Heloise' household," she says. Good thing, too. She has gracefully nurtured the beloved Heloise brand—and honored her mother's memory—for almost forty years.

3. Discuss her role models.

As so much has already been written about her mother, talk about her father. Though Marshal (Mike) Holman Cruse chose to take a backseat to the mother/daughter Heloise fanfare, Heloise is quick to tout his importance: "There would not be a 'Heloise' without my father. If he had not encouraged my mother, she never would have done it."

The benevolent Cruse would also steadfastly support his daughter's work for the remainder of his life.

4. Don't list any specific cleaning or organizational hints.

Heloise has already written several books on these subjects—let your reader buy them. Rather than obsessing over her potential to "clean your clock," focus on what makes her tick.

My first telephone conversation with Heloise lasted two hours—and that was simply to schedule an appointment. Why so long? Heloise is a hoot—she guides you from polishing silver to rollicking laughter in an instant. Furthermore, she lives in Texas—a state that understands what "a hoot" means.

5. Provide observations as to how she interacts with others.

It's critical for all business people to understand that the end-users of their products and services are very human, human beings. When Heloise comes face-to-face with her consumers, she shines brighter than vinegar-and-water-treated window glass. For example, at her book signing, she did much more than meet, greet, sign, repeat—she assumed the role of perpetual host. The four-hour event evolved into an anecdotal stand-up routine—one that played out in front of a rotating collection of euphoric neatniks.

Here are a few of my favorite bon mots from the day. Whether they are original to Heloise or repeated from other sources doesn't matter: it's all about her animated, spot-on delivery.

On her mother: *"We never called her 'mommy,' it reminded her of 'mummy.'"*

To techies: *"When I ask you what time it is, don't tell me how to make a watch."*

To picky eaters: *"You can be a vegetarian and still eat crap."*

To Corporate America: *"A camel started out as a horse that 'went to committee.'"*

Finally, to men in general: *"Housework is genderless."*

Heloise is universal. We all have something to clean: a house, a car, or even those proverbial cobwebs in the brain. *I'd like to think this book's hints help with the latter.*

In truth, Heloise's enduring success is not due to her knowledge of household cleaning and organization; it's a reflection of her genuine connection with—and respect for—the people tasked with those duties. Her process? "I am observant. I enjoy watching people," says Heloise. "I craft my column based on what I observe." The people actually drive the column, *and* the reverse.

ShowMeJones.com

"Housework is genderless."

—Heloise

Just as her content is meant to assist folks to care for their most personal possessions, Heloise is at her best when it gets personal—when she's in the presence of her beneficiaries. Even working alone at a computer, Heloise is emotionally tethered to her fans. Regardless of the forum, Heloise engages her audience by speaking to them—not about them. Her true talent is compassion—an act no one can accomplish with just a broom and a mop.

At the end of the day, Heloise and I overheard this comment: "She treats everyone as if they are her best friend." She quickly turned around and declared: "But they are!"

For Heloise, a friend in need is, quite literally, a friend in deed(s).

Reason for dinner invitation: This was a no-brainer. Let's say Vicki Gunvalson gets in a brawl with, for example, Jeffrey Hayzlett. (I can dream, can't I?) Heloise can clean up anything.

Derek Call Wakefield

Santa Claus
Worldwide Media Mogul

S anta Claus is coming to town—or, in this case, to dinner.
Plus, after decades in the global marketplace, the man knows more about maintaining a successful commercial enterprise than an industrial stocking full of Gates, Buffett, Bezos and Apple's seemingly omniscient "Siri."

Claus' impact can be found everywhere—and his business practices are substantiated by virtually every inspirational message we do-gooder business writers can dish up. As my friend Melissa Cunningham Phillips so cleverly noted: "I have never met a manager who doesn't keep some sort of list of who's 'naughty' and who's 'nice.'"

And just as dinner companion Michael Feuer wisely advised professional *adults*, "If you don't ask, you don't get," millions of *children*—quite ironically—have *no problem* asking Claus for exactly what they want each year.

When it comes to best practices, the staff at Claus Inc. have amassed—or Christ-massed—so much experience that "practice" has literally become "perfect." Let's face it: Claus is the undisputed king of the memorable customer experience. As for celebrating jolly old Saint Nick's powerhouse brand and enduring business model, my friends and I have a lot to say:

On regulatory compliance
"Santa's security status is classified, but it is fair to assume his annual mission is a complex global exercise that requires meticulous coordination with multiple intelligence, security and transportation agencies. He has never failed—a performance standard that is unmatched by any other aviator. And to think he pulls it off with reindeer."
—Bob Orr, Aviation and Homeland Security Correspondent, CBS News, retired

On risk management
"Santa has always had a big tolerance for risk. He continues his work—unfazed by potential chimney defects (all chimneys are not created equal, yet Santa assumes they are)—and remains willing to assume any potential downside rather than passing it onto consumers. This is a good counterbalance to the risk adversity of the elves. Their cautiousness can slow down Santa's distribution channels, yet they remain a positive aspect on the manufacturing process."

—Tanya Acker, judge, *Hot Bench*

On logistics
"Santa's North Pole HQ is centrally located—enabling him to reach North America, Europe and Asia with greater efficiency. Claus also reaches more customers on December 25th than UPS, FedEx and the USPS combined. He's a logistics genius."
—Craig Bouchard, *New York Times* bestselling author, *The Caterpillar Way*

On marketing and public relations
"Claus has revolutionized the concept of co-op advertising. Every consumer marketer on the planet seems more than happy to foot the bill for his PR. Though I would never divulge specifics, organizations sometimes pay big dollars for personal appearances by celebrities. Claus' P&L may surprise you."

—Phil Beuth, former president, *Good Morning America*

On an aging customer base
"Claus' ongoing challenge: how to be a leader despite a growing lack of support from an aging 'nonbeliever' customer base. The answer lies in his unwavering commitment to excellence. Customer service and quality products will always prevail."

—Pat Boos, former senior vice president of marketing, Time Life

On professional image
"I'll tell you what I like about Santa. I like anyone who is fatter than I am."
—Janet Evanovich, *New York Times* bestselling author

On brand development
"Santa is all about the magic that happens when you believe. If you have employees and a brand you believe in, MAGIC happens."
—Kassie DePaiva, daytime television actress

On a competitive spirit
"Claus has the spirit and determination of a true athlete. Don't let his appearance fool you. Magic Johnson and I once played him and Mrs. Claus in basketball—and lost."
—Jack McKinney, former head coach, Los Angeles Lakers and Indiana Pacers

On weathering the storm
"With the North Pole for home base, Santa is certainly accustomed to harsh weather conditions. Fact is, Santa is as tough as he is loving. Refusing to give in to the luxuries of modern-day travel, his sleigh still flies with no roof nor windshield. Like Steve McQueen on his Triumph, Santa's inner rebel laughs in the face of the world's worst storms. His minimalist trendsetting outerwear is both effective and the stuff of Brooklyn envy—a faux-fur trimmed parka protects the jolly jetsetter from the elements, and his incomparable hipster beard covers all but the top of his rosy cheeks. Sure, Santa's sled has onboard Doppler and computer models, but nothing can guide him through a blizzard better than that reindeer with a red nose."
—Rob Marciano, senior meteorologist, ABC News

On legal action
"If Claus and the FAA were in front of me in a case where he was being accused of violating a no-fly zone, now that's a dilemma. How do you rule against Santa?"
—Larry Bakman, judge, Hot Bench

On embracing your Mission Statement
"When your reason for being is 'to make children happy,' you are already a huge success. As a great leader, Claus sets an excellent example: Giving and being kind to others is a wonderful goal for children of all ages."
—Peggy Post, director emeritus, The Emily Post Institute

In summary, when it comes to applying the best of Claus' time-tested, generosity-focused business model, one lesson is abundantly clear: If it ain't broke, don't fix it.

Reason for dinner invitation: *He's jolly, kind, wise and warm. But even better, he'll eat anything.*

Meet The Press

While in college in 1983, I worked the overnight weekend shift as a DJ at 98 KFMZ. I felt like a celebrity—I was a real disc jockey with the requisite (yet fabricated) low-pitched voice to prove it. In my somewhat misguided mind, this late-night DJ gig qualified me as a member of the press despite the fact that, other than *still* providing mandatory updates to my mother on my whereabouts, I reported on nothing.

Though a really hip DJ name would have been preferable, I settled on boring "Randy Jones"—it was either that or "Spaz Nightowl," and the station's program manager didn't go for that.

"Randy Jones" also came with its share of problems. In addition to being far too common and excruciatingly boring, "Randy Jones" already belonged to the original cowboy in the Village People—an artist who had essentially stolen my name and, as he and I would later discover, my 9/13 birthday. That said, I do think Randy and I would have had BIG fun at the Y-M-C-A.

My on-air shifts were from 11 each Friday night to 7 on Saturday morning and from midnight to 8 on Sunday morning. For the most part, my DJ nights went along relatively smoothly at "the home of the Midwest's Best Rock, 98 KFMZ." I would crank up the studio speakers, put on my best Spaz Nightowl DJ voice, and take the occasional request call from the dorms. In the immortal words of the Stray Cats, I'd "Rock This Town."

Part of my job was also to play the station's weekly requirement of public service announcements and religious programming or "God Shows." But working alone all night, and with no sleep, had its downside. And sleep deprivation would almost always kick in about 5 on Sunday morning—just in time for the God Shows to air.

Powerline was one of my aforementioned God Shows and arrived weekly in a vinyl record album format. If you don't know what a record album is, I'm sorry, but you suck.

My task was simple. Put the album on the turntable, place the needle on the appropriate starting groove on Side One, and switch the turntable to "live air." Then, I'd pick up a Pat Benatar album and get paid to go rock out in the adjacent studio.

One memorable Sunday morning, I began *Powerline* right on schedule and retreated to the second studio for my Benatar fix.

We are young
Heartache to heartache we stand
No promises, no demands
Love is a battlefield...

If the phone at the station rang, which was rare during the God Shows, a small light would blink above the sound board to alert the "talent" of an incoming call. So, on this particular morning, if someone called I would certainly "see the light"—no pun intended.

As a result, there was absolutely no need to stifle Ms. Benatar's considerable vocal prowess, so I let her hit me with her best shot until about 5:24 a.m., when I returned to the *Powerline* studio to change to the next God Show.

Teachable moment No. 1: Record albums can "skip." Meaning: if the needle were to hit an imperfect or damaged groove in the album surface, there was a good chance the album would repeat the same single second of content...*indefinitely.*

When I returned to the first studio, based upon my swift calculations, *Powerline* had started to *skip* at approximately 5:07 a.m. and had repeated (and broadcast) **the same exact word** for approximately seventeen minutes:

"Jesus. Jesus. Jesus. Jesus..."

And no one had called. Why? NO ONE WAS LISTENING to 98 KFMZ *or* Spaz Nightowl or *Powerline*.

Being a broadcast professional, I immediately sprang into action. Even if one poor fool—perhaps a shut-in with no telephone—was listening, I had to respond quickly. Though I briefly considered Benatar's *Hell is for Chil-*

dren as a stop gap, I grabbed the first album I found: the von Trapp Family Singers. No, not Julie Andrews and the really cute kids from the movie but the *real* Maria von Trapp and her rather sturdy offspring. *Why a hard rock station even had a von Trapp Family Singers album remains a mystery.*

I ripped *Powerline* off the turntable—no point being subtle now. A few seconds of silence or "dead air" followed until my imaginary single listener was treated to a live broadcast of my *attempt* at lining up the needle with the von Trapp's first song groove. However, within two minutes, I decided the von Trapps had to say "so long" and "farewell" for good.

Riiiiiip!

I grabbed yet another record album and, after scanning the cover, knew I had found the perfect song to keep within the theme of God Show programming.

The artist was Adam Ant.

The record album was *Friend or Foe.*

The song was the previous year's mega-hit, "Goody Two Shoes."

And Spaz Nightowl was a God Show genius.

Teachable moment No. 2: It is not necessarily the record album that causes the skipping problem. It can be the turntable's partner in crime—the needle, a teeny-tiny apparatus that can choose to self-destruct if overused and/or mishandled. And, after seventeen minutes of repetitive "Jesus. Jesus. Jesus…," and *two live broadcasts* featuring careless needle ripping and album switching, the odds of a smooth transition were *not* in my favor.

Adam Ant sings:

Goody-Two
Goody-Two
Goody-Two
Goody-Two

Spaz pushes needle to a new grove:

Don't Drink
Don't Drink
Don't Drink
Don't Drink

Flabbergasted, Spaz pushes the needle again, harder and further into the song:

Don't Smoke
Don't Smoke
Don't Smoke
Don't Smoke

One last attempt:
Shoes, Goody
Shoes, Goody
Shoes, Goody
Shoes, Goody

At this point, the only thing left to do is ask: *What do you do?*
Spaz gives up—it is now 5:32 a.m.

With the next God Show *finally* playing, albeit two minutes late but from a reel-to-reel tape and *not* a record album, I was once again safe, although also exasperated and exhausted.

Finally, at 8:04 a.m., I was reunited with my beloved 1979 Ford Pinto. Despite the fact that most credit Carrie Underwood, I assure you it was actually an extremely distraught Spaz Nightowl who first exclaimed, "Jesus! Take the Wheel!"

NEAL CONAN

Though Neal Conan, the former host of National Public Radio's *Talk of the Nation*, was never a member of the Boy Scouts, he learned—the hard way—the importance of their legendary motto: Be Prepared. The same lesson budding broadcaster Spaz Nightowl began to learn at the hands of a joyfully mischievous God, his "shows" and his much-publicized master plan.

"As someone who was able to improvise my way through school, I never learned to prepare until I started as a broadcaster," Neal says. "In particular, I remember a man who called in after a newscast to ask about a story I'd written on a battle in Vietnam. After speaking with me for a few minutes, he concluded, 'You have no idea what you're talking about.' On reflection, I decided he was right.

"Later, I did an interview with the great reporter Neil Sheehan about *The Arnheiter Affair*, one of his books on Vietnam. Afterwards, he asked, 'When were you there?' I wasn't, but took that as a great compliment and a lesson on the value of preparation as a base from which to apply my improvisational skills.

"Preparation is command of the subject. My favorite moment of the day is when I get to stop worrying and just do it." Plus, he wrapped it up, "if you listen, the guest will take you to the next question."

Like so many other career quick thinkers who had to learn to balance preparation with extemporization, the mentally multitasking Conan often finds himself speaking thirty-seconds behind what he is actually thinking about. Of course, he has also earned the right to trust himself: "If I have half an idea, the other half will come."

SHOWMEJONES.COM

"Preparation is command of the subject. My favorite moment of the day is when I get to stop worrying and just do it."

—Neal Conan

It has often been said: "being good isn't good enough." Neal's commitment to a careful study of the facts is proof positive that he will always be much more than "good enough" at whatever he chooses to do.

Today, Neal Conan remains, in his words, "radio active"; however, he spends much of his time overseeing the operation of his macadamia nut farm in Hawaii. What's more, Neal may be the only man in history to move from an influential, high-profile position—one that assessed the nation's (sometimes chaotic) political and cultural landscape—to literally having a "nut job."

Think: irony.

Nonetheless, chances are good the perpetually prepared Conan is also the most informed Nut Jobber on the planet.

Kevin Randall Jones

WILLARD SCOTT

Willard Scott is the ideal restaurant companion.

If he gets the chance to insert a one-liner into a conversation, he does it. If he feels an amusing anecdote (Soupy Sales' shenanigans, meeting the Pope, Mayberry's Aunt Bee and her purported potty mouth, etc.) would add a little sparkle to the topic in question, he shares it.

In fact, Willard is such a masterful storyteller that prior knowledge of his subjects is not required. Through the twinkle in his eyes—yes, they truly twinkle—and his quite literal gift of gab, you appreciate his tales as if you had been there. And yes, if he happens to accidentally overhear something at the next table that inspires him to spontaneously croon "Indian Love Call," just sit back and bask in the glow of a master entertainer at work.

When I'm calling you
oo-oo-oo, oo-oo-oo
Will you answer too?
oo-oo-oo, oo-oo-oo-oo.

There's something funny about those who are funny. Some of our most memorable jokesters have been motivated by wildly different factors, including a desire for attention and/or to overcome feelings of insecurity. For many of us "class clowns," our often disruptive behavior is intended to rebrand our social image—to cast ourselves as socially relevant in the reality show that is puberty (and life). Yet, for a lucky few, humor seems to come as natural as breathing.

Looking for the fun in life is second nature to Willard. Above all, he lives simply to share that happiness with others. His personality is not forced; it's effortless. What's more, the yuks come from the huge heart of a man who accepts himself lock, stock and barrel: "I am hokey and I'm proud of it."

For Willard, his comic timing not only defined his career, it refined it as well: "A sense of humor goes a million miles, breaks the ice and makes people comfortable," he suggests. "As Popeye says. 'I yam what I yam.' I am accessible. People come up to me."

Willard Scott began as a page at Washington, DC's NBC station in 1950. That same year, he formed The Joy Boys broadcast team with lifelong friend Ed Walker. A comedy fixture on DC radio, The Joy Boys remained on the air until 1972.

During this time, Willard often portrayed Bozo the Clown at DC-area events but, as he explains, "there were other Bozos all over the country." He then pauses, cracks a wry smile and goes in for the kill: "Most of them are in congress now."

Willard also famously created and appeared as the very first Ronald Mc-Donald in TV commercials in 1963. As for the inspiration behind the now infamous redheaded pitchman, "I had such great luck with Bozo, I said, 'Let's stick with a clown.'"

In many ways, "sticking with the clown" has become a glorious metaphor for Willard Scott's career.

Perhaps most noteworthy, he made his debut as TODAY's amiable weatherman in March 1980. "The TODAY Show was having ratings problems. They brought me up from Washington to liven up the show," Willard recalls. "The first couple of weeks were touch and go—a couple of people wanted to get rid of me because I was too hokey." However, the ultimate validation came years later when TODAY Show creator Pat Weaver told him: "When I created the show, you were exactly what I had in mind for a communicator."

CNBC's Tyler Mathisen has known Willard for the majority of his life: "When I was growing up in Arlington, Virginia, Willard Scott was our neighbor. He's a great entertainer and, if possible, an even better guy. No one has a bad word to say about Willard."

Why? Perpetual "Joy Boy" Willard looks for the JOY in everyone and everything. This, of course, raises the question: Can unaffected celebrities like Willard Scott continue to exist?

Sure, even before the internet and social media, "bad press" existed. Scandals, lawsuits and public heartache were common. Nevertheless, there was also a somewhat greater sense that, on the other side of the turmoil stood a human being—not just an impersonal meme, hashtag or punch-line. Are we now forced to be so aware of others' interpretations of who we are that we have ceased to *be* who we are?

After all, #willardscottisnotontwitter.

Willard Scott rose to fame when the public was much more likely to ac-cept people at face value—especially those who wouldn't have cared if they were "trending" due to allegedly offending, defending or pretending. Those like rubber-faced Willard who understood only the concepts of laughter, benevolence and authenticity.

SHOWMEJONES.COM

"A sense of humor goes a million miles, breaks the ice and makes people comfortable."

—Willard Scott

However, Willard's greatest contribution may well be his time-honored commemoration of advancing age as a well-deserved badge of honor. For more than three decades, he appeared on TODAY with his wildly popu-lar 100th-birthday salutes. Though Willard retired in 2015, until that time he joyfully maintained: "Thank God for birthdays. If it weren't for birth-days, I wouldn't work."

Come to think of it, the above comment pretty much applies to everyone.

However, the big question is, what will happen on March 7, 2034—Wil-lard Scott's 100th birthday? Here's a thought: a national holiday, a tele-vised parade, free Big Macs and Smucker's Jelly for everyone and twen-ty-four-commercial-free hours on NBC dedicated to the legendary career of a national treasure—our communal Class Clown with class—Mr. Wil-lard Scott.

After all, this is the man whose whimsical reply to my question "What's special about you?" was a powerful, all-encompassing and profoundly en-viable one-word response: "Me!"

We should all be so lucky.

ROB MARCIANO

Although countless topics find their way into day-to-day conversations, one has toppled the competition for centuries. No, not politics: the weather—our universal go-to subject when banter is required and common ground has yet to be unearthed.

"Some weather we're having."
"Don't you just love this weather?"
"This weather is ruining my hair."

Or this enduring favorite: "Whether the weather be fine, or whether the weather be not, we'll be together whatever the weather, whether we like it or not."

One memorable Saturday morning, I discovered via my television that ABC News Senior Meteorologist Rob Marciano was broadcasting live from nearby Marco Island during Tropical Storm Erika (i.e. "whether the weather be not").

My inspiration-starved inner essayist rejoiced: if Rob Marciano is storm chasing a mere two miles away, wouldn't it be fun to chase the storm chaser and write about it? After all, isn't it important to constantly seek mutually beneficial connections? ("We'll be together.") To expect the unexpected? ("Whatever the weather.")

Or, to see a potential downpour of opportunity when others see only rain? In the end, what's life without a little invigorating storm chasing?

Though my subsequent tour of Marco's broadcast-friendly hot spots didn't produce a face-to-face Marciano meeting—he moves too fast—the appropriate use of another potentially weather-sensitive device brought us together: iPhone (+ Twitter app).

"Deep down I think everyone has a little 'weather geek' in them," Rob says. "Not only does weather impact what we do every day, but because all of our senses are engaged, everybody has an inherent interest in weather."

Weather is universal.

As for his dedication to debris clouds, dense fogs, dew points, diamond dust and difluence, Rob recalls: "Everybody in my business has a story of their epiphany. For me, it was the blizzard of '78. I remember lying in my backyard and looking at the snow coming down and wondering why it was falling on me."

The Glenville, Connecticut, native would go on to obtain a bachelor's degree in meteorology from Cornell University. After college, a yet-to-be-weathered Rob Marciano worked for a brokerage firm, an experience that suited his curious nature yet seemed to reflect the concept of "whether" rather than "weather." "There's a yin and yang in the market just as there's a yin and yang in the weather."

His subsequent career path has taken him from an exploration of Mother Nature to human nature and back to Mother Nature. The common thread? To make sense of the seemingly unpredictable—a skill possessed by few but beneficial to all. Then again, don't most of our jobs slide along a continuum connecting Mother Nature to human nature? Aren't most of us seeking some sort of universal acceptance of ourselves, our product and/or service? What's more, is anyone immune to the perverse power of the unknown?

Rob Marciano began working with CNN News Group as a news and weather anchor in 2003. His reports for CNN during Hurricane Katrina and the BP oil spill in the Gulf of Mexico earned him a Peabody Award.

Next up: he served as co-anchor of *Entertainment Tonight* from January 2013 to August 2014. However, Rob's decision to explore Hollywood's unpredictable (there's that word again) displays of human nature had nothing to do with our country's seemingly endless fascination with celebrity culture. For him, it was about curiosity and access, not actor and actress. "*Entertainment Tonight* allowed me into a world that very few people get to see—to learn things that were completely foreign to me," Rob explains. "The celeb side was not at all interesting to me."

Rob eventually returned to his shameless flirtation with Mother Nature as part of the broadcast team at ABC News. "You get in the elevator, you talk about the weather. The next thing, you talk about 'that movie,'" he suggests. "In a completely different way, Hollywood and entertainment are as prevalent as weather talk. It's just another way to be part of the national conversation."

"Rob is a unique blend of brains and brawn," says Paula Faris of *Good Morning America Weekend*. "He's like a chameleon in that he can adapt to any and every environment—whether it be chasing a tornado or hamming it up in the studio."

Colleague Dan Harris adds: "He is an approachable weather nerd. He truly loves this stuff, in a way that is infectious. It just leaps off the screen. And it all comes with a huge dose of humor and warmth. Which I can tell you, from experience, is not an act; he is even funnier and warmer in person."

Moreover, Rob Marciano seems to be one-part weatherman and one-part whether-man. After all, "whether" denotes investigation, inquiry, alternatives and choice—all Rob Marciano mainstays.

He appears happiest when surrounded by a whirlwind of activity—when trying to make sense out of the random, the intermittent and the ostensibly volatile. An enviable code of conduct in an increasingly restless world. Why? One word: survival. We don't say "weathering the storm" for nothing.

While it's true there are those who ache for structure, Rob's greatest fear may be a life that lacks surprise and adventure. His world appears to celebrate the cooperative coexistence—the thrill—of *risk and reward*, not *risk vs. reward*. "I've never really had a goal and that's worked out well," Rob quips. "I would never tell anyone to set their sights and hopes on one particular job because they are also closing the door on other opportunities to learn and to experience life." Not to dishonor goals, objectives, schedules and vision boards, but when do these tools cross over from creating our careers to abating our potential?

Of course, some insist that Mother Nature always wins. In the case of Rob Marciano, his inquisitive nature—a zealous exploration of the yin and yang and the unpredictable—toppled her royal slyness from her climate-controlling, barometric pressure-treated throne long ago.

"What I appreciate most about Rob is his sincere passion for what he does," adds Paula Faris. "His love of science is thick. His work ethic is ridiculously and ardently feverish."

"I have a curious mind," Rob admits. "My wife is annoyed at how I constantly interview people. I just want to know everything, so I'll never stop asking questions."

("Whether she likes it or not.")

Kevin Randall Jones

Bob Orr

If you visit the Society of Professional Journalists website at www.spj.org, you will find a lengthy "Code of Ethics", a detailed description of conduct meant to help an industry of (albeit, opinionated, passionate and flawed) researchers, writers, photographers, videographers and broadcasters to police themselves. Among the language presented: "Ethical journalism should be accurate and fair. Journalists should be honest and courageous in gathering, reporting and interpreting information."

Without question, we all seem to have an opinion about journalism and journalists—about fact vs. fiction. Still, it's tough to find fault with any man or woman whose life's work has been an ethical focus on our collective education—emphasis on "ethical."

Though a young Bob Orr always dreamed of being the play-by-play announcer for the Pittsburgh Pirates, he ultimately began his television news career in 1973 at WTRF-TV in his hometown of Wheeling, West Virginia, before working in Columbus, Ohio, and Philadelphia. Bob joined the CBS News team in July 1993 and remained there until his retirement in February 2015.

During his CBS tenure, he primarily focused on two beats. From 1994 to 2006, Bob was the transportation correspondent, covering safety and security issues. After 9/11, though he retained the transportation correspondent title, Bob began focusing more heavily on security and counter-terrorism. When the Department of Homeland Security was established, he formally added DHS to his coverage responsibilities.

In November 2006, Bob took over the justice beat as the CBS News Justice and Homeland Security Correspondent. In this capacity, he was the lead correspondent covering domestic and international terrorism as well as U.S. law enforcement issues. Bob was a primary contributor to special event broadcasts of major stories including the 2013 bombings of the Boston Marathon and the 2011 death of Osama bin Laden. As a journalist, he is the recipient of four Emmy Awards.

Bob explains: "For more than two decades, I had a front-row seat to just about every international event." However, to him, with such extraordinary access comes responsibility—and with responsibility comes obligation.

Bob Orr's journalistic focus essentially branded him as a "Master of Disaster." After all, how many of us have jobs that force us to face the darkest sides of the human condition on a near-daily basis? "I do feel that all of the awful events I witnessed and/or reported on over the years caused me considerable stress and angst. Reporters are human beings, and subject to the same kind of emotional reactions as anyone else. One simply can't spend twenty-four hours a day covering disasters, accidents and terror attacks without paying a personal price."

The next question is: what kind of man or woman does it take to be in the business of "handling the truth"? Certainly not those who believe the on-gain, off-gain love affair between Kermit and Miss Piggy is headline news. To begin, a healthy sense of humor doesn't hurt—even Bob jokes: "I am the worst person to be with at a cocktail party—I can depress people in ten minutes."

He also admits: "I had to put up a firewall to not get too emotionally attached." A firewall that he also confesses can easily go up in flames. "The shooting in Newtown, Connecticut, was the single worst story I ever had to handle. I still cannot fathom the senseless, cold-blooded killings of twenty defenseless first grade children," he recalls. The heartbreaking story is also one Bob found impossible to cover in a dispassionate way.

Though Bob and his team won an Alfred I. DuPont-Columbia University Silver Baton for CBS News' coverage of this event, he would joyfully throw said Baton in the trash if there was a way to turn back the clock and change history.

As for the very human need to protect one's emotions, don't many news consumers essentially do the same thing? Don't we put up firewalls around our over-sensitive, media-battered hearts? Hasn't the news become so emotionally challenging to digest that, for example, many news programs seem to have adopted a programming philosophy seemingly based on one-part gab fest and one-part fashion show with headline news sprinkled in?

Perhaps it's human nature to become somewhat dispassionate about the "bad news" that seems to inundate our daily lives, but it's downright unconscionable to ignore the contributions and the sacrifices made by journalists like Bob Orr—those who essentially live each day with our collective grief. In short, if you think it's hard watching the news, try reporting it.

"My family paid a higher price than I did," Bob says. "The counter-terrorism beat, in particular, is a 24/7 obligation—meaning: the correspondent is never really off."

Due to Freedom of Speech, we can all say—and post on social media—pretty much anything that makes us feel good about ourselves, even at the expense of another person. Bob agrees: "We live in the most connected time man has ever known; however, I would argue that we are also the most misinformed."

SHOWMEJONES.COM

"We live in the most connected time man has ever known; however, I would argue that we are also the most misinformed."

—Bob Orr

However, he also places journalistic endeavors into two distinct categories: "investigative" vs. "human interest." Regardless of where a journalist fits on the sliding scale between the two, every "journalist" shares the obligation to be ethical at all costs.

True, I have been blessed with having print and online vehicles to share my journalistic voice. However, that voice is one that unapologetically comes from a "rose-colored-glasses" view of the world. Be it right or wrong, I continue to place an emphasis on positivity in hopes to—in some small way—balance out the overwhelming amount of darkness found in almost every other form of media. My journalistic "firewall" attempts to shield readers from anything other than optimism and kindness.

I will always believe there is something constructive to be learned from everyone we meet—famous, not-so-famous, or *infamous*—even if that lesson must ultimately be classified as what to NOT do. True, I have even joked during my interviews: "If I happen to unearth a smoking gun, I'll help you hide it."

Bob Orr was not only tasked with unearthing the smoking guns, but—whether he will admit it or not—he also played a critical role in disarming the various offenders. "The most important thing for me was not 'what' I covered, but 'how' I covered it," he humbly states. "I gave the job my best shot and I am satisfied with that."

Like so many of us, Bob understands that, these days, "news breaks first on social media—social media drives the bus. Everyone is a reporter. Everyone is a cameraman." If it's true that we have all become pseudo-journalists, shouldn't journalistic ethics be a topic for national discussion—one with the goal of establishing user-friendly guidelines that apply to all?

"The whole point of journalism is to inform, so if I helped somebody get a little smarter about some issue, that's the only lasting dividend."

The First Amendment to the U.S. Constitution, says that "Congress shall make no law...abridging [limiting] the freedom of speech, or of the press...." Freedom of speech is the liberty to speak openly without fear of government restraint.

For Bob, the meaning is simple: "We must have a 'free press' because it's the only institutional check we have."

Is Bob Orr a supporter of the Free Press? Yes. However, is retired Bob Orr free of the press? No.

"I continue to read and watch a variety of outlets in an attempt to get a proper contextual understanding of the important issues," he says. "I won't be too interested in partisan spin or programs that openly advocate a single editorial opinion, but the rest of it...bring it on."

Though we will all retire from the *rat race* at some point, membership in the *human race* requires a lifelong commitment.

JEOPARDY

My bunny issues began when I was seven years old. In the middle of the night, *I swear* the Easter Bunny stood outside my bedroom door and observed me for what seemed like hours.

I should have taken this as a sign: When I grow up I am going to become a lobbyist for the Fur Information Council of America and begin a very personal bunny eradication process.

Besides, if the Easter Bunny was so benign, then what's the deal with the eggs? Bunnies do not lay eggs—chickens do. Bunnies and chickens don't have a history of just hanging out together.

So what does the Easter Bunny have to do to procure his annual egg inventory? My theory: He is in cahoots with members of the National Chicken Council and U.S. Poultry and Egg Association—a hypothesis that essentially makes Jim Perdue a mob boss.

Many years later, with numerous bunny-free Easters behind me, I was hired to perform a unique public service. I became a somewhat notorious singing-telegram messenger at Columbia's You Gotta Be Kidding store.

Though I was in college by this time, I must confess to being the source of other children's nightmares as one of my more popular characters was a six-foot-plus singing bunny rabbit. I can't say that all my young targets were fans of the mutant singing-bunny concept and, secretly, I respected their occasional screams of horror. Plus, on two occasions, I was hired to hop around the backyard of Wal-Mart heirs Bill and Nancy Laurie for the Easter Day amusement of their family and friends. I mean, if Wal-Mart was pro-bunny, then something was clearly wrong with me.

During my second year of employment at You Gotta Be Kidding, Vikki Morgan, the owner, decided she just had to have a French Lop bunny as a store pet. She subsequently purchased the creature and named him Benson. The store's new star attraction delighted the children, dutifully used his litter box, and showered everyone with love and affection. *Except me.*

The irony was that I loved animals: dogs, cats and pretty much all varieties of livestock. I never met an animal I *didn't* like—until Benson.

Vikki often joked that Benson was director of security for the flourishing You Gotta Be Kidding empire; however, based on what I know now, she underestimated his talent. For instance, had Benson been around during Watergate, I'm pretty sure he would have nipped that pesky breaking-and-entering thing in the bud pretty quickly.

My relationship with Benson started out fine. He tailed me every day as I toddled around the store. When I stood at the helium tank preparing balloon bouquets, he sat quietly and observed. Even as I changed into my various costumes in the back dressing room, the ever-present Benson was right there, occasionally nuzzling my lower legs in hopes of receiving affection, which I dutifully provided. After all, *I loved animals.*

But as time wore on, my personal and professional relationship with Benson began to deteriorate. If left alone with me in the store (meaning: no witnesses) Benson became more aggressive—almost herding me around and demanding my attention. And if I did not comply, Benson developed an annoying habit of nibbling my tootsies in defiance.

I expressed my concern to Vikki—not just because of toe discomfort, but due to the potential consequences if Benson ever took issue with a child visiting the store. As she cuddled the self-righteous beast, Vikki summarily dismissed my concerns and scolded me: "Randy, he's just a wuvable wittle bunny wabbit. YOU must be doing something to antagonize HIM."

Less than a week later, I arrived at the store, after hours (meaning: alone and unprotected), to prepare for yet another Flasher-Gram. And yes, by "Flasher," I am indeed referring to myself in a tiny G-string that barely protected my family jewels, topped off with the obligatory trench coat—that's pretty much it.

Benson had begun to pace irritably as I prepared my balloon bouquet. When it came time for me to change into what little costume I was to wear, despite the fact Benson clearly didn't want to let me pass, I negotiated a path around him and continued my business.

Once I retrieved my G-string and trench coat, I disappeared behind the dressing room curtain in the back of the store. Moments later, Benson pushed the cloth drape aside, entered the dressing room, assumed a seated position and glared at me. Then something must have snapped—I suspect in both of us. As if we were mortal enemies on the verge of a duel, we locked eyes. Of course, as the only *mortal* present, I began to feel a bit silly. After all, he's just a wuvable wittle bunny wabbit.

Out of some odd sense of modesty, I turned my back to Benson, dropped my shorts and underwear and stood there naked. As I bent over to step into my G-string, Benson jumped three feet in the air and took a big chomp out of my right butt cheek.

I yelped and quickly swung around—the force of my movement just strong enough to release Benson's death grip on my bottom and hurl him toward the floor again. He was slightly disoriented from the fall and, though my tush was aching a bit, I took advantage of his vulnerable position and nudged him out of the room with my foot. And, for a brief time, it appeared Benson had moved on.

Images of my childhood Easter Bunny stalker began to creep into my mind, but I dismissed them. I mean, this is absurd. He's just a pet bunny—not the spawn of Satan.

I was wrong.

Now completely dressed in the required minimalist attire, I exited the dressing room at the rear of the store and made a left turn up the small hallway that separated me from my balloon bouquet, the front door and freedom. Another quick left into Vikki's office to grab the recipient's contact information and I would be home free.

I picked up the necessary paperwork and turned to exit. But it was too late—Benson had already assumed a power position in the small office doorway. His labored breaths caused his entire body to heave and, as he exhaled, his little nasal flaps trembled from the pressure of the forced outbound air. I'm not sure I have ever seen so much hatred in a pair of eyes and I have lived through a divorce.

I was cornered. I knew it and Benson absolutely knew it. I decided my best alternative was to make a quick dash for the front door but, just as I started to make my move, World War III began. With teeth exposed, Benson charged and seized the top of my left foot. I screamed. My pained reaction seemed only to encourage him to alter positions and bite even harder. I screamed again and began to use both of my hands to try to pull the rabid creature from my injured foot, but he was resolute in maintaining his grip.

I then began to kick my injured leg into the air, hoping the movement would, once again, dislodge Peter Cottontail's deranged descendant and set me free. Yet I was powerless to release the rodent. Finally, having exhausted all reasonable methods of freeing myself from his grasp, I simply began to kick the shit out of Benson with my other foot.

Now, you would think the odds would have been in my favor, but when you're engaged in battle with an enraged Lagomorph, the balance of power is far more even than you would suspect.

Just minutes into combat Vikki returned and entered the office to discover me—well—kicking the proverbial poop pellets out of her "wuvable wittle bunny wabbit." Understandably, she began shrieking at me to stop beating the animal, but moments later, as she saw the blood streaming down *my* foot, she stood there shocked and speechless.

Yes, I did get cleaned up and yes, I performed my Bachelorette Party "flash" that night, albeit with bandages and thicker socks than usual.

The next day I marched into Vikki's office with an ultimatum, "Listen, I make you money and he doesn't. I am good and he is evil." And in the best B-movie Western voice I could muster, I lowered my tone, looked her dead in the eyes and growled: "It's…the…bunny…or…ME."

Benson left You Gotta Be Kidding that afternoon, never to return. And yes, he also left a small scar on my left foot, one which remains to this day. But other scars were even more permanent. Despite the good folks at Wal-Mart, between my disturbing childhood Easter Bunny encounter and my Benson experience, I ultimately developed a fear and outright hatred of all-things bunny rabbit. If one of those dirty hopping creatures crosses my path in the yard, I freeze.

When a family of bunnies moved into the bushes outside my front door, I used the back door for months. And when an *animated* bunny inadvertently scared Anne Hathaway's friends in the movie, *Ella Enchanted*, my then-fourteen-year-old daughter put her arm around me in the theatre and cooed, "Are you okay, Daddy? Did the wittle bunny scare you? Do you need to hold my hand? Do we need to go home now? It's okay, Daddy, I'm here for you!"

In the years since, I came out of the closet and began to openly discuss my overt "leporiphobia."

Obviously unfazed by my misery, my editor-friend Nancy Scott shared the existence of *Bunnicula*, a children's book series about a vampire bunny that sucks the juice out of vegetables. *(Ah—realism!)*

My Facebook friends are relentless: every single evil-bunny-themed image finds its way to my page *at least once*. Naturally, there's a significant uptick of bunny postings during Easter season. Forgive me for saying it this way, but it's almost like these images *rise from the dead* once a year to remind me of what a wuss I am.

Even Vikki recently re-entered my life: "Randy, you do understand that Benson was a *bunny*, right? Yes, a badass bunny but a bunny nonetheless. You live in Florida and I happen to know you've seen worse; you've had pythons on your street and alligators in your driveway before."

My reaction? "Unleash those pythons and bring on the gators."

Then there's my friend and pro-bunny maniac, Sharron Johnson, who has spent years trying to respect my distaste for the floppy eared evildoers, but even she couldn't resist sharing the existence of a 1972 B-movie cult horror film called *Night of the Lepus*. "I could never watch it but you may like it—it's a horror movie about giant mutant rabbits that terrorize the Southwestern United States."

To which I responded, "Horror movie? Don't you mean DOCUMENTARY?"

Moral of the story: *Professionally speaking, know when to be fearless, draw the line in the litter box, and stand up for yourself.*

Another moral of the story: *Personally speaking, bunnies suck (and bite).*

FEAR. THE REACTION MOST LIKELY to stand in the way of any sort of achievement. Whether real or imagined and regardless of its source, Fear is part of the Danger Family of emotions: Terror, Dread, Anxiety, Horror, Distress, Panic and Trepidation. Of course, Danger is a card-carrying member of a larger, seemingly unyielding group of kinfolk that include: Risk, Peril and even Jeopardy.

Without question, Fear, Danger and their various descendants seem to be hell-bent on ruining our lives. *At least "Risk" is often associated with "Reward."*

As a columnist, I have encountered those who dismiss danger *and* fear as well as those who crave and/or create it. Money—or a lack thereof—can cause an almost desperate level of fear and vulnerability. Though we sometimes fear another person, when we take the time to learn more about him, our fear naturally dissipates. FOMO—or Fear of Missing Out—becomes even more intriguing when juxtaposed against the fear associated with those things we have convinced ourselves we can *never-in-a-million-years* do.

And when it comes to bravely facing fear head-on, our nation's military men and women often put themselves in harm's way simply by going to work.

Can fear be all encompassing? Yes, but that's rare. Though there are many ways to look at it, and with my apologies to those who took part in the RMS Titanic's single Atlantic crossing, *fear* is often times just the tip of the iceberg.

SHOWMEJONES.COM

"A lot of people waste energy complaining that the 'rules of the game' aren't fair. Learn how to play within them or play another game."

—Brad Rutter

BRAD RUTTER

The answer is: The all-time, top-earning undefeated *Jeopardy!* Champion whose total career winnings exceed $4.3 million.

For those who have become *Jeopardy!* game show aficionados during its extraordinary fifty-plus-year run, the *question* response is easy: **Who is Brad Rutter?**

The Lancaster, Pennsylvania-native was too young to legally rent a car when, in 2000, at age twenty-two, he arrived in Los Angeles for his first *Jeopardy!* appearance. Since that time, Brad Rutter has shattered game-show records by winning *Jeopardy!'s* 2001 Tournament of Champions, the Million Dollar Masters Tournament and the Ultimate Tournament of Champions. More recently, he triumphed in the 2014 Battle of the Decades.

A competitive exhibition of mental acuity presented in a series of academic sound bites, *Jeopardy!* is arguably the ultimate intellectual Q&A—or, more accurately, A&Q.

Naturally, I began my conversation with Brad by disclosing a list of interview categories: preparation, game playing, competition and fear, the latter representing a reminder that "jeopardy" is, after all, synonymous with threat, difficulty and hazard.

Regardless of the question presented, cool-headed Brad provided effortless responses, so spot-on, in fact, that a printed transcript of our discussion would be equally compelling. With no oversized game board or cameras present, the totally Trebek-less Brad Rutter and his encyclopedic knowledge stood alone. His (swift and sound) sound-bite answers flowed seamlessly.

I'll take 'Preparation' for $400

As a child, Rutter—a lifelong bibliophile—visited the library once a week and always checked out the maximum number of books allowed. He subsequently "got into the habit of reading early and never got out of it." (Think: Brick Heck from ABC's *The Middle*, minus the attention-grabbing idiosyncratic behavior.)

On preparing for competition, Brad quickly offers: "To an extent, you either know it or you don't"—a concept that either relaxes or terrifies, depending upon your point of view. Though he points to some more commonplace *Jeopardy!* categories such as World Capitals, Shakespeare Plays and U.S. Presidents as worthy of pre-game review, it appears that a lifelong commitment to self-education is Brad Rutter's ultimate game changer.

True, it may be too late to change our childhood reading habits but, regardless of our fields, each of us certainly has a short list of categories that deserve our ongoing attention. (Mine is obviously gourmet cooking.)

'Competition' for $600

As for standing before headmaster Alex Trebek and adjacent to two other prospective know-it-alls, Rutter shares: "We are all nervous. The key is to be *less* nervous than the other contestants."

Nevertheless, in the business world, the eleven-character word, "competition," is often described using any number of less-than-favorable four-letter words. On this argument, Brad takes the high road and wins again: "Competition is good for you as you can test yourself. You learn you are capable of things you may not have realized before."

'Game playing' for $800

Whether fueled by legitimate strategy and/or personal agendas, workplace game playing is everywhere. If this concept is unfamiliar to you, you are, quite simply, not working.

To Brad: "You can always look a lot smarter than you really are if you just pay attention," a comment worthy of everyone's vigilant consideration. "If somebody's going to win, it might as well be me."

Finally, Rutter gamely suggests: "A lot of people waste energy complaining that the 'rules of the game' aren't fair. Learn how to play within them or play another game." Those words ring true in so many situations.

'Fear' for $1,000

Fear, specifically the fear of *losing* something, is a common motivator in almost every professional setting.

On this topic, Brad's credible sound bites continue:

"I have control over only one question at a time. I can't control the categories or the contestants."

"I can 'logic' my way out of fear. For example, I statistically proved to myself it was safe to fly."

"Most people are more afraid of what they shouldn't fear than what they should," he jokes, a reference to parents obsessed with sunscreen-glazing their child while a stingray unknowingly lurks nearby.

Brad has not squandered his considerable winnings. He lives simply in L.A. with two roommates and an ongoing commitment to working on both sides of the camera—a career focus resulting from the undeniable thrill of *Jeopardy!'s* media-rich environment.

Though most of us have been involved in high-stakes negotiations and business dealings, the vast majority of us have not had the added pressure of seeing our transactions hosted and/or televised. On the simplest possible level, intellectual powerhouse Brad Rutter and his spectacular-yet-unique success offer highly visible proof that, to be a winner, all you really have to do is think like a winner.

Game over.

> ### SHOWMEJONES.COM
>
> "I am very open to where the next opportunity is going to come from, but I'm also chasing the next opportunity at the same time."
>
> —Kathy Griffin

KATHY GRIFFIN

I know some of you are saying: "Seriously? Kathy Griffin is in a business book?"

But hold on now: like anyone who works hard for a paycheck, Griffin is *in business*. She keeps a keen eye on the court of public opinion, she is her own best brand ambassador, and she makes money for herself and other corporate giants. She also strikes fear in the hearts of countless celebrities simply by entering a room.

In truth, Kathy loves money—a fact she admits more easily than most of us. Well, she admits EVERYTHING more easily than most of us.

Griffin has won two Primetime Emmy Awards for her Bravo TV reality series, *Kathy Griffin: My Life on the D-List*. It could also be argued that Kathy's self-deprecating exploration of her D-List celebrity status catapulted her to the A-List.

An accident? Not likely. Kathy Griffin has proven she knows exactly how to care for her primary product: Kathy Griffin. Since 2007, Kathy has terrorized co-host/giggle guy Anderson Cooper as part of CNN's New Year's Eve special. In 2013, she was inducted into the *Guinness Book of World Records* for writing and starring in twenty televised stand-up specials—more than any other comedian in history. In 2014, she became one of only three women (Kathy, Whoopi Goldberg, Lily Tomlin) to win a Grammy Award for Best Comedy Album.

Her other honors include The Human Rights Campaign's Ally for Equality, Iraq and Afghanistan Veterans of America's Leadership in Entertainment honor, GLAAD's Vanguard Award and The Trevor Life Award from the Trevor Project.

In short, Chicago's Kathleen Mary Griffin has cashed in on our nation's obsession with pop-culture capers. How? Kathy, the proverbially plucky pal, puts herself on the same side of the table as her loyal consumer—a hard-to-achieve goal for anyone in search of the almighty dollar.

Spend one-on-one time with Kathy and she quickly proves she is much more than meets the eye. To her: "I get the business part of it." And she does—she's still here.

Interviewing Kathy Griffin is bliss: you don't have to do much. Simply wind her up—wait, she actually arrives pre-wound—sit back and enjoy the celebrity-skewering ride. "I'm a raconteur. My act is stories that are personal—things that have happened where I share a personal experience with jokes intertwined," she says.

Kathy has the power of observation, a matchless gift for storytelling, and an almost inexplicable ability to speak nonstop without losing focus. Though many fancy themselves to be storytellers, most (like me) tend to get lost in a tangent or two. Her laser focus can't be learned; it just "is." She owns her material because she literally *lives* it.

Not that Kathy moves in a straight line from point A to point B: her delivery is better described as line, turn, pivot, laugh, line, pivot, loop, leap, look, laugh, line—but she effortlessly gets you there without missing a beat. Then there's her razor-sharp wit—so acute, in fact, it's amazing that the folks at Gillette haven't tried to harness its power.

I began our discussion with an explanation of my platform: "My work is an exploration of positive business principles. Basically, I'm always nice."

Cue caustic Kathy: "You and I are in a very different field!" Then came the wry zinger: "You and your damn 'positivity.'" *Insert belly laugh here.*

But she understands her audience—a group she describes as "upscale gays and soccer moms"—and she wisely chooses her material to appeal to her demographic meal ticket. Kathy explains: "My stories range from being wildly inappropriate to a story where I'm the butt of the joke." More than anything, the public loves imperfection.

Conversely, she admits there *are* lines she does not cross. Don't believe it? Then you should have been with me at Griffin's performance at Merriwether Post Pavilion in Columbia, Maryland, on June 25, 2009—the day Michael Jackson died. Though Jackson had comedy's target on his back for decades—one many feel he placed there himself—I personally witnessed

Kathy's respectful handling of a family's tragedy, a scenario other comedians undoubtedly exploited.

For Kathy—and all of us—it's about seizing *control* of opportunity. "I'm very willing to go with the flow and go wherever the 'love' is," she says. "Sometimes I have a good year making money on television. Sometimes I have a much better year making money touring. I do 'funny.' I can do it in a book. I can do it on stage. I can do it at a charity function. I can do it in a television show." And the music to an executive's ears? "I can make you a lot of money doing it."

That's called confidence, my friends.

What's more, Kathy understands the concept of a fair price based upon what the market will bear. She prides herself on her ability to go with the flow—day by day, gig by gig—yet remain aware of her primary sources of income. "I am very open to where the next opportunity is going to come from, but I'm also chasing the next opportunity at the same time."

She has also achieved a special balance in her act due to her parents' participation. "I have always known that my mom and dad were naturally funny. When it came time for a reality show, [including them] was a no-brainer."

Though her beloved father, John, passed away in 2007, Kathy Griffin has elevated her ninety-something mother, Maggie, to semi-star status. She regularly shines a spotlight on her mother's opposing points-of-view and recounts mother Maggie's various admonishments for daughter Kathy's ongoing "bad behavior." Like mother, (un)like daughter.

When Kathy Griffin is in the room, *proceed with caution*—any misstep could land you in her act. Nevertheless, Kathy wouldn't have a career if it weren't for a babbling Bieber, a loose-lipped Lohan, or supposed she-man Ryan Seacrest. The real lesson here? Just as you should never write anything you don't want on the front page of the *New York Times*, don't say or do anything you don't want Kathy Griffin to use in her act! Advice that actually works regardless of your social or business circles.

Yes, she may regale the planet with a celebrity's faux pas, but what about the non-Kathys in our lives who observe our behavior and, *without us knowing*, take a negative view into the world. Think about it. Is there a more disturbing fear of the unknown?

However, for Kathy, it's all about the funny: "The nice thing is that a lot of the people I've 'made fun of' are finally coming around and realizing I'm 'having fun with.'" And when it comes to providing material to "have fun with," it seems our beloved yet naughty celebs are the gift that keeps on giving.

For those who had hoped that this piece would contain one Griffin one-liner after another, I'm sorry to disappoint. Though dazzling in person, Kathy doesn't tell "jokes" and, as is the case with anyone we encounter, there's much more to Kathy Griffin than a punchline.

Funny how that works.

SHOWMEJONES.COM

"Young women should not fear any societal stereotype that tells them they do not belong. We need our young women to have the confidence and willingness to reject 'labels,' and pursue all of their interests and passions."

—Robin Hauser Reynolds

ROBIN HAUSER REYNOLDS

As a nation, we have become a technology-obsessed culture—a society with more electronic thingamabobs, gizmos and doodads than most of us believed possible just twenty years ago. And though this may be stating the obvious, jobs in the computer-related field are only going to rise over the next decade. Nonetheless, less than one-third of these positions are likely to be filled by Americans and an infinitesimal percentage of those American workers will be women. And yet, we've all heard the news: girls can do anything boys can do.

"We bring girls home in pink blankets—boys in blue blankets," says filmmaker Robin Hauser Reynolds, director and producer of cause-based documentary films at Finish Line Features LLC. "Then we make the assumptions that girls don't want to get dirty, play in the sandbox or play with blocks."

So what's the problem? "To begin, it's gender bias. We bring our daughters into the kitchen more. We give more scientific explanations to our sons," Robin suggests. "I am the first to admit there are differences between men and women, but there are no differences between men and women and their ability to succeed in the field of computer science."

The opportunity costs to our nation are clear. First, more technology jobs will be filled overseas and second, our daughters and granddaughters are missing the chance to be part of a field that promises extraordinary opportunity.

For Robin, inspiration began at home. "My daughter called and told me she was going to drop her computer science major," she recalls. "'I'm really bad at it,' she told me. 'I'm the worst in the class; I don't fit in.'" Holland Reynolds was one of just two women in a class of twenty-five. After taking three computer science classes, she dropped the major. As it turned out, she was earning a B.

Robin's maternal—and ultimately her external—reaction came in the form of the documentary: *CODE: Debugging the Gender Gap.* "Robin has taken a topic she doesn't have firsthand experience in and provided a lot of information in a very compelling way," says Danielle Feinberg, director of photography at Disney/Pixar. "She is a true filmmaker in that way." Feinberg also appears in the film. One of Robin's goals is to get a copy of *CODE* into every school in America.

This is not the first time her cinematic Mama Bear response has been on public display. In 2013, Robin produced and co-directed *Running for Jim,* an award-winning documentary that chronicled the story of Jim Tracy—the revered coach of the San Francisco University High School cross-country team. Tracy and his team gained international attention when its sixteen-year-old captain, Robin's daughter Holland Reynolds, collapsed and crawled across the finish line at the 2010 California state championship race. At the time, Jim Tracy was battling Lou Gehrig's disease.

Holland's determination helped to secure Tracy's legacy as the most winning track coach in California history. Her mother's dedication cemented it by putting his story on film. Jim Tracy passed away on April 7, 2014, yet Robin's cinematic retelling of his powerful story is guaranteed to stand the test of time.

If one of the universal messages of *Running for Jim* is to "finish the job"; then *CODE* circles back to an equally powerful lesson: "begin the job"—not just in terms of women studying computer science, but in society's responsibility to actively encourage young men and young women with equal zeal. "I hope to inspire our audience to begin that change," Robin explains. "Change in the way our school system values computer science education. Change in the way we think of a programmer. Change in the way women and people of color view themselves in the tech field."

In a world seemingly ruled by WIFM—or "What's in it for me?"—Robin Hauser Reynolds seems to suggest a more selfless point of view: WIFU or "What's in it for US?" It's a concept that works equally well for "us," the pronoun, and U.S., the nation. "There are those of us who want to be champions for gender equality, for ethnic diversity, for LGBT," she says. "However, this issue has huge economic and financial ramifications. And what's the one thing that everyone seems to care about? Money."

Few would deny that the "good old boys network" still exists. And the stereotypes associated with coders—i.e. the *brogrammer*—don't help matters.

"I have never been intimidated by living in a man's world," Robin says. "We need to empower our daughters to solve problems for themselves, to have confidence, to be assertive and to know they can do anything they set their mind to. They do not need to be rescued by boys or men."

When asked why she was so driven to use her voice for the eternally needy greater good, the characteristically eloquent director/producer didn't have an answer. Why? She had never thought about it. Then again, isn't it better when the desire to give is based on instinct—maternal and otherwise—as opposed to personal gain? WIFU wins again.

Perhaps the biggest shock is that equal opportunities for women is a topic that still requires our collective attention—and likely will for the foreseeable future.

"My work is not fear-based; it's the opposite," Robin declares. "Young women should not fear any societal stereotype that tells them they do not belong. We need our young women to have the confidence and willingness to reject 'labels,' and pursue *all* of their interests and passions."

Now, consider this: Where would computing be today without Grace Hopper? Don't know who she is? Fire up your computer and look her up. Because chances are, without Hopper, your computer wouldn't have much to say.

Derek Call Wakefield

CARL EDWARDS

For business professionals, networking is essential. More specifically, when two people share similar interests, goals, and/or backgrounds, a win-win situation is more likely to emerge. For example:

NASCAR'S Carl Edwards—born in Columbia, Missouri, in 1979—graduated from Rock Bridge High School in 1997 before attending the University of Missouri.

NAPLES' Randall Kenneth Jones—born in Columbia, Missouri, in 1962—graduated from Rock Bridge High School in 1980 before attending the University of Missouri.

Bingo!

Though my original interview request was presented to my hometown hero when he was racing at nearby Homestead-Miami Speedway, by the time the meeting took place, a full year had elapsed. In this case, the vanishing art of patience proved more beneficial than our society's desire for haste. Just like Edwards' No. 19 Toyota Camry, we sure do love to move fast.

For the self-described "kid from Rock Bridge" who dreamed of a career in racing, an age-old Midwestern saying would ultimately take on brand new meaning: Carl's "get up and go got up and went"—all the way to the NASCAR circuit.

The one-time substitute teacher was noticed by Jack Roush in 2003 when Edwards was in the NASCAR Craftsman Truck Series. In 2005, he became a full-time driver in the NASCAR NEXTEL Cup Series. Carl's natural charm has afforded him almost as many opportunities off the track as on. A very popular pitchman, he has endorsed products for Subway, Xfinity, Goodyear, Ford, Claritin and Office Depot. He has even co-starred in commercials with the persnickety AFLAC Duck. On television, Edwards has appeared on *Chicago Fire, The Grinder, Royal Pains, 24* and in the ironically titled *Slow Me Down* video with fellow Mid-Missouri native, country music's Sara Evans. Nothing seems to slow down Carl Edwards—then again, speed is his business.

SHOWMEJONES.COM

"I have noticed that looking out the front windshield and keeping my eyes off the rearview mirror helps a lot. Don't worry about the people behind you; just go forward."

—Carl Edwards

Unlike so many of us professional risk-takers and mistake-makers who move too quickly through our daily tasks, Carl is part of a profession that doesn't offer a do-over option—efficiency, performance and speed must work together like, *you guessed it*: a well-oiled machine. To him, speed isn't a knee-jerk reaction; it is the result of a plan of action.

"For me, it's about preparation. I try to execute perfectly when it's time," Carl says. "There are no excuses. When it's time to go, you have to be able to do it. The only way you learn that is through all the trial and error—and all the frustration."

Just as our collective speed is constantly in overdrive and "trading paint" has increasingly moved from the racetrack to the boardroom, Carl's NASCAR-driven workplace analogies kept coming at every turn:

On management
"If you get angry or frustrated—or you feel insecure—you have to stick to: 'I've just got to keep working. I know what works. I have to relay the information. I have to trust my crew will make the car better.'"

On strategy

"Strategy changes throughout the race very quickly. We have a full plan, but we have all these if/then scenarios. 'If this works, then we go to this set up.'"

On science vs. instinct

"I sit in the car and my job is to relay exactly what the car is doing. There's this interesting melding and meshing of what I feel and what we do technically to the car."

On maintaining control

"The hardest thing in a race car is to control your emotions. You can't just 'try harder and go faster.' It's not like playing the piano or the guitar—it's not like you just try harder and make it sound better."

On focus

"I have noticed that looking out the front windshield and keeping my eyes off the rearview mirror helps a lot. Don't worry about the people behind you; just go forward."

On maximizing your time

"There's a start and there's an end; when it's over—it's over."

Now, consider this challenge: name one profession where the aforementioned thought processes do not apply.

Nope, you can't.

In Carl Edwards' case, failure to heed his own advice is dangerous—to him and those who travel in his circles. But are the rules of the professional road really all that different for the rest of us? Most of us have been on the receiving end of inadequate work due to an assignee's decision to rush through the process. *Do-over*

Consider those times you have received an email response that contained an answer to, for example, two questions rather than the requested three. *Try again*

Of course, we've all sped through our to-do list only to leave someone waiting—haphazardly racing around in an attempt to salvage a successful day. *Disaster*

The lesson: speed without thought can backfire. No one wins when our speed exceeds our ability—and the ability of others—to achieve peak performance.

More than anything, Carl understands his job description: "I am here to drive that car, make sure it's as fast as it can be, and not make any mistakes. I have to do everything well and make sure—at the end of the race—I have done everything I could." Then again, what else is there?

Yes, Carl Edwards wants to WIN—and he has, many times. Unlike so many who seek the easiest possible route, he welcomes the challenge—the responsibility—that accompanies the speed and unparalleled attention-to-detail his profession requires: "Once the race starts, you're all out—100 percent. You're giving everything you can—every lap—trying to get as far to the front as you can."

So the next time you navigate our ever-accelerating professional landscape, heed Carl's warning: "There are a thousand ways to lose a race." You may think that, despite a harried mishap or two, you have 999 or 998 chances left, but the fact is, you just lost.

Sure, embrace your inner speed demon; however, think, prepare, pay attention, *understand what drives you* and—just like the highly successful, freewheeling Carl Edwards—backflip for joy at the Finish Line.

GENERAL BARRY R. MCCAFFREY

Experts agree: preparation is everything. However, somctimes our homework is more challenging because we lack the personal experience and/or insight to comprehend the critical importance of the topic at hand. Nonetheless, we soldier on in the hope that no one will notice our ignorance.

And the worst-case scenario: completing a project or exchange thinking we nailed it when, in truth, we failed at it. The daunting task before me? An interview with one of the most influential military officers of the last century, General Barry R. McCaffrey.

The role of those in our nation's military is decidedly hands-on. Their daily activities reveal an emotional, physical and, often, spiritual connection to "service" that many civilians cannot grasp. Like many Americans, I have very little contact with those whose job is to protect and defend my very way of life. After all, only one percent of Americans serve in the military. With the exception of my father—a U.S. Air Force veteran—no one in my immediate family has served. And my father's self-effacing quip: "'I flew a desk' in Cheyenne, Wyoming, during the Korean War."

Notwithstanding, there is nothing common or "general" about the opportunity to speak to a four-star general, retired or otherwise. My approach: own my ignorance, be respectful, listen and learn. The result: a thoughtful, inspiring and universally relevant education.

General Barry R. McCaffrey, USA (Ret.) served in the United States Army for thirty-two years. He retired in 1996 as a four-star general. At retirement, McCaffrey was the most highly decorated serving general. He has been awarded three Purple Hearts, two Distinguished Service Crosses and two Silver Stars for valor.

After leaving the military, General McCaffrey served as the Director of the White House Office of National Drug Control Policy for five years during the Clinton administration. Next, he served as the Bradley Distinguished Professor of International Security Studies from 2001 to 2005; and as Adjunct Professor of International Security Studies from 2006 to 2010 at the United States Military Academy at West Point. He is currently a military analyst for NBC and MSNBC and president of his own consulting firm.

Though retired from military service, McCaffrey still appreciates a well-structured day. Our interview began promptly at 8 a.m. First up: a Q&A on how to appropriately address a retired, high-ranking military officer. McCaffrey's swift suggestion: "You can call me 'Barry' or 'Your Excellency.'"

Though he credited Henry Kissinger with the whimsical one-liner, generally speaking, the ice was broken. *All that said, I did not call him "Barry," nor will I ever.*

When asked to share the most important characteristic of our military men and women, McCaffrey did not hesitate: "The talent level. They are able to pass all of our screens. They are an incredibility select lot—the young women more than the young men."

> SHOWMEJONES.COM
>
> **"Never lose sight of why you are there; whom you are speaking for—or the impact of your decision."**
>
> —General Barry R. McCaffrey

In total, the United States Armed Forces is a massive institution with 2.3 million men and women combined among the Army, Marine Corps, Navy, Air Force and Coast Guard. "The kids you see in uniform in an airport essentially came out of the top 15 percent of American youth," the general says. "They are happy to be serving something greater than themselves." Regardless of your place of employment, it is uniformly beneficial to first consider "we" over "me."

Though some of us still believe in supporting the Office of the President regardless of who occupies the Oval Office, our group is clearly diminishing in size. According to McCaffrey, the majority of servicemen and women are not registered to one party or another. "My dad served for thirty-seven years—he never voted until he was out of the Armed Forces. He thought it was inappropriate. We serve whoever the American people have elected with equal vigor." A position as noble as it is selfless—and one worthy of additional public consideration.

Next, McCaffrey on diversity: "If you walked into a meeting and looked around the room, guaranteed, the room would have substantial numbers of women and minorities." He then adds: "The central ethos of the Armed Forces is: until the commander has made a decision, everyone is under pressure to independently hash out their viewpoints of how to make things work."

Diverse minds and backgrounds will always produce diverse thought—a win-win scenario in any professional endeavor.

"I find there is more confidence in adjudicating conflict (in the military) than there is in civilian business," McCaffrey says. "The military is dealing with decentralized units. You have to listen to the people on the ground. You can't dictate."

Ask almost any member of the U.S. Armed Forces about their job and the concept of discipline will likely arise. Not necessarily in terms of the control gained by enforcing obedience or order, but the learned and enviable skill of self-control. "It's not an authoritarian institution. They aren't being hammered to do things right; they are in charge. They are used to making decisions on their own."

And why do soldiers fight when they might get killed? To McCaffrey, it has nothing to do with an authoritarian ability to punish them. The answer is more closely aligned to anyone who occupies the role of caregiver. "A sense of pride—a sense of responsibility to each other. The bonds of comradeship, friendship and loyalty in combat are extraordinary. It's as powerful as a mother and her child."

McCaffrey is also quick to note that the public's trust in our congressional leaders is typically low; however, regardless of the poll, the most trusted group is the U.S. Armed Forces. Whether the setting is the military, commercial business or home, what is life in the absence of trust? "People learn they can either trust your word or they can't. At the end of the day, are you willing to work hard? If yes, the word spreads. Pretty soon, people want you as part of their team."

McCaffrey's ongoing use of "us," "we" and "our" ultimately reveals his heart. Just as I owned my ignorance, he continues to own his interminable commitment to his beloved military colleagues. "I wear a tiny lapel pin with two oak leaf clusters on my civilian suit," explains McCaffrey. "I wear that Purple Heart point to remind the current serving members of the Armed Forces—and the veterans—that my mindset is not at a four-star, strategic level. In my mind, I'm an infantry company commander in combat."

Why?

"Never lose sight of why you are there; whom you are speaking for—or the impact of your decision." True, many claim to have been "on the front lines" of some sort of skirmish, but winning a battle of wits is quite different from winning a battle for freedom.

SUZE ORMAN

It's practically impossible to write about time spent with personal-finance wizard Suze Orman using a detached, third-person journalistic voice. Why? Suze Orman excels at leaving no financial or emotional stone unturned—she lives to get personal. And if there's one thing with the potential to put any number of us in jeopardy, it's money.

Suze's response to my first question ("How do I make this interview interesting for you?") set the tone for all that was to follow: "Ask me things that really mean something to you and will transform your life financially and emotionally," she instructed. With "you" and "your" prominently displayed at the forefront of her directive, "I" started to get anxious. Suze Orman expected to talk to flawed-human "me," not probing-writer "me."

As a devoted viewer of CNBC's *The Suze Orman Show*—which ended its thirteen-year run on March 28, 2015—I could only wonder if Suze's I-can-see-right-through-you on-screen persona now had me in its sights. My internal questioning mechanism was all a-twitter: #helpme.

As the erstwhile villain/catalyst in her financial life was a smarmy broker named "Randy," was I to suffer guilt-by-first-name association? Will I be forced to disclose my lackluster annual 401(k) contributions? And finally, on a personal level, will I metaphorically be "approved" or "denied"?

Suze Orman may be an Emmy Award-winning television host, a *New York Times* mega-bestselling author, a columnist and one of the top motivational speakers in the world, but she is much more than that. Simply put: she's 100 percent genuine. Suze is a tireless teacher, faithful friend, consummate confidant and a powerhouse brand—a person who never thought she was building "Suze Orman," the empire. "I followed the signs, the path and the doors in front of me," she recalls. "And I wasn't afraid to walk through them."

In fact, the one-time restaurant employee maintains: "I loved every second of being a waitress. I loved serving every one of those people a plate full of joy. I loved every moment of every day."

She also celebrates her bygone eatery days by "the love that I had for the life that I had, not the life I dreamt of having." How many of us can say that?

Clearly, businessperson Suze Orman had the elusive "it" and served it up on a plate. "It" eventually served her—and countless financial information seekers—right back. As a result, it's hopeless to avoid Suze's razor-sharp, personal focus—and one would be a fool to try.

As expected, her various comments explored a litany of extraordinary self-help topics:

"People First. Then Money. Then Things." (I certainly know that one.)

"Who you are and what you have are synonymous." (I agree.)

"Always do what is right, rather than what is easy." (I try to.)

"Every new moment you spend with anybody and anything has to be a new moment and not just a recreation of the past." (I never thought of it that way.)

"When we deflect a compliment onto someone else's greatness, we are denying ourselves the greatness we deserve." (I inadvertently "deflected" and found myself on the receiving end of one of her patented—yet glorious—Suze smack downs. *A memory I will always treasure.*)

It would be easy to say that Suze is a force of nature, but nature is nothing if not unpredictable. Or is it? Especially when one considers the power of human nature.

Take a look at the trajectory of her career and one can't help but wonder: do the interests and qualities we display in our youth offer an even stronger glimpse into our future than we realize? Even those like Suze who, despite being blessed with "it," have doubted their intellectual abilities?

As a child, Suze dreamt of becoming a brain surgeon. When her high school transcript didn't support an educational focus on medicine, she chose to pursue social work. Either way, a young Suze Orman seemed intent on getting inside other people's heads—a goal she clearly managed to achieve.

Included in the National Association of Social Workers Code of Ethics is an entry that seems to have followed Suze from the classroom and into her multimedia spotlight: "Social workers respect the inherent dignity and worth of the person." Suze agrees: "If you define a social worker as one who wants to work for the good of all human kind, then yes, I am most definitely a social worker. You cannot teach somebody net worth unless they value their self-worth. Money flows in through your hands and flows out through your hearts."

SHOWMEJONES.COM

"Every new moment you spend with anybody and anything has to be a new moment and not just a recreation of the past."

—Suze Orman

Without question, Suze Oman is also the most intuitive person to ever take up residence in the interview spot opposite mine. There's no better example of her penchant for curiosity—and subsequent intuition—than her trademark skill with questions. She is intent on understanding "you" first—your methods and motivations.

Her voracious line of questioning flows naturally until she is satisfied your truth has been exposed. Why? "One can never fix a financial matter with money," she advises. "Always speak in truths, rather than in words." After all, in Ormanland, "Money has no sex, no race, no religion. Money is the universal language of the world." Money demands truth.

Even her answers can come in the form of questions. As with anyone who stands before her knows, Suze wants to challenge us to think, not just listen. Questions demand thought.

With facts, experience and tough love as her weapons of choice, Suze gets to the heart of the matter. In the process, she touches the hearts (and minds) of those she counsels. If, like me, you're bent on throwing your hat in the ring to speak with (the thought-full) Suze Orman, make sure it's a "thinking cap." She'll accept no less than your best effort, and you can absolutely expect the same in return.

WHETHER SUZE COULD SENSE my vulnerability or not, I was at a very low point when I first received her unscheduled (therefore *unexpected*) return phone call. Despite my tireless effort creating these columns and stories, their journey from Naples to the Nation was moving at slower-than-glacial pace.

For me, perhaps the most eye-opening discovery is how extraordinarily hard we do-gooders have to work just to—well—do good. If social media is any indicator, the public seems to respond best to funny, touching, shocking or (sadly) unkind. "Thought provoking" doesn't always seem to provoke a lot of thought—*or* attention. Basically, if you put a Kardashian on top of a glacier and pelted him or her with water balloons and filmed it, you'd be a hit. But dare to talk about how it may feel to *be* that very same irrigated Kardashian, and your message would likely have an uphill battle. *My fear* wasn't that I was doing all of this work for nothing, but that no one cared.

Suze Orman's innate sensitivity + her *very personal* advice + the aforementioned "Suze smack down" was *exactly* what I needed. At the risk of appearing to be the biggest crybaby to ever sit at a keyboard, I confess: I hung up the phone and blubbered—but not for the reason you may think. After years of consciously trying to *give to the universe*, for the first time, I was acutely aware that *the universe had responded in kind.*

In hindsight, the universe has given me *more* than I could ever wish for—but it took a shockingly well-timed phone call from Suze to force me to, quite literally, learn to view this "universal" concept though a brand new pair of eyes.

I once said to my father: "People don't want to discover *new ideas or talent* any more. They only seem to want to discover *money.*" Isn't it ironic that Suze Orman, a former waitress and the ultimate champion of money matters, ideas *and* talent would serve up a day of personal discovery I would never forget.

LYNN TRAVIS STENDER

N ot long after my Orman-themed column ran, Suze's wife, Kathy (K.T.) Travis remarked: "I want you to meet my sister, Lynn. You would love her painting classes." Despite my recent *SuzEpiphany*, a reflex reaction kicked in: "Help! I can't paint."

The tragedy: despite a platform based, in part, on dismissing our self-perceived limitations and accepting our innate creativity, **there are things we continue to tell ourselves we cannot do**. For example, those who maintain they can't write, speak in public, stay organized or, most detrimental of all, be creative.

Based in Boca Raton, American artist, teacher and lecturer Lynn Travis Stender has been teaching painting workshops for almost two decades. She is also known for her "Plein Air" workshops (painting outdoors), which she conducts in Napa Valley, Provence, Venice and Tuscany.

Though I whole-heartedly support Lynn's mantra: "If you have a soul, you have creative expression," her sister, Kathy Travis, caught me with my editorial pants down. After all, if I talked the talk, I must walk the walk—and acquaint with paint. Though I would have much preferred Venice or Tuscany, with my husband, son and daughter in tow, we were off to Boca!

Now seated with paintbrush in hand, Lynn taught while I listened, learned, painted and translated—and the double meanings exploded. After all, if art requires creativity—and creative thinking begets innovation—then art, imagination and success are inextricably linked.

Lynn: "What sets the mood of all landscape painting is the sky." Randy: The sky isn't the limit. Creatively speaking, the sky is the beginning and not the end.

Lynn: "When the artist sees the layers in the subject, perspective is applied." Randy: Without perspective—an understanding of the details—business leaders cannot lead.

Lynn: "Whatever you're creating your art on is called your support." Randy: Without the proper support, art—and its progenitors: imagination, originality and innovation—cannot exist.

Lynn: "The exact same materials and instruction result in unique individual expression." Randy: Collaboration rules. Everyone brings something different to the table.

SHOWMEJONES.COM

"If you have a soul, you have creative expression."

—Lynn Travis Stender

Did my time with the extraordinary Lynn Travis Stender expose my inner Monet? Well, I have yet to receive an invitation for a gallery exhibition. Did I conquer a deep-seated fear? Absolutely. How did I feel? Like Monet, Manet and *buffet*, all rolled into one!

Upon seeing my finished product, Suze's *face* said it all: "Don't quit your day job," but her verbal reaction to my watercolor masterpiece filled my intellectual canvas: "It doesn't matter what other people think. The only thing that matters is how it made you feel while doing it."

True, we have all heard the advice to reject our fears and be our authentic selves; but here's where the rubber meets the road, where the paintbrush meets the canvas: how you wish to be perceived and who you are may not be the same. Letting go of your fears and bravely facing your truth is the tricky part.

For those *fearless* enough to look in their philosophical mirror and accept what they see, I congratulate you. To be a student of one's self is our definitive life's work and—may I also suggest—a true art form.

WILD KINGDOM

M ary Lou Boggs Jones, my paternal grandmother, was the kindest, most loving woman I have ever known. My fondest childhood memories are the special weekends spent out in the wild on my grandparents' small farm just north of Columbia, Missouri.

With my beagle-mix, Snoopy, and my very special barnyard pal, Henny Penny the chicken, I spent many a wonderful weekend at that farm on North Murray Lane. Roaming the woods, scaling fences and playing catch: a ball gingerly tossed to Snoopy; a stray grasshopper lobbed to Henny Penny. The three of us were inseparable.

A little fat boy;
A little fat dog;
A little fat chicken;
And a grandmother secretly *plotting big trouble for Moose and Squirrel.*

As Mary Lou's death on January 23, 1990, coincided with my former wife's unexpected positive pregnancy result, I must extend my heartfelt appreciation to Grandma Jones, who, no doubt, used her newfound influence with *Him* to bring my daughter, Mary Elizabeth Jones, into my life on September 19, 1990, a little less than nine months later.

As for Snoopy, though my obsession with Charles M. Schultz and his Peanuts characters led to your uninspired name, you were the epitome of boy's best friend. Just understand that, if not "Snoopy," your name might have been "Barnabas Collins" or "Dark Shadow," so please count your posthumous puppy blessings.

And Henny Penny—yet another unimaginative name, courtesy of my grandmother this time—your untimely death in 1970 "at the paws of a wild coyote" was sad, very sad indeed. However, the mysterious circumstances of your death eventually came to light when, at age forty-three, some thirty-five years later, I learned from my older sister, Paula Perfect, that there was no ravenous coyote, *only a family meal that lacked an entrée.*

First, to my husband Derek: Your somewhat-well-intentioned assessment that *Henny Penny will always be part of me* did NOT make me feel better. Second, to my evil-secret-keeping sister Paula not-so-perfect: You suck.

And lastly, to my Grandma Jones: I know one day we will meet again and you will hold me in your arms as you did when I was a boy. And I will, once again, know that feeling of complete safety and unabashed affection. And, of course, we'll discuss *how I named my daughter after you.*

Then God, you and I will sit down and have a little chat about, for example, politics, art, childhood memories and oh, *I know*, this Henny-Penny-as-food situation. As our family wasn't poor, and Jell-O alone would have made for a fine Sunday meal, *you*, Mary Lou Boggs Jones, can finally explain to me, *and God*, why you couldn't be bothered to make a trip to the poultry department at Nowell's Supermarket on that Sunday oh so long ago.

Because, trust me, *I would die* to know your answer.

ShowMeJones.com

"Most people who say they don't like animals don't like people much either."

—Jack Hanna

JACK HANNA

Though some would argue Grandma Jones was simply following Mother Nature's time-tested guidelines, my forever-altered intestinal tract does not agree. This dining debacle also served as a reminder to me that the animal kingdom has long been instrumental in teaching children about appropriate—and sometimes *wildly inappropriate*—behavior.

A rabbit named Peter educated us on the importance of conflict resolution. For better or worse, monkey George was habitually curious and, in separate incidents, three bears and three pigs taught us about the importance of home security. Plus, despite a literary reputation as "big" and "bad," according to wildlife luminary Jack Hanna, "A wolf will feed the sick, the old and the young first." Pretty impressive character traits for a creature so oft maligned.

But we've learned to expect Jungle Jack Hanna to set the record straight on a world most of us will never experience firsthand. Inspired by wildlife pioneer Marlin Perkins, Jack Hanna parlayed a fascination with animals and a position leading the Columbus Zoo into a television empire spanning thirty-plus years and countless TV appearances—most notably, his frequent guest spots on *Good Morning America* and alongside David Letterman.

Hanna's high regard for the animal population is also reflected in his view of the public's acceptance of the animal kingdom. "Most people who say they don't like animals don't like people much either."

By all accounts, Jack Hanna seems to be a "what you see is what you get" kind of guy—a genuine gentleman. Jack has set a very simple benchmark for appropriate professional behavior. "I operate by The Golden Rule—do unto others as you would have them do unto you."

When I first published this column, it accidentally read: "do onto others as you would have them to do onto you." Uh, not quite the same. Though much of what animals do onto each other they brazenly do in public.

Of course, humans are animals too—complete with instincts, genetic predispositions, unique skill sets and laws to keep us from acting like predatory animals. Yet, prey we do—through such actions as leveraged buyouts, hostile takeovers and foreclosures.

When asked about lessons human worker-bees can glean from the animal kingdom, Jack enthusiastically responds, "Just look at ants and termites, they each have specific jobs to do." By performing specific tasks every day, these creatures work solely to serve the greater good—ostensibly without complaining.

Animals = 1; Humans = 0

However, Jack also points to an innate respect in the wild that does not always translate into the land of the bipeds. "The animal world does not waste food and animals do not abuse their own children. For example, gorillas may fight, but they still work together."

Working through issues to achieve top performance is apparently part of the natural order of things. It's about survival. As the concept of business survival has never been more prominent, shouldn't cooperation receive equal billing?

Animals = 2; Humans = 0

Though Jack Hanna also marvels at the mysteries behind the instinctual and highly effective way animals communicate, many in workplace settings marvel at some people's overwhelming lack of communication skills.

Animals = 3; Humans = 0

Specifically, according to Hanna, "The elephant is one of the most intelligent creatures on the planet." So yes, it seems that without the benefit of iPhone, Twitter or Outlook, an elephant truly never forgets.

Time to hire me an elephant. The Laws of Nature win every time.

NICOLE & ALANA FELD

The word "circus" has fallen upon hard times. In recent years, this seemingly happy child-focused event has often been subject to less-than-favorable use in describing such activities as a "media" or "political" circus. Essentially, a beloved symbol of childhood has become an oft-used synonym for "chaos."

If you think your office is like a circus—probably because you and your co-workers struggle to keep several balls in the air simultaneously—try actually keeping several balls in the air simultaneously and *think again*. In the case of Ringling Bros. and Barnum & Bailey Circus, chaos would be the last word to describe its time-honored business practices. The meticulous planning and preparation necessary to transport hundreds of people and live animals from town to town is nothing short of a creative and logistic miracle.

Feld Entertainment has owned and operated The Greatest Show on Earth® since 1967. In fact, the Feld family has maintained the legendary brand longer than Barnum, Bailey *or* the Ringlings.

They operate by a sophisticated mix of traditional business savvy coupled with a new generation of creative thinkers—sisters Nicole, Alana and Juliette Feld. And that's what keeps it relevant, fresh and engaging.

Regardless of your age, the circus evokes a sense of wonder that few experiences can ever emulate. My visit with the Felds also offered a glimpse of a tour-bound cast in rehearsal. Still, take away the make-up, costumes, lights and sound, and you're left with an equally compelling experience. However, the spectacle is replaced by a stunning display of humanity— the unwavering commitment visible in the very real faces of each athlete, comedian and player. Few of us will ever be as uniquely defined by our professions as those who choose a life in the circus.

The Feld sisters grew up with clowns, acrobats and animals serving as a backdrop for their childhood. As parents, Kenneth Feld and wife Bonnie wisely stressed the importance of education and encouraged their daughters to discover their individual passions.

While Nicole insists she and her sisters were not groomed to follow in their father's and grandfather's footsteps, Alana whimsically suggests, "Perhaps we were groomed our entire lives and didn't know it." Kenneth's most important lesson was one of respect—for the business, the employees and the audiences. Even when the young sisters asked to perform, the practical patriarch insisted upon a regular three-show performance day. "We were not circus brats; we were taught to respect what everyone did," recalls Nicole.

For many of us, lines can easily blur between parental and managerial skills. However, when one is in the "people business" with a focus on family values, nothing beats good parenting.

Though many family businesses struggle to balance the old guard with the new watch, Nicole, Alana and Juliette literally bring a lifetime of experience—as both impressionable children and educated adults—to a business whose sole purpose is to celebrate a child's imagination. Nicole acknowledges the pressure: "It's a huge responsibility to take care of a brand that is a national treasure."

As with any business, there will undoubtedly be challenges—but what good is a circus without a balancing act?

ShowMeJones.com

"Everything in nature has the same importance."

—Clyde Butcher

CLYDE BUTCHER

One who is categorized as a "black and white" thinker has been said to see only yes or no, right or wrong, good or evil—and nothing in between. Some suggest black and white thinkers view the world without emotion and practice only logical thought. Naysayers sing the praises of the various shades of gray—and the nuances that lie in between.

As for our more colorful personalities, even our children are taught that color represents creativity. Just ask any child about their reaction to their first big box of Crayola crayons. Black may work well for an outline but what child can resist the temptation of Shocking Pink, Midnight Blue or Jungle Green?

Before you decide where you lie on the color/thought spectrum, celebrated landscape and nature artist Clyde Butcher is likely to turn your "black and white" belief system on its ear. With a passionate fan base and more awards than you can shake a bald cypress tree at, Clyde has built his career on challenging what it means to be a black and white thinker while redefining the importance placed on color. As an internationally renowned nature photographer, he works exclusively in black and white.

Responding to the tragic death of his seventeen-year-old son Ted, killed by a drunk driver in 1986, Clyde made a career-changing decision to honor his child—and life itself—and shun the commercial trends of photography. "It became more important to pursue what I loved—not what 'sells,'" he says.

Henceforth, Clyde's artistic joy—his soul—would forever be expressed in black, white and the seemingly monochromatic rainbow that lies in between. Why? "Color gets in the way of seeing what is really in the picture. When all you look for is color, you miss the details." To Clyde: "Everything in nature has the same importance."

Though maintaining focus is essential in business, of equal importance is the ability to stop and reconsider what shaped that focus in the first place— or Clyde Butcher's beloved "details."

An advocate of seeing the "Big Picture," he prefers his work displayed in large formats. "When it's big, you can't really see it all—you have to feel it. Your eye can't take in the entire image, which forces you to step in and study it," he says. A basic thought process that metaphorically applies to any type of big picture investigation—artistic, business or otherwise. After all, what may initially seem to be of critical importance could ultimately end up clouding your judgment.

As Clyde sees photography as both science and emotion, he ultimately dares the left-brained (analytical) and right-brained (creative) public to do something profoundly simple: think.

Whether you see the world in black, white and/or nifty shades of gray....

Or if you prefer the colorful Land of Oz to Dorothy Gale's Kansas....

Butcher's lesson is clear: no matter what you do in life, a little extra thought as well as an attention to—and respect for—detail goes a very long way.

IF YOU THINK ABOUT IT, "WILD" is an interesting word. But no matter how you look at it, when *wild* appears in a sentence, a certain amount of energy—positive *or* negative—is sure to follow.

Untamed: a wild animal.

Enthusiastic: a child at the circus.

Fierce: a bunny rabbit.

Overwhelmed: me in the presence of a bunny rabbit.

Rowdy: a Republican in the presence of a Democrat, *and vice versa.*

Outrageous: American politics.

Yep, I'm going there. And as part of this process, I'm going to quote myself from earlier in this book:

It's so important we don't play it safe and simply interact with those with whom we agree. It's essential to look for common ground with those who have alternate points of view.

As the senior vice president of Manhattan Construction's Southwest Florida Operations, Bruce Fields became part of an extremely elite group of those blessed with unprecedented presidential access. Not only was Bruce afforded the opportunity to work hand-in-hand with former President George W. Bush, he was present at the dedication of the George W. Bush Presidential Center. Bruce scored his invitation based on a personal career milestone: he served as Manhattan's project executive in charge of the construction of the new $250 million facility in Dallas.

On April 25, 2013, as Bruce Fields listened to five presidents—each representing different generations and belief systems—he experienced a flashback to a beloved bygone era. A time when the impact of the nation's accomplishments was regarded with greater awe than the challenges faced in getting there.

Though we have certainly seen modern-day examples of our country coming together in a *crisis*, Bruce observes, "I witnessed five presidents put aside personal politics and demonstrate an authentic and sincere support of each other. They came together in celebration of a national achievement."

They varied from Carter's heartfelt listing of Bush's accomplishments to Clinton's overt appreciation for their cooperative efforts on behalf of Haiti. From George H.W. Bush's joy at honoring a son to Obama's acknowledgment of W's support, the spirit of cooperation and camaraderie was palpable.

"We all know there are differences in the ideologies of the two political parties," Bruce explains. "However, on this particular day, it was both unexpected and refreshing to see these prolific gentlemen focused instead on *what we have in common*."

SHOWMEJONES.COM

"One of the best things you can do in life is struggle—those days are seared in my memory. It's the best thing that ever happened to me."

—Sean Hannity

SEAN HANNITY

The day before I was scheduled to chat with conservative talk-show host Sean Hannity, I happened to be on the phone with my buddy "Kurt": a fair-minded, well-educated professional. And Kurt's curt response to my interview news? "I don't like Sean Hannity." As Kurt is one of my regular go-to sources for intelligent conversation, I probed a bit more: "Well, have you ever *watched* his show?"

The answer was "no." What's more, I discovered that his opinion had been formed solely from "news programs" on—*wait for it*—Comedy Central. When it comes to the soundbite-driven ways in which we seem to form our opinions, it truly must be noted: *#HoustonWeHaveAProblem.*

But as they say: Opinions are like—ahem—noses; *everybody has one.*

Conservative talk-show host and opinion purveyor Sean Hannity is the first to admit: "I make my living off the First Amendment." Sean serves as host of FOX News Channel's *Hannity.* Based in New York, he joined the network in 1996. Additionally, *The Sean Hannity Show,* syndicated to more than 500 radio stations nationwide, boasts a loyal audience in the millions.

What gets him worked up? (Part One): "I like passionate debate. All discussion is good because we learn from it." The result: enthusiasm, wordplay, dialogue.

What gets Sean worked up? (Part Two): lack of preparation. The result: interrogation, confrontation, hullabaloo.

With the understanding that "passionate debate" is instrumental to growth and development on a variety of professional fronts, wouldn't the real tragedy be if these discussions never took place?

Despite Sean's goal that his words not be taken personally—people do. And controversy ensues. Search "Hannity" online and the third-party opinions are varied. So wide-ranging, in fact, "Kurt" likely isn't the only one who has never tuned into Hannity's actual programs. After all, many have been guilty of surrendering their minds to hearsay on both sides of the political fence. In a world where the mouth often engages before the ears have completed their due diligence, this may come as no surprise.

Sean is so easy to talk to that I felt comfortable expressing some of my personal views. For example, I candidly shared that he loses me when he blatantly "makes fun of" a sitting president. As we Americans don't seem to always enjoy worldwide popularity, I question whether this type of media coverage ultimately does more *international* harm than *stateside* good. Did I expect my pronouncement to change Sean's on-air process? No. Did he *respectfully* listen to me? Yes, he absolutely did.

In fact, Sean Hannity places a premium on listening. "I'm not in the position of reading people's minds," he says. Clearly, Hannity's content targets conservative America; however, he suggests a wider appeal: "I'm all about solutions. A big part of the mission of my show is to teach—to provide news and information you won't find elsewhere." With his eye on education, Sean has, for example, committed significant on-air time to issues such as Sharia law and freedom concerts.

Though some occasionally show pride in their blue-collar roots, Sean maintains an ongoing relationship with his working-class background. As a young man, he was employed as a dishwasher, construction worker, waiter and bartender. His takeaway: "One of the best things you can do in life is struggle—those days are seared in my memory. It's the best thing that ever happened to me."

To Sean Hannity—as opposed to "is greater than"—the whole may be the sum of its parts. "I was happy poor and I'm happy now. I don't think about whether or not I'm successful. I read, I prepare, I keep my head down and I work."

Although he insists that "all opinions need to be heard," Sean dismisses the proliferation of self-proclaimed authorities popping up daily on the web. "I don't read comments from anonymous people sitting around in their underwear pounding on a computer. It's much easier to demonize somebody from afar."

A certain amount of respect should always be extended to those who have the courage to stand behind their convictions. You may not always agree with what Hannity has to say, but his face, name and reputation are inextricably linked to his belief system.

Sean Hannity *owns his opinions*. If only "PitBullMom7," "Mysteryman1956," "Listen2meFL" and countless others typing away in their underwear would do the same.

Kevin Randall Jones

CARLY FIORINA

In case you haven't heard, Carly Fiorina is a Republican. Despite her considerable success in other areas, many refuse to see anything other than Carly's politics. Alas, we live in a world where one's political affiliation seems to trump all else—a world where the "left" and the "right" have been accused of placing an emphasis on being right as opposed to doing right. It's a world where the skill of *listening* has tragically diminished.

Carly offers a more sensible view: "From my experience, people agree on about 85 percent of the issues and politicians argue about the rest of it. Politics magnifies differences." However, she skillfully focuses less on differences in favor of areas of agreement: "Everybody actually wants to live a life of dignity, purpose and meaning, but they have to believe they have a chance to."

In 1999, Fiorina was named chairman and CEO of Hewlett-Packard, thereby becoming the first woman to lead a Fortune 20 business. Much has been written—both positive and negative—of her time on the job. Lest we forget the swift exit often faced by those sitting atop the corporate ladder, Carly's departure came with more media fanfare than would likely accompany most male C-suite partings.

Gender-bias aside, as a leader, she has fashioned a refreshingly simple platform: "Unlocking the potential of the people I work with is the highest calling of leadership. In my experience, no matter what the setting is, people have far more potential than they realize—so organizations have more potential than they usually utilize."

Since leaving Hewlett-Packard in 2005, Carly has served in a large number of advisory and policy-making positions and lent her support to several civic organizations.

Though she is keenly aware of being a woman in a male-dominated world, in 2009 Carly was physiologically reminded of this reality. Yes, she lost her senate bid to Barbara Boxer of California the following year, but she triumphed personally: Carly became a breast-cancer survivor—an act that elevated her fearless factor to new heights.

> ## SHOWMEJONES.COM
>
> "One woman can change the world because one woman changes the lives of everyone around her."
>
> —Carly Fiorina

"Before I had cancer, it *looked* like I was fearless," she says. "Courage is not the absence of fear; it's acting in spite of fear. I'm not sure I would have [run for president] before I had cancer. There actually isn't anything to be afraid of."

Carly is understandably still mourning the 2009 loss of her thirty-five-year-old stepdaughter, Lori Ann—a situation she thoughtfully explains: "She struggled with addictions and they overcame her." However, Lori Ann Fiorina's life is celebrated every day her stepmother moves forward to support women's issues. Through heartache, Lori Ann added even more fearlessness to her stepmother's agenda.

"Her death is probably why I am so passionate about wasted potential because death is not the only thing that wastes people's potential," Carly says. "Many people's potential is wasted or overlooked or dismissed or never given a chance."

Carly's commitment to Lori Ann's memory was also found in her (albeit unsuccessful) 2016 run for the White House as well as in her role as founder and chairman of the women-focused Unlocking Potential Project.

"Women are half the nation," she says. "Women also represent the most underutilized potential in the world. If we want to solve problems, women have to play."

Just as I was about to leave a whimsically adorned room at Golisano Children's Museum of Naples, Florida, our interview host, Carly called my attention to a sign on the door and playfully inquired: "Do *you* know the words to the 'Clean-Up Song'? Because I do."

Clean up, clean up, everybody everywhere.
Clean up, clean up, everybody do your share.

Did I ever anticipate that a presidential candidate would sing Barney the dinosaur's "Clean-Up Song" to me? No. Did I metaphorically look skyward and exclaim: "Thank you Journalism Gods?" *Yes!*

Though TV's *Barney & Friends* showcased young boys and girls working as equals, the demonstrative Tyrannosaurus rex's lesson of equality hasn't always transferred into the professional woman's reality. In fact, shouldn't today's intellectual "clean up" revolve around the rethinking of our biased preconceptions and prejudices—especially when those ideologies negatively impact the women in our lives?

Despite the adversity-ridden slippery slope of the campaign trail, Carly maintains: "One of the things that always drives people apart is when someone is judgmental. If we judge others, we are going to separate ourselves from one another. No one of us is any better than any other one of us."

Now, listen up: Forget about politics. Forget about what you thought you knew about Carly Fiorina. Instead, think of your grandmother, mother, sister, wife and/or daughter. What's more, any male whose résumé includes the job title of "father" also has a 50 percent chance of having a daughter. Regardless of your political beliefs, your daughter needs you to passionately defend her right to reach her potential. In Carly's words: "One woman can change the world because one woman changes the lives of everyone around her."

Does Carly Fiorina expect you to always agree with her? No. However, placing a greater emphasis on the power of *listening* works in every professional setting, political or otherwise. Just as there is a gap between reading and comprehending, there is a chasm between *listening*…and just *hearing*.

> ## SHOWMEJONES.COM
>
> "You don't change anybody's view of politics; you can only change their view of YOU."
>
> —James Carville

MARY MATALIN & JAMES CARVILLE

I recently took a vacation from my normal editorial crusade for real human contact and posted a question on Facebook—one I frequently ask in person, too. Yes, Facebook: the technological tool that has often reduced the concept of a "friend" from flesh and bone to, often times, little known.

The question: Considering how divided we seem to be as a nation, has "hate" won? Is there hope for compassion, collaboration, discussion and compromise?

Whether the answers came via cyberspace or in person, the candor was undeniable.

"I'm not sure 'hate' has won, but intolerance seems to be the new normal." —*Kevin Kenneally, Naples, Florida*

Though not included as part of my question, governmental politics received most of the attention.

"I prefer to not know the party affiliation or political beliefs of anyone in my circle of friends. What I literally don't know can't hurt me." —Tammy Wyatt Roberts, Potomac, Maryland

Politics: The word most likely to induce fear, elicit groans and disengage human edit buttons the moment it's injected into a public forum.

My favorite definition of "politics" comes from Merriam-Webster:

The total complex of relations between people living in society.

Why? Politics are undeniably in play practically anywhere power is desired. Political maneuvering can be found inside all levels of government and in the office, on volunteer boards and within homeowners associations, in the classroom and even at Little League games.

I also chatted with politics' dynamic duo, the pair who have come to symbolize the ultimate marriage of left and right wing ideologies: Mary Matalin and James Carville. It's not just that the pair has successfully navigated a twenty-plus-year marriage and raised two children, but their professional lives have provided them collective access to all corners of our nation's political arena.

As an author, television and radio host, political contributor, pundit and public speaker, Mary Matalin is one of the most popular conservative voices in America. She served under President Ronald Reagan, made her mark as George H.W. Bush's campaign director, and most recently served as assistant to President George W. Bush, and as assistant and counselor to Vice President Dick Cheney.

Her liberal husband, James "The Ragin' Cajun" Carville, is a political consultant, bestselling author, actor, producer, talk-show host and speaker. James' list of electoral successes suggests a knack for steering overlooked campaigns to unexpected victories and for turning political underdogs into winners. His most prominent victory was the 1992 election of William Jefferson Clinton to the U.S. Presidency.

If James is correct that part of our collective disconnect stems from members of one party not coming into personal contact with those in the other, then what happens in Mary and James' polar-opposite scenario? Spoiler alert: it ain't hate.

"Our marriage isn't a democracy. We have a higher calling and responsibility to our family," Mary says. "Considerations in marriages are way different than considerations in politics."

Couples can certainly disagree on any number of issues, but when it comes to politics, James proposes: "It's a learning process. Sometimes, you just have to understand you are going to disagree. You're not going to change anybody's mind so why talk about it? You just have to let things go."

And one let-it-go method? The couple intuitively knows when to leave politics at the office: "You don't want to come home at night and clean your own toilet," Mary says.

"Hate has not won but stupidity is inching up the scale and nonsense is overtaking a good portion of the country. Whatever happened to The Golden Rule?" —*Karen Gentry Manning, Gladstone, Missouri*

Yes, "Do unto others as you would have them do unto you": a staple of childhood education that some of us feel disappeared alongside Dick, Jane, Sally and their enthusiastic canine, Spot. So, I repurposed "do unto others" into "what do you admire about each other?"

"I like that he's relentlessly honest in the projects he chooses to work on. He's ethical; he's well humored; he's rational. He honestly believes his opinions," Mary says. "What I most love about my husband has nothing to do with politics. He helps everybody. He's a giant soul."

And now, James on Mary: "She is very smart and very loyal. She has a really broad skill set. She almost likes to go against the wind."

Nonetheless, is cooperation dead? "Compromise has become an empty word—it means capitulation," Mary says. "I find that where political conversations break down is when somebody is arguing on emotion and not facts. If there is data to support your argument, I'm all ears. I have changed my mind on many things."

And James? "There is a lot of acrimony and people talking through or at each other, but the public kind of demands it. Negative partisanship is pretty proven. It's not so much that they like their own party, but that they detest the other party." Yet so many of us were taught to fight *for* our beliefs, not *against* the values of others.

Matalin and Carville also choose to focus on areas of agreement. For example, to these two residents of New Orleans, civic responsibility has no party affiliation.

In truth, as someone who has *chosen* to remain somewhat politically neutral, I was intimidated by the couple's intellects—but I openly admitted that and chose to listen and learn. But what about the extraordinary number of Americans who refuse to accept what they don't know and fail to take steps to educate themselves? The elusive *ideal world* aside, Mary proposes: "There's a reason we all believe what we believe—because we think it is right *or* we've seen it work."

That said, "hate" is not part of her platform. "The answer is to sit down and talk about it. The answer is not to scale up; it's to sit down. Shouting doesn't close potholes or rebuild schools. I like to light candles, not push the darkness." And one of Mary's primary decision-making tools? "You have to rely on your gut. Your gut is only as good as your preparation." To Matalin, the best gut reactors are those who have invested time in thought.

In the end, Matalin and Carville enjoy a tremendous benefit: they automatically challenge each other's belief system and, in turn, strengthen each other's resolve. However, their real (shockingly simple) secret? They compartmentalize: they keep their work—and political beliefs—in proper perspective. Politics is simply one part of a much bigger, glorious household picture.

Lest we forget, a person's politics is not the sum total of attributes that make up his or her character. In fact, to James: "You don't change anybody's view of politics; you can only change their view of YOU."

Now, reread this entire section, not just as a profile of Matalin and Carville, but as a means to study your approach to compassion, collaboration, discussion and compromise—as well as politics' influence in all areas of your life. Become a student of YOU.

> **"I am a believer that love always wins. Those lemons may need a lot of sugar, but there will always be lemonade on my screened-in front porch." —Ronna Rothenberger, Portland, Oregon**

Of course, here's the clincher: "We have an advantage over a lot of people because we're in love with each other," James says. "You know, at the end of the day, that's kind of a big advantage."

Besides, didn't someone once tell us that "love means never having to say you're sorry"?

This column was originally published in the Naples Daily News on Saturday, June 11, 2016. In the early morning hours of Sunday, June 12, 2016, a gunman killed forty-nine innocent people in a gay nightclub in Orlando, Florida.

THE FACTS OF LIFE

*M*arcus Welby, M.D., starring Robert Young, premiered on television in 1969, and quickly gained my rapt attention. So at seven years old, I immediately knew I just had to be a doctor like Dr. Welby on TV, or even chain-smoking Dr. G., my ear, nose and throat doctor in Missouri.

Though much less was known about the dangers of smoking in *those days*, and despite his medical specialty, curmudgeonly Dr. G. would light up between each patient until, by roughly 10:15 each morning, an actual cloud hovered throughout his '50s-era office.

But it was his birdlike assistant, Mrs. H., who fascinated me. *(Long sentence alert!)* Clad in a conventional white nursing uniform and platform shoes, sporting a traditional nurse's hat covering vibrant henna-red hair tucked oh-so-carefully under a hairnet, Mrs. H. hastily fussed about the office, ushering patients safely through the smoky haze.

In retrospect, I suppose Mrs. H., who appeared *to me* to be about 103 years old at the time, was my first real exposure to a multitasker. The woman never stopped moving. And between my Virgo astrological sign, and early Type-A tendencies, it's no wonder she was so interesting to scrutinize. One never quite knew when Mrs. H. would emerge from the smoky haze, grab an unsuspecting patient by the arm and whisk him or her away to Exam Room One. It was basically a medical *Phantom of the Opera* but without the music or disfigurement.

But mostly, I was captivated by TV's Marcus Welby and staff. Every week, I watched in wonder—forcing myself to memorize the medical terms I heard on the show. Another side benefit: I could provide my family and friends a comprehensive recap of every single episode. On the other hand, my Welby-inspired medical knowledge proved to be occasionally hazardous as I would somewhat carelessly diagnose diseases in my neighborhood. "Uh…Scott, you really should show this to your mom—you may have a diphyllobothrium infection—I'm pretty sure you could die."

Late one night my medical competence was to be put to the ultimate test when I was suddenly awakened by a blood-curdling scream. I vaulted out of bed and entered my mom and dad's room to determine the source of all the ruckus, whereupon I discovered my dad doubled over in—dare I say it?—hemorrhoid-related pain.

Sorry for this, Dad. Please just keep in mind I dedicated this ENTIRE BOOK to you.

To begin, how on earth does one simplify the concept of hemorrhoids relative to a seven-year-old's mental capacity? Yet my brave mother managed to channel her inner Welby to elucidate as best she could during our brief triage consult. Though I now understand that pain of that intensity would likely have been caused by a *thrombosed* hemorrhoid, in—uh—*hindsight*, I am pleased my mother did not have that specific terminology at the ready. No doubt I would have heard *trombone* hemorrhoid, which would have confused the situation and hindered my ability to provide accurate counsel.

But now that I think about it, trombone hemorrhoid is actually a pretty accurate description for that particular malady.

As soon as my mother finished her rather awkward explanation, I deliberated for a moment, paused briefly, looked my thrashing father straight in his bloodshot eyes and stated candidly, "I am sorry, this is something I don't know anything about. I am afraid I can't help you." I then returned to my room and went back to sleep.

Of course, children are supposed to explore many different areas of interest. It's always been my belief that the characteristics leading to a child's most rewarding career path emerge early. It's equally important for parents to look for these signs in a child's initial development.

As I'm not sure actual doctors should have an "oops" option when it comes to treating patients, it was clearly in everyone's best interest that I moved on to consider alternative career goals. And I did.

Now I'm a SPIN Doctor!

SHOWMEJONES.COM

"There is always a window of opportunity."

—Bob Emfield

BOB EMFIELD

Whether the source is my presentations or essays, it's pretty much guaranteed I'm going to get on my soapbox and stubbornly champion a concept I view as *fact*: **we are all creative.**

I recently asked seminar attendees for a show of hands as to "Who has a teenager living at home?" (<25 percent) "Who has raised a teenager?" (>70 percent) "Who has *been* a teenager?" Oddly enough, only about 90 percent confirmed their prior teen status, leading me to believe that, for some, it's just better to completely block out the teen years.

But my point? **You cannot** *raise* **a teenager or** *be* **a teenager without developing a keen ability to think creatively.** Of course, not everyone can be as lucky as me. My mother would actually create scenarios to justify my more dubious adolescent activities, especially when my late-night, return-home condition was, shall we say, fueled by more than just a Double Whopper with Cheese.

MOM
(noticing my listless behavior)
Randy, do you feel okay?

TEEN RANDY
Well, now that you mention it, I am a
bit—uh—*lightheaded?*

MOM
(pause)
What did you have to drink at your Burg-
er King employee party?

TEEN RANDY
Uh…Hawaiian Punch?

(technically, this was a true statement)

MOM
(pause)
Randy, *do you think* someone put *alcohol*
in your Hawaiian Punch when you weren't
looking? Well, we better get you to bed.

Though she likely didn't believe her ridiculous *teen-boozehound-Randy-got-Hawaiian-punched* scenario, as evidenced in the way my mother has lived her entire life, she was the definitive *creative thinker*. And if she chose to *creative think* her way out of the possibility she was raising a juvenile delinquent, who was I to argue?

Keep in mind this was the same woman who, in 1974, loaded me, my best friends Suzi and Scott, and their mother Nancy, into our enormous Electra 225 convertible and drove us to the University of Missouri campus to watch the streakers: "I never thought I'd live to see that day that people would run around nekkid. But now that they are, let's go!"

Without her unconditional love and inspired lifelong thought processes, would I have grown up to become—well—a *professional creative thinker*? I say "no."

IF THERE IS ONE CASUALTY of our increasingly frenetic business lives, it's the decline in time devoted to simply think, listen, inspire and create. After all, can any business thrive without a healthy infusion of fresh ideas and creative thinking?

In the late 1980s, friends, beach enthusiasts and retail-industry veterans Bob Emfield and Tony Margolis took the aforementioned time to embrace their love of Florida's Gulf Coast—going so far as to fashion a fictional character symbolizing their appreciation for the idyllic tropical lifestyle. They created Tommy Bahama.

Emfield and Margolis understood what their creation ate and drank as well as how he spent his free time in his quest to live life as one long weekend. Their lives and the lifestyles of countless consumers changed when the following idea surfaced: "Why don't we dress this guy?" A chance meeting between Margolis and fashion designer Lucio Dalla Gasperina resulted in a newly-formed management trio ready to introduce Tommy Bahama to the national retail landscape.

Though the three founders shared leadership responsibilities, another man stood above the rest. "At every meeting, we always added a fourth chair for Tommy," Bob says. The invisible presence reinforced the notion that all business decisions had to be based on the question, "What would Tommy do?"—a brand marketing play absolutely brilliant in its ingenuity and simplicity.

Tommy even took a seat at our lunch meeting. Okay, laugh if you want at the image of Bob and I repeatedly referring to an empty chair, but Tommy gave an entire brand—and now our fascinating discussion—a highly unique yet very beneficial focus.

To Bob, "there is always a window of opportunity," but his own window may never have opened if he and Tony hadn't taken the time to be creative visionaries on a grand scale.

> ## SHOWMEJONES.COM
> "You cannot raise a teenager or be a teenager without developing a keen ability to think creatively."
>
> —Randall Kenneth Jones

Then again, isn't creativity ultimately the cornerstone of any successful business? Creative thinking has been responsible for many of the images, brands and cultural icons we take for granted today. The publishing industry gave us Scarlett O'Hara and Rhett Butler; the food and beverage industry gave us Coca-Cola; the health care industry gave us penicillin; and the entertainment industry gave us Mickey Mouse.

Menswear's Tommy Bahama has certainly earned its place on this list of truly inspired accomplishments. This also raises a very important question: As a business leader, are you doing everything possible to create environments where your teams can think creatively and speak openly?

Absolutely no organization can afford to miss out on an inspired thought or imaginative concept that may revolutionize its business.

Though all three founders retired in 2008, Bob's ongoing passion for the brand is apparent—and, metaphorically or not, Tommy himself is never far from his side. As Bob puts it, "There's a little bit of Tommy in all of us."

If a *beachcomber* is defined as somebody who looks for valuable things at the seashore, then Bob, Tony and Lucio are arguably the three most imaginative beachcombers of all time—finding extraordinary value in the coastline by cleverly looking beyond the seashells and spare change.

So is Tommy Bahama real or imagined? Just ask the millions who have bought into his ongoing search for the endless weekend, and the answer is clear. Like Virginia and Santa Claus—I dare say, there too is a Tommy Bahama.

BILL DONIUS

Bill Donius wants people to think; (some might say) twice as hard as they normally do. In fact, Donius' professional focus is the placement of one's Left Brain (commonly known as the analytical side) in direct competition with his Right Brain (typically credited with creativity, imagination and intuition).

If his theories hold true, the Right Brain may just win or—at a minimum—significantly challenge the (often dominant) Left Brain's insatiable need for logic, analysis and computation.

Bill spent thirty years toiling in high-profile, left-brained pursuits supporting the health care, television production, retail food and banking industries. However, what began in the late '90s as a personal journey to better understand his "lack of success with personal, intimate relationships" led to Bill's current role as a popular corporate speaker/trainer and author of the *New York Times* bestseller, *Thought Revolution*.

Though he credits Dr. Roger Sperry's (1981) Nobel Prize-winning research on the independence of brain function between the left and right hemispheres as inspiration, Bill saw another potential application. He spent the next six years conducting research with hundreds of test subjects to determine if a methodology for unlocking innovation, intuition and creativity could be applied to Corporate America. The answer: a resounding "yes."

Look at it this way: "The most overused saying in business is 'think outside the box,' but how many know how to do it?" he asks.

Bill employs a hands-on method of coaching a meaningful right-brain response—one best experienced in person. For example, when he asked my "Left Brain" to describe my "Business Class" column, my memorized response seized control: "'Business Class' is an exploration of positive business principles selected from interviews with high-level executives, newsmakers, business leaders and business-savvy celebrities."

Conversely, when Bill engaged my "Right Brain," the result was short, sweet—even shocking. My non-verbal, imaginative brainwaves delivered an emotionally-based yet infinitively more accurate answer. In fact, so powerful was the image in my mind's eye, it appeared in bold neon lights—like the Las Vegas strip of the frontal lobe.

My Right-Brain answer: "VALUES."

SHOWMEJONES.COM

"How can we embrace the power of the *creative process* if some of us still fail to respect the power of the *creative person*?"

—Randall Kenneth Jones

With the understanding that *imagination* and *children* seem to go hand in hand, Bill Donius points to traditional education as almost adversarial to creative thinking: "We are taught to not daydream, to follow specific rules and to color inside the lines," he says. Bill also observes: "Sir Isaac Newton, Bill Gates, Steve Jobs, and even Madam Curie had their most defining creative breakthroughs before they were thirty years old. Even brilliant minds get trapped."

Today's primary Right-Brain trap: "Reliving the same day over and over again." If the Right Brain's primary foe is redundancy, then the Left Brain's primary excuse is: "I don't have enough time."

Much has been written about the business world's lust for creativity, but how much of that is really true? Just ask around and the concept of creative thinking seems to represent *freedom* to some, and *panic* to others. Those who love facts and figures fear the Right Brain's muddled fodder—the alleged whirlwind of overcharged neurons and electrons battling over synaptic access to reason. Many also view the Right Brain as more frivolous and less focused—more of a tool for fantasy than problem-solving.

What's more, look at the terms and phrases often associated with corporate "creative types" such as marketers, copywriters and graphic designers: erratic, distracted, "all over the place." Our creatives have frequently been accused of lacking an attention-to-detail just because their Right-Brain proclivities provide the ultimate "Big Picture" of inspiration.

Then again, look at how we traditionally devalue our creatives. I am personally all-too-aware of how many people wish to gain access to a "creative" for free. *(Oh yes, my words magically transport themselves from my head to the page on their own. Here, please take some. I'll make more.)* And just ask a graphic designer or photographer and he/she will likely scream when describing the number of times their labor has been reduced from dedicated effort to a finger-snap of activity.

The next question could be: How can we embrace the power of the *creative process* if some of us still fail to respect the power of the *creative person*?

Per Bill, the Right Brain is (perhaps even more) likely to deliver clarity and order. In fact, it can provide the same immediate gratification so often associated with the Left Brain's love of sequencing and facts.

Finally, for those of you have always viewed the Right Brain as the creator of slapdash thoughts sent over to the Left Brain for processing and clarification, think again: By literally keeping an open mind, you may discover that Bill Donius' *Thought Revolution* connects the two divergent sides of our brains by cleverly building a thoughtful bridge over muddled fodder.

Yes, Simon and Garfunkel fans, my Right Brain hoped you would notice.

Kevin Randall Jones

COLIN MOCHRIE

Many of us feel we're asked to do seemingly crazy things—all for the sake of getting a paycheck. However, very few will ever be called upon to act like, for example, a lead-poisoned beaver, an Opera-singing bovine or an intelligence-deprived handyman. Fewer still will find themselves professionally seduced into publicly assuming the characteristics of the opposite sex. And though it may sometimes feel like it, most don't spend their workdays tip-toeing blindfolded through 100 fully loaded mousetraps—each ready to prey upon our professional missteps.

So if your workday is compromised by an annoying up-and-comer nipping at your heels, try spending a day walking in the shoes of comedian and improviser extraordinaire Colin Mochrie. *Crazy* is his stock in trade.

A one-time honor student and wannabe marine biologist, the quiet, shy Colin was coaxed into auditioning for a play at school. "Once I got my first laugh, I was hooked," he says. After all, laughter is the drug that enslaves many who seek the comedic limelight.

Colin Mochrie is perhaps best known for the various incarnations of the popular TV show, *Whose Line is it Anyway?* After nine years on the British series, he appeared from 1998-2007 on the Drew Carey-hosted U.S. version on ABC and ABC Family. The show was revived in 2013 on The CW with host Aisha Tyler.

It could be said that Colin Mochrie's line of duty possesses perils akin to walking on a tightrope—potential disaster looms with every step. As an artist, he wouldn't have it any other way. His unshakable acceptance of improvisation's inherent dangers—including the aforementioned mouse-traps—raises the bar, stimulates the creative process and enhances not only his product, but the creative output of those around him.

Unlike Colin, most don't intentionally try to make their jobs *more difficult*. "We go out of our way to make it tougher," he says of his stage and television appearances. "It makes it more interesting."

ShowMeJones.com

"My thing has always been to make sure the people I am working with are having as much fun as possible. Making sure that I'm there to give them whatever they need."

—Colin Mochrie

Because his job is to expect the unexpected—to unconditionally accept the suggestions and scenarios tossed his way—Colin is understandably more fearless than the Average Joe. "You just have to do it," he says. "That's when you learn your strengths and your weaknesses." And just like a tightrope walker, Colin excels through fearlessness, focus and faith—and finally, by flagrantly throwing caution to the wind.

Colin Mochrie is ultimately a talented-yet-unassuming guy who simultaneously puts the *face* in *facetious*, yet—in person—reveals the *human* in the *humor*. At his core, Mochrie is a team player—one who appreciates the benefit of having worked with many of his colleagues for decades. The result: they (quite literally) finish one another's sentences. "I don't really do 'jokes,'" Colin says. "I work with great people and together, we come up with 'funny.'"

To suggest that Colin simply "makes stuff up" is a disservice to him and those in his inner improv circle. Truth be told, it takes a lot of commitment and mental prep to appear so hilariously ill-prepared.

The fundamental rule for improvisation is to literally and figuratively say "yes" to all suggestions rather than blocking the creative process with the imagination's ultimate buzzkill: "no." The same could easily be said of any creative pursuit.

Furthermore, by following "yes" with "and," one not only validates the suggestion provided but expands upon its potential. For example: "*Yes*, I am Charlotte, the spider from the web…*and* I've always wanted to dance like Gene Kelly." *Cue spontaneous Spider in the Rain dance.*

Business organizations have also come to appreciate the value of improvisation training to enhance communication skills. Improv helps to break down barriers, build self-confidence, overcome negativity, encourage trust, bolster cooperation, foster creative thinking and boost morale.

For more than twenty-five years, Carol Nissenson, managing/artistic director of Washington, DC-based NOW THIS!, has taught improvisation techniques to Corporate America. "I've heard the phrase 'think outside the box' hundreds of times. I prefer: improvisation teaches you to look inside the box, see what's there and use it in different and more effective ways," Carol says. "Even if your initial response is 'that's an awful idea,' try looking at it this way: remember the Pet Rock? An 'awful idea' that became a huge success."

Colin recalls: "Brad [Sherwood] and I did a workshop for GE executives in New York. Their natural inclination was to *not* listen." Once the participants said "yes" and (here comes the magic word again) *listened*, according to Colin: "The scenes started to move forward rather than being stopped by one person's negativity."

Besides, everyone improvises on a daily basis anyway. In fact, isn't the ability to be quick on one's feet typically considered a benefit? None of us is going to have an answer prepared for every question. Like it or not, the art of improvisation is a must-have professional tool.

For Colin: "My thing has always been to make sure the people I am working with are having as much fun as possible. Making sure that I'm there to give them whatever they need." Professionally speaking: is there a more powerful and/or honorable goal?

He also takes his work home with him: "My wife is also an improviser. It's amazing how often you can be negative in your day-to-day life," observes Colin. "Now, we try to say 'yes' to new experiences and see where they take us."

Is there value in imitating Colin Mochrie, the master of imitation, spontaneity, dependability, collaboration and positive, productive professional peril?

YES, and—now it's your turn.

DESIGNING WOMEN

PEGGY POST

A ccording to legendary author Emily Post: "Whenever two people come together and their behavior affects one another, you have etiquette." And here I was, on the verge of experiencing the ultimate test of that theory.

Considering my editorial focus on courtesy and respect, my first meeting with Peggy Post of The Emily Post Institute was emotionally on par with my filmmaker son Kevin's desire to hook up with Steven Spielberg. In my world, Peggy Post was a rock star—albeit one I visualized in white gloves and a perfectly placed fascinator atop her noggin.

With the knowledge that I was about to come face-to-face with the nation's guardian of manners and etiquette, I wasn't surprised that *anxiety* entered the equation. Will I embarrass myself? Will my stomach start to growl? Will a four-letter word force itself to the surface and fly out of my mouth without my consent? And perhaps most horrifying of all: Will I accidentally place my elbows on the table?

Having mentally prepared myself for a protocol disaster of epic proportions—and fearful of keeping an Emily Post-successor waiting—I arrived at our designated meeting place, Barnes & Noble, thirty-two minutes early. I proceeded to select a table, move, select another, move, and select yet one more, and move again. *(A lady deserves to be seen in her best light.)* Then, just in case, I pulled out a sanitized handy wipe and cleaned the chosen table *again*.

Now, a bit more relaxed, I ordered coffee. *I think the size was Gargan-tuo—Starbucks always confuses me.* But at this point "Murphy"—you know, the guy with the "Law"—managed to wriggle inside my head and taunt me: "If you don't finish that now, you're going to get all excited and knock that hot coffee into Peggy Post's lap." Thirty-seven seconds later, my *coffee bowl* sat empty.

And next? Just minutes before Peggy's anticipated arrival, my absurd-ly quick intake of *Gargantuo* coffee seized control of my bladder and the men's room was—of course—upstairs. After all this effort, was Peggy Post destined to arrive without a proper greeting? Not on my watch! In a scene reminiscent of a silent movie, I jumped into action: Run. Go. (Wash hands!) Run. Return. Sit. The only thing missing was a pratfalling Mabel Normand. And yes, I pulled it off just in time to *calmly* greet Peggy as she walked toward me.

Bypassing my extended hand, Peggy gave me a warm, natural smile and an even more heartwarming hug. No white gloves, no stylish cap, no ani-mated birds circling above her head—just a lovely yet unpretentious wom-an with the innate ability to light up any room she enters. In truth, Peggy is used to meeting nervous people.

With the 1922 publication of the book, *Etiquette,* Emily Post would for-ever be known as the official matriarch of social conduct and the origi-nal figure identified in the pop culture catchphrase: "What would *Emily Post* do?"

As spokesperson, author and director of The Emily Post Institute, Peggy's life revolves around answering that very same question. Though the words "manners" and "etiquette" may conjure up fears of a burgeoning behavioral brouhaha, "nervous" is the last reaction she wishes to elicit. Emily herself was an advocate for making people comfortable regardless of the situation. According to Peggy: "It's all about building relationships based upon trust and respect."

I knew this before, but coming from her, its impact was much more pow-erful despite its profound simplicity.

Next, Peggy on electronic communication: "There is a real human being at the other end of electronic messages—a person with feelings." Lesson: (irony alert!) THINK before you "post."

More specifically, Peggy is the author of more than a dozen etiquette books. In addition, she writes a monthly column in *Good Housekeeping* magazine and a bimonthly wedding etiquette column in the *New York Times.* Her media appearances include *Oprah, Dr. Phil, The View, Live with Regis and Kelly, TODAY, Good Morning America, Dateline,* VH1 and CNN.

Even Dr. Phil emailed me to offer his personal Peggy Post praise: "When I need an expert on manners, there's one person I look to and that's Peggy Post. Her books are must-reads for anyone looking to improve the way they conduct themselves in society. Peggy is down to earth, commonsensical and has a great way of delivering her message. She has also taught me a few things about manners, for which my wife Robin is forever grateful." When Robin gets involved, you know Dr. Phil means business.

After two delightful hours, Peggy and I parted ways and promised to keep in touch. Even if I had committed an egregious etiquette faux pas, she would never have said a word. "A guest never points out the bad behavior of their host."

SHOWMEJONES.COM

"There is a real human being at the other end of electronic messages—a person with feelings."

—Peggy Post

Once home, as I reflected on my personal relationships—those that have stood the test of time—one common theme emerged: a respect for each other's work, passions and beliefs. Perhaps this also explained why so many of my long-term friendships originated in some sort of workplace.

When Derek asked the obligatory: *How did it go?*—still thunderstruck, I recited a list of glittery adjectives before I stopped, thought a moment, and declared: "Peggy Post is so perfect she makes Mary Poppins look like a hooker!"

Emily Post once wrote, "Certainly what one is, is of far greater importance than what one appears to be." While many superlatives can be used to describe Peggy—charming, smart, warm and witty—more than anything, she is disarmingly genuine and delightfully "normal."

For her and those responsible for Emily Post's legacy, of primary importance is remaining relevant and applying Emily's core principles to the norms of today.

Now, as our friendship has grown, I view Peggy in a more complex light. She accepts my faults—of which there are many. She knows I am likely to get over-excited during a spirited conversation and interrupt her. She understands I will invariably lean in during dessert and deposit my elbows on the table while making a point.

Though not typically a "spiller," I have managed to douse myself with a beverage practically every time we meet. I even dumped an entire cup of hot coffee down my shirt just minutes before she was to take the stage at a speaking engagement. Naturally, I wasn't satisfied by just *looking* stupid; I also let go a rather loud expletive and ended up *sounding* stupid too. Peggy's response to hearing my tale of ill-mannered woe: "I wish I had been in there to see that!"

Best of all, my *friend* Peggy Post teaches me to celebrate my authentic self. Because, when all is said and done, she looks for the *good* in people and not just signs of *goodness* in their actions.

Though she has now hung up her white gloves and retired as Emily Post's spokesperson, Peggy's impact on my life is never-ending. Today, as I consider how best to react to life's various hurdles, I no longer just look to Emily Post for the answer. Knowing that friends should ultimately bring out the best in each other, I simply ask myself: **What would *Peggy Post* do?**

And animated birds fly in the room.

Keith Isaac

CANDICE OLSON

N ot only is the word *design* an essential part of the creative toolkit, once we factor in its various uses and meanings, it is downright powerful.

We can *design* a space: a room, a home, a building. We can have *designs on* another person, a more rewarding profession or a different lifestyle. Some of the more enlightened take a *design* approach to life as seen in our educational choices and carefully crafted career paths. And others feel things happen *by design*: a meeting, a relationship—perhaps a deranged bunny rabbit feasting on our feet.

The best part: As design is one of the creative superpowers, it can be fluid and ever-changing. Don't like what you see? Refresh, repurpose, revitalize and reinvent.

CANDICE OLSON IS LATE FOR OUR INTERVIEW. After a day jammed with air travel, meet-and-greets and presentations, she's been held up by an accident on I-75 South. Finally, as Candice's elegant, statuesque frame enters Robb & Stucky Interiors' showroom, I look at my watch—only twenty-two minutes left.

Of course, on shows such as HGTV's *Divine Design* and *Candice Tells All*, Candice has performed miracles in twenty-two minutes. For someone with her pedigree, this limited time could arguably be used to erect a second showroom in the parking lot. In her world—where *creativity* meets *structure*—flexibility is everything.

Thankfully, I am prepared, and the charming, effervescent Candice Olson is, in a word, "on." It's show time.

In a story that rivals Hollywood fables of the past, Candice was discovered due to illness. Someone else's, that is. Clad in work boots, baggy pants and a tank top, she served as a last-minute replacement in the presentation of one of her award-winning designs on a Canadian design program.

Today, unexpected-understudy-turned-TV-design-mogul Candice Olson also safeguards "The Candice Olson Collection"—a thriving brand of home decor products, including upholstered furniture, fabrics, wallpaper, lighting, bedding and more.

Not surprisingly, many of the design techniques she champions also represent the way she has styled her career. For newcomers: "Work hard for the opportunity and try to beat it to the door before it knocks!" Candice then quips, "When my time came, I knocked those friggin' doors down!" For a woman who has participated in demolishing countless door frames, non-load-bearing walls and dated kitchens, one suspects this act came pretty naturally.

She also has a healthy respect for the *business* of design. Take a closer look and her celebrated approach effortlessly translates into excellent advice for the design of a successful business. According to Candice, "It's not all puppies and kittens. It is a *business*. Treat your client's money as if it were your own."

To illustrate her point, Candice cites a cash-strapped couple from her early days as a designer. By honoring their budgetary limitations, she went on to design three more of their homes. Yes, the budgets did increase, but the relationship the trio built on mutual trust and respect was priceless.

Devotees of Candice's signature style live by her enviable vision: "My work is a fusion of traditional form, scale and proportions, with the clean, crisp, simplistic beauty of modern design." However, with modern technology often seen as an adversary to traditional business values, the same could be said of her professional style. "There's something comforting about the traditional—such as a handshake and a personal meeting," she observes.

Whether she's eliciting belly laughs from a story about renovating a former frat house she once helped to "trash," or weighing the pros and cons of my impromptu *throw-pillow-fight* request, in twenty-two minutes, Candice Olson proved to be a natural, both on-screen and off.

Kevin Randall Jones

BARBARA CORCORAN

W e can all approach critically important business meetings with a certain amount of anxiety. For the more imaginative among us, this painful situation can even be musically underscored. (Insert *Jaws* theme here.)

Duhhhh uh

Our hearts race. Our heads swim in anticipation.

Duhhhh uh

Our bodies—our spirit—preparing to be devoured.

Da da dahhhhh

Take the above scenario—multiply it several times over—and prepare to meet television's most feared business beast, the SHARK.

dun dun dun dun Dun dun Dun dun DUN dun DUN dun DUN DUN DUN DUN

(SFX: Entrepreneurs screaming. Music out.)

In truth, a shark tank—televised or otherwise—can't possibly contain all that is Barbara Corcoran, one of the stars of ABC's *Shark Tank*. To begin, look up the words associated with "shark" and they appear tailor-made for television: tough, ruthless, deceitful. However, as most of us seek a workplace with less spectacle, take comfort that the real Barbara is markedly less "shark-ful" than her male co-stars—men who seem to revel in the smell of entrepreneur blood.

Growing up as one of ten children in a two-bedroom home in Edgewater, New Jersey, young Barbara witnessed her parents navigate practically every developmental, behavioral and financial obstacle imaginable. However, according to her: "My mother could find the positive in anything, focus on it—and make it grow." As for the "nature vs. nurture" debate, the success of Barbara Ann Corcoran proves: Florence and Ed Corcoran won on both counts.

Sure, her bio proudly highlights: "straight Ds in high school and college" and "twenty jobs by the time she'd turned twenty-three." What is not written is easier to understand: Barbara Corcoran doesn't respond well to boredom. As a young adult armed with a $1,000 loan from her boyfriend, she quit job number twenty and opened a small real estate firm in New York City. This very personal project evolved into a $5 billion real estate business—a company she sold in 2006 for $66 million.

> ### SHOWMEJONES.COM
> "Tough love is the most essential tool in the box."
>
> —Barbara Corcoran

Equal parts mother, mentor, teacher and taskmaster—with a hint of "party animal" thrown in for "good leisure"—Barbara celebrates the parallels between parenting and management. "Tough love is the most essential tool in the box," she says. After all, she has witnessed this pillar of parental power work equally well in the living room and in the boardroom.

Option One: "Sit down and figure this out or you're both grounded."

Option Two: "Sit down and figure this out or you're both fired."

Her secret: Barbara manages to achieve an enviable balance between professionalism/respect and honesty/candor—a skill desired by many but mastered by surprisingly few. She describes her style as "the truth, wrapped up with a bit of courtesy" and feels equally passionate that "Nothing replaces sincerity and a smile."

According to *Shark Tank* entrepreneur and Barbara Corcoran mentee Brett Thompson of Pork Barrel BBQ, Barbara's televised authenticity follows her into real life. "She makes us feel like a part of her family. She creates a connection that goes well beyond business," says Thompson. As Barbara puts it: "I'm more inspired by the people involved than I am by the product." Though she understands the emphasis placed on the bottom line, she heralds a different view: "It's actually all about the people, not about the numbers." Take that, Wall Street.

When choosing projects, Barbara says, "I'm old enough and successful enough to stay away if I'm not 150 percent committed to the person and their product. I also ask myself: 'When they become successful, are they going to be appreciative?'"

After spending time with Barbara Corcoran, one quickly realizes: her warmth, self-confidence, laser focus, fearless sense of humor—and above all—extraordinary knowledge base can never be adequately illustrated in the media. Why? She is a "people person." To fully appreciate her, you must experience her, (symbolically) hold her close and never let go of her—or her principles.

Just like her beloved mother Florence—a woman too busy to waste time and too caring to not give of her time—Barbara is a shark with a heart. After all, it's not just business—*it's personal.*

Photos by Kevin Randall Jones

ERIN BROCKOVICH

When statesman Gouverneur Morris penned "We the People" for the preamble of the U.S. Constitution, he helped to define the United States as a single entity—created by and for a group of *individuals*. Renowned consumer advocate Erin Brockovich loves the word "we." In fact, she whips it out—as well as its close allies "us" and "our"—with great regularity. For example: "Today, **we** look to someone else to give **us** the answers and lead **us**. **We** stand in **our** own way. I think **we're** all born leaders."

Though she has no problem using the first-person "I" when taking responsibility for her actions, Erin celebrates her ability—*our* ability—to loudly and proudly proclaim membership in the constitutionally defined coalition of "we." She also wonders if "we" have forgotten about the individual responsibility that comes with being a part of Team U.S. and/or Team "us."

True, Erin's people-first platform endorses positive character traits such as honesty, integrity and respect. However, like so many of us, she wonders when these overworked nouns will be permanently transformed from *buzzwords* to *action items*. "I am seeing lost hope and when that hope is renewed then 'we the people' can speak and we can lead."

In the '90s, Erin spearheaded an investigation revealing that Pacific Gas & Electric had been poisoning the water in Hinkley, California, for more than thirty years. As chronicled in the 2000 film *Erin Brockovich*, PG&E was forced to pay out the largest toxic tort injury settlement in U.S. history:

$333 million. The beloved movie may have launched Erin Brockovich, the brand, but the film's heroine, the real-life Erin has quite literally been keeping American heads above water ever since.

One doesn't really "interview" Erin Brockovich. If you're lucky, face time with Erin allows you to absorb her natural charm and time-honored belief system while preserving another endangered natural resource: active listening. It will also come as no surprise to those familiar with the Kansas native that she loves another (flawlessly Midwestern) word: stick-to-itiveness, the very basis of her pop-culture persona.

With the knowledge that she is sometimes viewed as aggressive, Erin explains: "I'm very kind and compassionate. I believe people feel they can confide in me. It helps when we put down our armor and realize none of us is perfect. We open up more. But don't mistake my kindness as a sign of weakness."

Despite her ongoing commitment to her principles, her words—her passion—come forth as if presented for the first time. "It's never about Erin; it's about us. We have so much more in common than we realize. At the end of the day, we all care about our health, our welfare and our children," she says. "I'm just a foot soldier on the ground." In fact, she summarizes her successful action plan very simply: Erin Brockovich's primary goal is to "right wrong."

Erin's No. 1 obsession has not wavered since *before* her high-profile battle against PG&E. It's still all about "Water, water, water, water and water." In fact, her father warned a young Erin: "In your lifetime, water will be a commodity."

Erin Brockovich is one of the most requested speakers on the international lecture circuit. In 2016, she also launched The Erin Brockovich Foundation, a nonprofit organization meant to educate and empower even more communities in their fight for one of the basic foundations of human survival: clean water.

Professionally, Erin is also in a unique situation: she essentially shares her personal brand with her cinematic doppelganger, *Erin Brockovich's* Julia Roberts. With a business world now obsessed with developing "branded content"—the careful blend of entertainment and marketing— the film *Erin Brockovich* stands as a shining example of early content marketing. Ironically, the film was released long before anyone had conceived of the notion of a YouTube video as a platform-building sales tool.

Spend time with Erin and you can't help but appreciate Roberts' brilliant, Oscar-winning film portrayal. However, in person, Erin Brockovich actually accomplishes the seemingly impossible: she almost makes you forget about Julia Roberts entirely. Julia's Brockovich is frozen in time in the late 20th century, whereas Erin's Brockovich is fixated on the issues of today. She is older and wiser, yet wickedly funny and refreshing. Nonetheless, like her cinematic Ghost of Brockovich Past, she is still a force to be reckoned with.

As is almost always the case with efficacious people, there is no substitute for the original.

"I'm more than fifty now and I feel stronger and wiser than I have felt my entire life," Erin says. "I feel more empowered by myself, my decisions and my confidence, than ever before." Proof that advancing age should generate the aforementioned sense of purpose, not a sense of entitlement.

"People think I'm this big, bad person who comes in to stop something, but I'm more of a motivator. I'm about personal empowerment," she says. "The people have given the power to government and to businesses. The people have forgotten to give the power to themselves."

SHOWMEJONES.COM

"I'm very kind and compassionate. I believe people feel they can confide in me. It helps when we put down our armor and realize none of us is perfect. We open up more. But don't mistake my kindness as a sign of weakness."

—Erin Brockovich

Erin also has a very clear message for those sitting atop our nation's environmentally precarious corporate ladders: "You can be the hero. You have the means to be morally responsible. You have the ability to be the solution. Industry and consumer can join forces. They need each other and they have pulled away from each other."

So the next time you hear someone quip that Hollywood has nothing to teach us, consider this: Erin Brockovich and *Erin Brockovich* continue to be powerful educational tools—on action and compassion, on humanity and morality. Or, as she puts it: "the power of being human."

Now, with the understanding that our country was formed by unparalleled displays of *stick-to-itiveness*, stop and take action. Seize your Brockovich-identified *born-leader* status and renew your focus on a historically significant, all-inclusive and perpetually powerful pronoun: **We. The people** will thank you for it—and so will Erin Brockovich.

LAW & ORDER

I recently found a foolproof way to get out of jury duty: be myself.
Our story begins with my receipt of a personal invitation to attend the coveted jury selection process at the exquisite Collier County Courthouse in Naples. How could I refuse such a lovely, legally binding offer?

Ironically, this was my first dip into the jury pool. Although I have heard multiple stories as to the best way to be voted off of Jury Island, I honestly didn't mind finally having the opportunity to go. Call me a traditionalist, but I actually believed it was my civic duty. I was also well aware that the case would likely be fairly lightweight. It's not like the average retired-senior resident of Southwest Florida was going to be in court for knocking off a 7-Eleven.

I have to say, the Collier County Court has got it going on. The bubbly clerk who greeted us at the door seemed to regard us more as her special guests as opposed to what one might expect from repeated viewings of *Boston Legal* or even *Night Court*—more Rachael Ray than Judge Judy.

With copious amounts of coffee at our fingertips, each of us waited patiently for our number to come up while Bubbles the Clerk provided concierge-style care, including periodic yet thorough updates as to the day's judicial progress. Actual judges would also occasionally enter the holding area and thank us *personally* for our time and service. For my part, I love meticulous communication and courtesy so I was quickly trying to figure out how to parlay this jury duty assignment into a regular paying gig. After all, Bubbles was basically my dream assistant.

After two hours or so, a dozen or so juror names were called, including mine. Bubbles efficiently directed me and my potential juror pals into a single-file line before we marched off to an upstairs courtroom. Though this mobile queue was reminiscent of my days at Fairview Elementary School, I resisted the urge to pull the pony tail of the girl in front of me. Nonetheless, I am almost positive I heard the guy behind me mutter under his breath, "Move it, lard ass." *Ah—memories.*

Upon entering the courtroom, the serious but cordial Judge Dapperdan immediately imposed a twenty-minute limit for the prosecuting and defense attorneys to interview the jury pool in an effort to select the lucky seven who would spend the balance of their day in court. *So far so good— they run a tight ship!* My anal-retentive Virgo side was overjoyed.

The problems first started when the prosecuting attorney opened his mouth—let's call him "Doogie." By my estimation, Doogie was about seventeen years old. And Doog had not even completed his first sentence before committing faux pas No. 1: "...I ask you to return a verdict of NOT GUILTY."

Huh? Aren't you the prosecutor?

Having realized his egregious mistake, Doogie quickly recanted—admitting to having only recently changed from the defense to the prosecution side of the table. *Oopsie! And where did he work before that? The GAP?*

But my mind was open and my sense of duty clear as Doogie asked if any of us had any strong opinions regarding the legality of prostitution. Honestly, I had never thought about it. Though I have certainly known my share of loose women (and men), to the best of my knowledge, none had ever charged a fee for their time or attention. When I was younger, most of us were so stupid we gave it away for *free.*

After one awkwardly skinny, mature gentleman shot his hand in the air to renounce *all-things-sexual,* the room sat awkwardly silent. Asexualman had proven to be a legal-system buzzkill.

I carefully considered my options. Knowing that honesty was the best policy, I tentatively raised my hand and was acknowledged by D.A. Doogie. "I must admit, I have an issue any time the government tries to tell any woman what she can or cannot do with her body." Although I realized I was shooting myself in the jury-selection foot, I had to tell the truth. Plus, if we were going to get any traction on this topic, someone had to fire the first volley. *Bang! Let's get this party started!*

An *adult* would have thought Doogie would leave me alone at that point. Though I certainly have no fear of speaking in public and/or sharing my opinions, I candidly thought my comment would liven up the room a tad and I'd be forgotten. It would surely only be a few minutes before I would be graciously dismissed by Judge Dapperdan, whereby I would rush back into the comforting arms of Bubbles for a final cup of joe and a fond farewell. But for some inexplicable reason, Doogie kept coming back to me:

"What do you do for a living?"

"Uh…sales." *My typical one-size-fits-all response.*

"And do you close every sale?"

"Uh…no, I don't."

"But even if you don't close the deal would you argue that the sales process took place?"

OMG—Doogie is going to try to convict based upon an incomplete transaction. Way to tip your hand on that issue, Doog! After a comment or two from other jury candidates, an even more determined D.A. Doogie returned to face me: "Mr. Randall, let me ask you this."

Though, in my mind, it takes a special kind of person to mess up "Jones," I chose to not correct him. Believe it or not, I was not enjoying the attention.

"Mr. Randall, don't you feel you would be less likely to uphold the law in this—uh—specific situation?"

"No, I don't."

"Mr. Randall, do you feel you can—uh—address this alleged crime with the—uh—seriousness it deserves?"

Starting to get miffed…

"Yes I do. I am a law-abiding citizen. I understand the concept of legal vs. illegal."

"Mr. Randall, you don't—uh—think you'd—uh—take, for example, a murder trial—uh—more seriously?"

Officially pissed now…

"I WOULD HOPE WE WOULD ALL TAKE A MURDER TRIAL MORE SERIOUSLY!"

At this point, I started to ask myself: What would Erin Brockovich do? But that was no good. Erin is probably not afraid to go to jail for the sake of a worthy cause. Though some have referred to me as "the male Erin Brockovich," by comparison her *cojones* make mine appear weak.

So let me recap the situation: Both the prosecution and the defense had a total of twenty minutes to question the jury pool. D.A. Doogie chose to not only take up almost all of the allotted time, but attempted to go head-to-head in a battle of wits with me—the feisty gay guy/positive communication advocate who publicly admits to fearing nothing except for bunny rabbits, my dental hygienist, Cerise Pierce and ABC News' Elizabeth Vargas. What turnip truck did this guy just fall off?

And why would the defense attorney want to get involved at this point with Doogie doing such a bang-up job clumsily trying the case in advance of an actual trail? Nonetheless, once again I thought I was in the clear. But like the Energizer Bunny of the Florida Legal System, Doogie came back for more.

"So Mr. Randall…"

Obviously aware of my mounting frustration—and probably sensing that I was about to launch into a very different style of name-calling—Judge Dapperdan stepped into the fray:

"Excuse me; it's Mr. Jones, correct? Not Mr. Randall?"

Exasperated, I loudly declared: "Yes—but, you know, at this point, I'll answer to anything."

I don't know if it's rare for a jury pool to *giggle*, but this one proceeded to do so as Doogie morphed from a light red to deep crimson in color. I swear I even saw Asexualman crack a smile.

But here's the kicker: I heard yet another solitary snicker coming from the other side of the courtroom. I briefly glanced over and, to my amazement, it was the defendant—Ms. Alleged-Lady-of-the-Evening herself—expressing her amusement.

Now Doogie, I'm not a lawyer, and I certainly couldn't do your job, but I also have respect for the legal system and the trial-by-jury process. I can't even imagine a court system more organized or respectful than that of Collier County, Florida. And I even get that, from a professional standpoint, we all have to start somewhere. Everyone is entitled to have a bad day at work. But in any situation, *when the hooker laughs*—you're in deep shit.

Though I genuinely feel we all have a civic duty to perform jury service, I was (gasp!) not selected to be part of this specific panel of adjudicators. And in the relatively small town of Naples, I have yet to even run into D.A. Doogie at the theatre, a consignment shop or even IHOP. Imagine *that* reunion.

However, I do plan to ask Bubbles if she's free for lunch next week.

Kevin Randall Jones

G.W. BAILEY

W<sup>e are simply not going to get along with everyone we meet—no matter what we do, some people are not going to like us, and vice versa. Yes, we can attempt to be nice and attentive. We can craft thoughtful emails and draft handwritten notes. We can send flowers 'til the cows come home; however, when personalities collide, it's likely to end in behavioral road kill.

What's more, the words used to describe us aren't always going to come out of love. Take G.W. Bailey, for example. During his forty-year career, he has been described as lazy, slovenly, manipulative, arrogant, ignorant, power-hungry and curmudgeonly—and that's just the beginning.

No, these adjectives have not been targeted at Bailey *personally*, but to his work. To clarify, Bailey is an enduring character actor who has often appeared as—shall we say—"disagreeable" characters on film and television. In fact, G.W. Bailey has made a career out of exploring some of the workplace's most undesirable personalities, many in law enforcement. And his job performance has been impeccable.

When politely asked to justify his somewhat nefarious character choices, Bailey simply states: "I have always wanted to do work I'm proud of." He smirks and continues, "Though you may question my judgment." His primary yardstick for script approval: "I tried to never do anything my grandmother couldn't see." Judging by his rib-tickling résumé, it's also safe to say his grandmother had a great sense of humor.

Though much is presumed about the so-called "glamorous" business of show, G.W. quickly warns: "Don't think that what I do is not a 'business,' it's very much a business; I pay taxes like everyone else." He also relates to those among us who work for ourselves: "My business is me. I have to maintain integrity or I won't get work."

Despite his lengthy résumé, three outstandingly ornery characters stand out: Staff Sergeant Luther Rizzo *(M*A*S*H)*, Captain Thaddeus Harris *(Police Academy)* and Lt. Louie Provenza *(The Closer* and *Major Crimes)*. However, what others may see as character flaws, G.W. sees as flawless characters. How? In his work and in his life, G.W. Bailey looks for—and celebrates—humanity.

G.W. on Rizzo: *"He was an adorable scoundrel, but he was also a survivor."*

G.W. on Provenza: *"He is the most human of all three, but he unapologetically sees the world as he sees the world."*

G.W. on Harris: *"He was a blowhard—a classic case of a character you 'love to hate.' He represents people you know in your own life, those you can openly hate from afar and rejoice when they get what's coming to them."*

When looking for humanity in his work, G.W. also plays by one alarmingly simple rule: "I understand that all the characters I've portrayed—every one of them—has a mother or someone else who loves them. Thaddeus Harris would melt into a puddle of tears if he saw his mom."

Nonetheless, G.W. Bailey's most authentic displays of humanity are best seen in his actions off the screen. Though he reports the public is sometimes surprised to learn he actually has a loving family of his own, he insists that interviewers discuss his No. 1 passion, the Sunshine Kids Foundation.

Established in 1982, the Sunshine Kids Foundation is committed to providing positive group activities and emotional support for young cancer patients and their families. Bailey serves as executive director, his participation representing an ongoing tribute to his goddaughter, Brandy Aldridge, who succumbed to leukemia at age seventeen.

Many still ask: Can I really find selfless, bona fide examples of humanity in today's workplace? Well, what if we all used our mother's or grandmother's *approval* as a be-

> ## ShowMeJones.com
>
> **"Everyone is loved by someone."**
>
> —G.W. Bailey

havioral benchmark for business? Better still, imagine what would happen if more of us focused on the *humanity* as opposed to the *insanity* in others. Finally, what if every organization's mission statement proudly declared support for the needs of our nation's children?

Sure, if you want to cut a deal with *M*A*S*H*'s* Rizzo—*do so at your own risk.*

If you want your corporate trainer to be a Captain Harris wannabe—*be afraid, be very afraid.*

If you want to work hand in hand with Lt. Provenza—*make sure you can handle* his *truth.*

But, if you're selected to be on the same team as G.W. Bailey—you've just been voted "most likely to succeed." After all, he has no shortage of characters or character.

As for those inevitable personality clashes—despite the various reasons you may concoct to dislike someone—always remember G.W.'s mantra: "Everyone is loved by someone." Focus on solving the mystery behind the man and you may discover you actually *like* keeping your friends close and your enemies closer.

SEVERAL MONTHS PASSED before I ran into G.W. again—this time, at the annual Sunshine Kids gala fundraising event in Naples. Though he recognized me immediately and we exchanged pleasantries, G.W. was there for a purpose: to raise money for his charity. Sunshine Kids was not just a cause *near and dear* to his heart; it had become an integral part *of* his heart.

As much as I enjoyed spending time with G.W., I understood I was not an essential part of the evening's activities. Besides, I had done my (albeit small) part already. By writing the column, I had raised awareness of G.W. Bailey's Sunshine Kids crusade and *that* should be enough for anyone.

Later in the evening, as Derek and I were passing through the silent action area, we happened to cross paths with G.W. and a companion walking in the opposite direction. To my surprise, I suddenly felt something touch my shoulder. As I looked to the right, I discovered the source: tireless philanthropist Mr. G.W. Bailey. Without losing a moment's focus on his existing conversation, he pulled off one of the classic moves of positive reinforcement and recognition: G.W. Bailey *literally* patted me on the back.

Forget Leonardo DiCaprio: for at that brief moment, I was King of the World.

THE JUDGES OF TV'S HOT BENCH

Without question, we are a society of rules and regulations. Whether we refer to them as directives, decrees, acts, edicts or laws, these principles allegedly spring from the goal of applying an agreed-upon behavioral structure to our comings and goings as well as our actions and reactions—all for the benefit of the greater good.

When part-time Naples resident Judge Judy Sheindlin traveled to Ireland in 2013, she discovered a unique Irish spin on applying the law of the land. The president of the High Court may decide that any cause or matter—or any part thereof—may be heard by three judges. Sheindlin subsequently found herself with three reasons to create a new court program—one that would showcase the legal process in a brand new collaborative light: Three Judges. Three Opinions. One Verdict.

Co-produced by Sheindlin's Queen Bee Productions and CBS Television Distribution, *Hot Bench* premiered in September 2014 and featured a trio of thought-provoking judges: Judge Patricia DiMango and attorneys Tanya Acker and Larry Bakman.

The term "hot bench" is used to describe a court where a bit of brouhaha often accompanies frequent interruptions from a judge—or, in this case, judges. This same judicial ruckus is also the likely reason for *Hot Bench's* rapid ratings rise.

Of course, beginning with early childhood, we are taught to "share," "play nice" and "follow the rules." As the basic tenets of the law are introduced at an early age, let's travel back to childhood and explore DiMango, Acker and Bakman's wide-ranging backgrounds in terms of the roles they might have played in the legal aftermath of *Goldilocks and the Three Bears.*

Bakman would likely have been cast as the district attorney leading the prosecution of Goldilocks on criminal charges of felony breaking-and-entering. DiMango could have assumed the role of presiding judge in the small claims court action for trespass brought against the trio of out-of-the-house wandering bears by their ill-tempered neighbor. And Acker might have filed a $100 million products liability class action on behalf of Goldilocks and other plaintiffs against the porridge manufacturer. Their failure to provide a warning label about the dangers of "too hot" gruel had recklessly and negligently caused irreparable damage to Goldilocks' taste buds.

Nevertheless, to the *Hot Bench* judges, the legal process is far from child's play. In fact, Acker suggests: "You don't always need to be in court if you act like a grown-up."

True, the legal profession is often accused of lacking both rhyme and reason. In notable contrast, Judges DiMango, Acker and Bakman quickly became a well-oiled, collaborative and, yes, highly reasonable machine—one with a mission Bakman succinctly states: "We want to make the best product out there."

"We listen to each other with an open mind. We respect each other's intellectual abilities and embrace our differences," DiMango says about the three-judge panel. "Each of us comes in with a different perspective. These differences also reinforce the mantra we have been told from the beginning: be yourself."

Acker offers another benefit to their diverse résumés: "We have different legal backgrounds. As a consequence, we tend to cover all the bases."

For his part, Bakman points to the delicate decision-making balance that is based on "the interaction between credibility and burden of proof"—a situation not uncommon inside any number of courtrooms and boardrooms.

There's also no better example of the transfer of *respect* into *collaboration* than when the judges retire to deliberate. Though the litigants do not witness the debate, the viewing public does. In Acker's view, "It's invaluable for people to see how legal professionals come to their decisions." Some might also suggest that Washington take note of the judges' talents for fact-finding, listening and compromise.

DiMango adds: "The most interesting part is what each of us has placed our emphasis on—what we have taken from the courtroom and into deliberation."

As he often does on the show, Bakman summarizes: "We love it when we can educate the viewer with our ability to teach and explain."

The lessons to be learned also apply across a wide spectrum of legal, business and even lifestyle scenarios. For example:

DiMango on listening: *"You cannot lose a word. That one word can change an entire sentence and that sentence can change an entire verdict. Every word has meaning. You have to hear what people don't say as well."*

Bakman on believability: *"Credibility is always an issue for me. I will judge the plaintiffs in terms of their demeanor, how sharp they are with the facts and whether they met their burden of proof."*

Acker on accountability: *"People need to take responsibility for what they do. Too often the legal system is used or abused by people trying to skirt their way out of an obligation."*

The importance I personally place on honesty and candor is no mystery. And for the judges, candor is no problem; it's the cornerstone of their job description. However—and perhaps most astonishing—Acker, Bakman and DiMango are forced to approach each workday with the knowledge that X number of people will unapologetically stand before them, look them in the eye, and *lie*. More than that, plaintiff X or defendant Y will sometimes go to great lengths to concoct a narrative with the sole purpose of pulling off a televised deception.

It would be foolish to think that everyone we encounter will be completely honest with us, but imagine if your world was partially defined by other people's calculated, shameless deceit.

True, many of us may find it challenging to understand our *truth*; however, by recognizing and respecting one another's inherent veracity, Acker, Bakman and DiMango work cooperatively to separate fact from fiction. Every. Single. Day.

With their skill at demonstrating the meticulous thought processes behind legal decision-making—DiMango, Acker, Bakman and their mentor Sheindlin have brought an increased focus on *value* and *values* to daytime television. *Hot Bench* is all about professionalism and respect—subjects that often seem like the journalistic equivalent of "beating a dead horse"; yet, we editorial altruists continue to plead our cases and hope for the best.

Thankfully, DiMango, Acker and Bakman represent proof that the aforementioned horse won't actually die without putting up a fight. Why? *Hot Bench* upholds the notion that respect, collaboration and staying true to oneself are not mutually exclusive concepts.

What's more, our tenacious trio of adjudicators are pretty darn likely to expose who tried to kill the poor horse in the first place.

RYAN FERGUSON

E ach year in July, great fanfare envelops our nation as we join together in celebration of a basic human right: freedom. For Ryan Ferguson, the concept of freedom resonates more now than ever.

Around 2:10 a.m. on November 1, 2001, Kent Heitholt, sports editor for the *Columbia* (Missouri) *Daily Tribune* was murdered in the newspaper's parking lot. Two years later, a young man named Charles Erickson began publicly sharing recurring *dreams* that he and his former classmate Ryan Ferguson were involved.

What followed was viewed by many as a series of finger-pointing, confusing confessions, questionable police work, awkward eyewitnesses and a prosecution team hell-bent on solving the case at any cost. The result: nineteen-year-old Ryan Ferguson was sentenced to forty years in prison based almost exclusively on "eyewitness" accounts from teenage dreamer Erickson and *Tribune* janitor Jerry Trump, who, at trial, miraculously gained the ability to positively identify Erickson and Ferguson. Erickson, through a plea bargain, received a twenty-five-year sentence.

Though assisted by renowned civil rights attorney Kathleen Zellner, Ferguson unsuccessfully returned to court several times. However, in April 2012, Trump and Erickson faced possible perjury charges and admitted on the stand they had lied at Ferguson's original trial. His conviction was vacated by the State of Missouri on November 5, 2013, on the basis that the prosecution withheld evidence from the defense team.

At age twenty-nine, he was released on November 13, 2013, after spending almost a decade in prison. Just like the millions of other Americans who pursue careers, make their own choices, and stand by their ideals, Ryan Ferguson had his freedom.

For more than a decade, Erin Moriarty of CBS News' *48 Hours* covered the Ferguson case. "In my mind, there just wasn't enough evidence to convict him. There was plenty of physical evidence at the crime scene but none of it belonged to Ryan," Moriarty said in a telephone interview. So thin was the case against Ferguson that one could easily wonder to what extent the concept of *show me* applied to the Show Me State's judicial system.

Once confined, Ryan ultimately learned to look inside himself for inspiration: "Though there are many things you cannot control in prison, you do have control over your mind and your body," he said. Words that ring true in so many situations—and in so many metaphorical "prisons."

Ryan began to focus on physical fitness and became a voracious reader. Some of his favorite (and most influential) titles included: *Who Moved My Cheese?* by Spencer Johnson (lesson: accepting change); *Your Erroneous Zones* by Wayne W. Dyer (lesson: conquering negativity and taking control); *A New Earth* by Eckhart Tolle (lesson: living consciously).

SHOWMEJONES.COM

"For many of us, understanding our innate freedom will often become an exercise in bravery."

—Randall Kenneth Jones

He is certainly not the first "Business Class" subject to tout the significance of reading as it relates to mental acuity, nor is he the first to promote the correlation between physical and mental fitness. However, Ryan has the *street cred* that others lack.

Moriarty observed: "Having covered these types of cases a long time, I discovered that those who turn out to be innocent never really 'connect' to life in prison. They survive by maintaining their own space and own world. That was Ryan."

Ferguson's ordeal has subsequently been covered by numerous national media. A documentary, *dream/killer*, produced by filmmaker Andrew Jenks, was released in 2015. Ryan's first book, *Stronger, Faster, Smarter*, also hit bookstores in 2015 and highlights his self-awareness, healthy living and fitness evolution. "It's about strength, survival and fearlessly creating your own path in life regardless of your circumstances."

It would be difficult to experience circumstances more dire than those of Ryan Ferguson. His book title was inspired from advice a nineteen-year-old jailed Ferguson received from his father, Bill. Words that focused on self-preservation and served as the backbone of Ryan's journey of personal (and subsequent professional) growth.

In 2016, Ryan and co-investigator Eva Nagao (from the Exoneration Project) headlined MTV's docu-series *Unlocking the Truth*. The program examines three controversial cases of convicted men fighting for their freedom.

An author, speaker and advocate for the wrongfully convicted, Ryan is equally passionate about the importance of establishing greater accountability in the judicial system. He explains: "I lost ten years of my life—years that will mean nothing unless I bring about change. If not, it will always haunt me."

As for Moriarty: "I hope Ryan doesn't allow himself to always be defined as 'wrongfully convicted.' I want him to use everything he has learned: courage and humility, the ability to overcome adversity, and the leadership skills he gained from dealing with different types of people. I just want him to become the best person he can be."

For many of us, understanding our innate freedom will often become an exercise in bravery. But as Ryan says, "Without growth, nothing else matters."

I BECAME FRIENDS WITH RYAN when he left Missouri and moved to Southwest Florida. We not only shared the same hometown, but considering we attended the exact same public schools, we practically shared the same life, albeit twenty years apart. In a different time, what happened to Ryan could easily have happened to me.

As he was closer in age to my children than me, I couldn't help but adopt a bit of a paternal outlook on the relationship. I even made arrangements to take Ryan to a photographer to get professional headshots to support his burgeoning work as a writer, speaker, advocate and fitness expert.

Just as Ryan had completed changing his clothes, I heard him call my name. As I turned around, he was standing there, right arm outstretched, something draped across his hand. His subsequent comment affected me more than I could have anticipated: "I don't know how to tie a tie."

Though I was aware he had been robbed of ten years of his life, at that moment, I was shattered by the true magnitude of the loss. As I reached around from behind Ryan and prepared his tie, I realized I was now a criminal of sorts: I was stealing a moment from Bill Ferguson, Ryan's extraordinary father. It was Bill's job to teach this essential skill to his son, not mine. In many ways, *the tie* is a rite of passage we fathers get to pass along to our sons—and Bill Ferguson likely never got that chance.

No, it wasn't just the tie that upset me, it was my newfound understanding of the cruel way in which our legal system had shattered the *ties that bind* us together—and the Ferguson family would never be the same.

Then again, neither would I.

SHOWMEJONES.COM

"For me, there was a transition from victim to victor. You begin to redefine yourself and your life."

—Beth Holloway

BETH HOLLOWAY

Many of us are not fans of the theory: "It's not personal, it's just business." Others put forth the notion that this old-school rhetoric simply serves as a ramshackle justification for bad behavior. Have people amassed fortunes using this brand of self-centered logic? Yes. Are they fulfilled? Possibly. But for those who worship at the throne of the bank account, fulfillment is likely defined by a rather short list of criteria.

The point? One's *work* and one's *life's work* should never be confused, misaligned or misunderstood. Sadly, the first is often "just business," but the latter is almost always extraordinarily "personal." The lucky ones manage to combine the two.

Achieving success at one's life's work doesn't necessarily lead to a burgeoning income. Nevertheless, what does come in can provide much greater value—a connection to our hearts. Or in the case of Beth and Natalee Holloway, the hearts of millions around the world.

At one time, Beth Holloway was a public school speech pathologist for children with special needs and a devoted mother of two. She lived a self-described "quiet, somewhat uneventful life" just outside of Birmingham, Alabama. All of this would soon change—under the worst possible circumstances.

In the summer of 2005, Beth's daughter Natalee disappeared on the last night of her senior high graduation trip to Aruba. The exhaustive search and widespread media coverage made Natalee Holloway a household name. Now living every parent's nightmare, Beth Holloway was thrust out of her Alabamian comfort zone and into the public eye.

As part of her unrelenting search for Natalee, Beth has been interviewed by countless national and international media. Even Barbara Walters selected her as one of the most fascinating people in 2005. Though a primary suspect in Natalee's disappearance has long been identified, his name has been intentionally omitted. It's a gross misuse of ink—and justice—to add fuel to his self-perpetuating, attention-starved fire.

Natalee was declared legally dead in 2012. Her whereabouts are still unknown.

For Beth, her unexpected life's work may have been tragic in its origin; however, today, business as usual is about as personal as you can get. "I found myself asking—since I've been a teacher and an educator—what can I do for others? What can I teach others from our tragic life?" she says. "I made the commitment early on in 2005 that I would share Natalee's story in hopes that others can learn how to endure in the face of adversity." Once a teacher, always a teacher.

Beth has most assuredly kept that promise. She has delivered her message of hope, faith and personal safety to thousands across the country. "It was cathartic in the beginning, but I think that's a normal process," she suggests. "For the last eight years, it's been personally rewarding and fulfilling to me to deliver the personal safety message to our young adults. It's very heartwarming to see that Natalee's story makes a difference in their lives—even though many are too young to remember it."

However, to spend one-on-one time with Beth Holloway—to hold her gaze as she discusses her beautiful daughter's hopes, dreams, charm and appeal—is equal parts uplifting and shattering. You feel your heart continue to break, one little piece at a time.

Beth's life's work is a celebration of all-things Natalee—complete with *what was* in equal billing with *what could have been*. "She wanted to go to medical school," Beth recalls. "I have no doubt she would have made it. She had big plans for her life. She was going to the University of Alabama. She was very disciplined and driven. She had an amazing network of friends. She had an amazing balance in her life."

This interview was easily the most challenging of my career. Mental images of a would-be Dr. Natalee Holloway—juxtaposed against the faces of my own two twenty-something children—created a cerebral rebellion that mocked my ability to focus, to comprehend.

In time, my course of action became clear: assist Beth Holloway in paying it forward—to tell the story of her noble mission. To honor Natalee, her family and the millions who continue to support—and learn from—

Natalee's legacy. Is there a more compelling reason to advocate for the education, welfare and safety of others? To look outside ourselves for purpose, fulfillment and courage—for our life's work?

"There are a lot of transitions that you make in your journey," Beth says. "For me, there was a transition from victim to victor. You begin to redefine yourself and your life." For those who have faced any kind of adversity, the spirit of this message could not be more universal.

Want to know more? You might run across news updates about the mission to bring Natalee's murderer to justice. Perhaps you can read *Loving Natalee*, Beth's bestselling book. Or you might watch the Lifetime movie based on it. Regardless of how you choose to learn about—and celebrate— Natalee Holloway, Natalee's beloved mother's all-too-personal objective is quite simple: protecting our children.

Even in its selfless simplicity, could there be a loftier goal?

THE DAY I SUBMITTED THE HOLLOWAY COLUMN to my editor, I felt as though I had run a mental and emotional marathon. Though Beth had been forthcoming and polite, she was also somewhat distant and reserved—as if a wall had been erected around her heart to protect her from the reality of her life's work. However, none of us should judge the actions or reactions of *anyone* who has lost a child.

Beth's job was to speak; my job was to respect her words. *Our* job was to honor Natalee and bring her message of travel safety to the public.

I finally came to understand why Natalee and Beth Holloway's story presented such a challenge to me. From the time the public first learned of her disappearance in 2005, my greatest fear has been that Natalee, the *flesh-and-blood person*, would get lost in Natalee, the *news story*. Natalee Holloway was *real* and, to this day, I beg historians not to reduce her incredible life to a series of film clips and footnotes.

Given the opportunity, what would Natalee have accomplished? How many lives would Natalee have touched? Though we will never know the full extent of her potential, Natalee's other lesson today is clear.

Every child's life has meaning.

Every child's gifts are immeasurable.

Every child—is everyone's child.

IN 2002, I WAS A CASH-STRAPPED, startup business owner in Leesburg, Virginia, and the parent of a thirteen-year-old boy and eleven-year-old girl.

In 2009, just a few months before we left Northern Virginia and moved to Florida, I answered an unexpected phone call relating to *another* phone call I had answered in 2002. I was apparently on the verge of being served a subpoena to appear in Loudoun County, Virginia, court to testify in a criminal fraud case.

Naturally, my staff rejoiced at the opportunity to tease me about the dramatic potential of my upcoming testimony:

Karyn: *"Are you going to break down and cry on the stand?"*

Robynann: *"Will you stand up and scream: 'That's him—he did it—I'll never forget that face.'"*

Virginia: *"Don't say anything stupid or you'll end up in the BIG HOUSE."*

However, I had never heard of the man on trial.

To make matters worse, I didn't recall my alleged actions in 2002 that were now leading me toward the witness stand. Making jokes was simply covering my real emotions—I was embarrassed because I didn't recall the specific events that linked me to the case.

SHOWMEJONES.COM

"Every child's life has meaning.
Every child's gifts are immeasurable.
Every child—is everyone's child."

—Randall Kenneth Jones

On July 29, 2002, a fourteen-year-old Ashburn, Virginia, girl, Erica Heather Smith, went missing. More than a week later her body was discovered in a shallow grave.

At some point in 2002, a telemarketer persuaded me to donate money to Loudoun Crime Solvers for the purpose of establishing a reward fund for information leading to the arrest and conviction of Erica Heather Smith's murderer. With obvious gratitude for the health and safety of my own children, and a heavy heart over the impact Erica's death undoubtedly had on her family, I wrote a $25 check and mailed it.

Seven years later, as a direct result of this 2002 donation, I was being served a subpoena to appear in court.

At issue? The reward fund manager had allegedly embezzled the unused money. My role was simply to tell the court that I had intended for my donation to be used for the specific purpose of "crime solving." Kind of a "duh," but apparently a necessary part of the proceedings.

As instructed, I appeared at the courthouse on Thursday, April 1, 2009, at which point I learned I was actually not needed; they planned to settle out-of-court. This was no April Fools' Day joke either. Though I was the only witness they had neglected to call, I was fine. I had literally just walked across the street to get there.

The Smiths' attorney wisely requested that I stay "just in case." After a short wait, he and three other people exited the courtroom. I was immediately aware of the quartet's sense of relief:

"It's finally over."

"We can get back to more important things now."

"It's been seven long years…"

Having spotted me sitting quietly on the bench outside the courtroom door, the Smiths' attorney turned to me, extended his hand, politely thanked me for my time and walked away. I began to gather my things and when I looked up again, he had returned. But this time, he was not alone: "Mr. Jones, I want you to meet Mr. Smith, Erica's father."

Despite my limited memory of the events that brought me to the courthouse that day, I knew I was now face-to-face with the intended benefactor of my modest contribution. A man, and father, who had suffered more in the past seven years than I could possibly ever imagine. I was polite, but also embarrassed by his unexpected gratitude. "I'm not sure I deserve all this attention. All I did was write a check," I stammered.

Moments later, standing on the steps outside the courthouse, I was suddenly able to comprehend the special attention given my presence that day. To the Smith family, I represented every unknown, faceless stranger who, upon hearing the story of their daughter's tragic death, had picked up a checkbook, reached into their wallet or volunteered their time in hopes of bringing a child's murderer to justice.

As I was about to turn and walk away, Mr. Smith reached toward me once again. I extended my hand for a second time, but Erica Heather Smith's father had a different plan. He bypassed my hand and hugged me—right there on the steps of the Loudoun County, Virginia, Courthouse.

I am aware that the emotions that lead to active charitable giving are often based on being touched by a tragedy in a personal way. Yes, I was touched that day, both literally *and* figuratively. That embrace from Erica's father was one of the most profoundly meaningful moments of my life. I assure you, I have not hugged my own children in quite the same way ever since.

Part of me will always ache for Erica, but all of me is honored to have briefly crossed paths with her extraordinarily brave father.

In July 2014, Erica's murderer was finally identified, though very few details were made public. The assailant had evidently committed suicide during the course of the investigation.

I think about Erica and the Smith family quite often. Her passing still haunts me, yet I always find myself thinking: I am so grateful I answered that telephone call in 2002. Though the act of philanthropic giving is supposed to be entirely selfless, seems to me I got quite a lot for my $25 donation.

Every child's life has meaning.

Every child's gifts are immeasurable.

Every child—is everyone's child.

FRIENDS

When it comes to a child's brand loyalty, it's best to expect the unexpected. Though my young children were devout Disney and Pixar consumers, once the film *Titanic* entered the picture in 1997, their cinematic best friends became Jack, Rose, assorted iceberg-mishap victims and a really big boat with a very limited lifespan.

My personal watershed moment occurred the day I realized I would have to watch *Toy Story 3* by myself.

It was during this transition from Disney animation to tween mentation that my children started to think—ahem—"like adults." They also decided we needed to act more like "friends."

Now, one might believe the neighborhood McDonald's would be a safe zone—a place where children would continue to act like children and parents still called all the shots. McDonald's, a beloved enclave where jovial Mayor McCheese ruled with an iron fist: "You Deserve a Break Today!"

Think again, Kemosabe. It's dinner time.

KEVIN
(finishing a fist full of French fries)
Dad, what is an alibi?

What? An alibi? Why does my son need to know what an alibi is? What the hell did he do?

DAD RANDY
(fishing)
Why do you want to know about alibis,
Kevin?

KEVIN
(flippantly)
I've just been thinking about it a lot lately.

Oh Good Lord, he's misappropriated money from his soccer team's end-of-season party fund. Or even worse, he's become Sterling Middle School's most-powerful-slash-most-feared drug lord. My baby boy is doomed!

Okay, I admit, I'm prone to jumping to conclusions and this day was no different. As both of my children were voracious readers, Kevin had simply entered a new crime-novel phase and was attempting to educate himself on the nomenclature. Thinking I was now safe from non-sequitur-imbued interrogation, I proffered a brief "alibi" definition and returned to my Quarter Pounder.

Alas, I somehow overlooked the fact that *she* was there too…

MARIBETH
You know what I keep thinking about?

Expecting to hear more about the life and times of Britney Spears…

MARIBETH
(with great candor)
All the different kinds of cheese.

Huh?

Kevin and I froze—a half-eaten French fry fell from his mouth. In my bemused state, I had managed to swallow my Diet Coke incorrectly and the fizz made its way north through my sinus cavity and into my nasal passages, causing me to gasp for air.

What would cause a child to make time to ponder the quantity and/or quality of a dairy product? What on earth have I done to my daughter? And the words I never thought would enter my mind: Maribeth, please, please, please, can we talk more about Britney?

Kevin and I slowly turned to face her—and yes, I could literally see my McNugget-munching munchkin dreaming of a wonderland of cheddar, sbrinz, mountain goat, Gloucester and Gouda.

As has always been the case, it's Maribeth's world and we're all just taking up space.

So here's the deal, regardless of where they sit on the friend spectrum, we're not always going to understand every aspect of someone's personality. But more important is having the ability to respect, appreciate and celebrate the various idiosyncrasies that each brings to the table.

Today, Kevin and Maribeth are two of my best friends—though they took me kicking and screaming into this terrifying new world of parent/child equality. In fact, I would have taken seven consecutive years of two-year-old behavior if we could have skipped ages eighteen to twenty-four altogether.

Since my children were very young, I have emphasized to them the importance of long-term friendships. On a basic professional level, most of us appreciate the profound accuracy in the expression: "It's not *what* you know, it's *who* you know." That being said, true friends often outlast any number of doomed career choices and/or romantic affiliations.

But more than that, our most trusted, beloved confidants will continue to open doors for us. And our most loyal friends take it one step further—they personally usher us through, assorted cheeses and all....

Peter Berec

PHIL BEUTH

I'm fairly proud of my ability to spin a whimsical yarn, but it's my good friend, the incomparable Mr. Phil Beuth, who I suspect invented yarn in the first place. For Phil, a ten-minute chat is just a warm up—a sort of opening act for the dazzling array of whimsical anecdotes and poignant narratives that are guaranteed to follow.

Though his Ego Wall is filled with photos of him alongside celebrities such as Oprah Winfrey, Paul McCartney, Mohammad Ali and Audrey Hepburn, ego had very little to do with Phil Beuth's success. He was, and still is, one of those rare people who actually have a "magnetic personality."

It is often said that a man is measured by the company he keeps. Let it also be said, when you are on the receiving end of a phone call beginning with, "Hello Randy—Regis Philbin here," it becomes difficult to measure the impact as the potential business lessons skyrocket. Regis graciously called to comment on the prolific career of his friend, Phil Beuth.

In fact, the celebrated television icon treated our conversation as if it was the most important task of his day. Though I applaud Regis for helping me honor his pal, our chat evolved into an unpredicted tutorial on enthusiasm and focus. As a captive audience of one, I was on the receiving end of Regis' trademark charming wit and unexpected personal attention. If I learned anything from Regis Philbin's behavior that day it's that, to him, we are not an audience of the masses; we are a mass of individuals.

However, Regis also kept his focus squarely on Phil: "People were attracted to him. People wanted to work with him. At that time, many tended to shy away from network executives, but his people wanted to hear his stories and his ideas."

Phil rose to the heights of the media and entertainment industry, most notably as president of *Good Morning America* (1986-1997). During this time, he also maintained active involvement at the highest levels of ABC-TV management. In Phil's words, "The most remarkable thing about my career is the people I got to work with. I was blessed with the best leadership in the business."

Lucky for us, Phil Beuth's memoir, *Limping On Water*, has captured his glorious career. A rare find, the book is essentially a love story of Phil's forty-year career with the much-heralded Capital Cities Communications. His former employer may have been "the minnow that swallowed the whale" when it purchased ABC in 1986; however, Phil's loyalty to his long-term associates is unwavering. "Everything was an open book with Cap Cities," he says. "We understood that owning a TV station was not only a *privilege* but also a *public trust*. Even Warren Buffett often stated that the balance sheet should include a line item for 'integrity.'"

Though willing to accept credit for his best ideas, Phil quickly defers to his mentor, Capital Cities CEO Tom Murphy, for establishing a timeless management philosophy: "If you hire the best people you can and leave them alone, you don't have to hire very many." Regis concurs, "Capital Cities had a way of producing executives who knew how to get the best out of people."

Born in Staten Island, New York, with mild cerebral palsy, Phil Beuth was reared by a single mother. The family's lack of health insurance resulted in young Phil having to straighten out his feet by tucking them under the radiator and doing sit-ups. Rudimentary, yes—but also a likely influence on a problem-solving philosophy based on taking control of the situation, using the resources available, and getting the job done.

Specifically, Phil takes pride in a 1988 decision to develop a series of prime-time specials on AIDS—produced without the guarantee of advertiser funding to support the initiative. According to Jessica Stark, former colleague at *Good Morning America*, "Phil has been, and always will be, the great crusader. Phil operated on his wits—which were considerable." In Regis' words, "Phil Beuth was a great executive—always up and ready to hear new ideas."

And then there's his storytelling.... True, most of us can point to a handful of special moments that defined our lives. My challenge to Phil: Can you pick just one life-altering snapshot?

Without hesitation, Phil launched into a story that would redefine the meaning of the "sweet spot" in baseball.

Buffalo, New York, 1984

A lifelong baseball fan, Phil, then president of WKBW-TV, would finally realize one of his boyhood dreams as part of a children's hospital fund-raiser pitting his Channel 7 Prime Timers against a crew of local police and firemen fielded by Buffalo's mayor. Of the fans present that day, most memorable to Phil were the children seated in wheelchairs alongside the first base seats.

Due to the effects of cerebral palsy, batter Beuth was not challenged to *hit* the ball; however, runner Beuth had difficulty arriving at first base *in advance* of the ball. Earlier in the game, the opponent's brash right fielder had already thrown him out at first base.

During the final inning, Phil came up to bat for the home-team Prime Timers with two outs and the winning run on second. As the aforementioned right fielder smugly moved closer in, a determined Phil belted the ball over his head as the announcer exclaimed: "The boss wins the game! The boss wins the game."

However, it was a subsequent encounter with a wheelchair-bound, nine-year-old boy that would ultimately enter Phil Beuth's Storytelling Hall of Fame. At the request of the boy's mother, Phil stepped over to meet the young fan.

The boy looked up and quietly asked: "Do you think I could ever do that?"

With the trials of his own childhood rushing through his mind, a highly emotional Beuth leaned in, embraced the boy and assured him: "Yes, you can."

A home run of generosity by anyone's standards.

"Winning the game was fine," Phil recalls, "but giving that child hope was the winning element that put everything in proper perspective."

P-E-R-S-P-E-C-T-I-V-E.

This powerful word—just eleven characters in length—provided Phil Beuth, and now countless readers, an emotionally charged memory guaranteed to help cover all the bases.

And Beuth's most important lesson: **live a life that creates great stories to tell.**

ONE OF THE GREATEST GIFTS we can extend another person can only happen as a result of familiarity and earned respect. Though each individual has a unique set of valued contacts, one of the most potent signs of our esteem is when we choose to share these connections with others; when we act upon an inspired notion that two strangers stand to benefit from knowing each other.

In addition to his introductions to Charles Gibson and Jack Hanna, Phil Beuth would take me under his wing on many occasions. Frankly, had Phil been college pals with Jesus—and there's a rumor running around that he was—he would undoubtedly have set the two of us up for a private tete-a-tete.

Jesus notwithstanding, **Phil introduced Randy to Randy.**

And this new Randy had quite the story to tell.

Long before sports columnist Mitch Albom celebrated some very special Tuesdays with a sociology professor named Morrie, Randy Antik was enjoying monthly lunches with a lifelong mentor—a prominent Dallas businessman named Stanley. Randy's first encounter with Stanley happened—completely by chance—when he was an eighteen-year-old intern in New York City. Years later and still hungry for stimulating conversation, the pair ended up living in the same city and shared regular meals over a period of ten years.

Stanley, who aged from his mid-eighties to mid-nineties during this time, had only one requirement: every three months Randy was to bring an interesting "young person" to join them. His preference: someone under fifty to help him "understand what the young people were up to."

The lunches ended with Stanley's death on January 22, 2002.

"Stanley," a.k.a. Harold Stanley Marcus, was the one-time president (1950–1972) and later chairman of the board (1972–1976) of luxury retailer Neiman Marcus.

His protégé, Randy Antik, is founder and CEO of the Imagine Solutions Conference, an annual thought leader forum that brings up to fifty world-class thought leaders to engage an audience of 500 private sector leaders on today's most relevant issues.

Though there's little doubt that Stanley Marcus' mentoring spirit is a significant part of Randy Antik and his character, Antik credits Marcus—and many other teachers—for inspiring his ceaseless urge to promote education, best practices and social issues. For when it comes to making introductions, Randy Antik has ultimately honored Stanley's influence by introducing, not just an impressive roster of thought *leaders*, but an inspired series of *thoughts* to hundreds of individuals each year.

KC Schulberg

Next, Phil introduced Randy to KC.

KC Schulberg's grandfather, B.P. Schulberg, produced *Wings*, the first film to win the Best Picture Oscar in 1927. His grandmother, Adeline Schulberg, was Hollywood's first female talent agent. His father, Stuart Schulberg, was an independent producer/director and executive producer of NBC's TODAY for ten years. His uncle, Budd Schulberg, was the Oscar-winning screenwriter of *On the Waterfront* starring Marlon Brando.

Prior to forming his own production company in 1998, KC served as worldwide production supervisor and then senior vice president of worldwide marketing for New York-based Hallmark Entertainment, a preeminent producer of television mini-series and movies.

His family's influence is probably most evident in the emphasis KC places on quality, artistry and humanity over personal financial gain. "At the end of the day, there are many ways to measure success," he says. "But class in business affairs is of primordial importance to me." After all, it was his Uncle Budd who famously wrote, "Having a conscience in Hollywood is like driving with a hand brake on."

Simply put, KC wants to "embellish the world with a little bit of magic." More specifically, *magical realism*: a literary and film genre where magic elements are a natural part in an otherwise mundane, realistic environment—a term which could easily describe his enviable approach to life.

His longtime friend, writer-director-producer David Paulsen (*Dallas, Dynasty, Knots Landing*) adds, "There is a lovely, magical quality about KC. He's a true producer—he has a dream and he finds a way to get it done." After all, "magic" doesn't happen by *magic*—it's the result of vision, hard work and an ironclad belief that each of us has the power to, as KC says, "bring joy and beauty into the world."

In any case, wouldn't our business world be a better place with a little more magical thinking? In fact, what would happen if more of us would reject the mundane in favor of a fresher, more visionary approach?

Whether you define magic in a more traditional "abracadabra" sense, or by its first cousins—spontaneity, creativity, inspiration and surprise—take a tip from Hollywood, and KC Schulberg, and try to work a little magic today.

AS I HAVE SPENT THE MAJORITY of my life as a part-time actor, I have frequently been compared to prominent performers. However, until I met KC, the comparison qualifier seemed to be based only on physical appearance. If the actor was tall and/or had brown hair, that seemed to be enough for most to declare doppelganger status.

Over the past thirty-five years I have been compared to Tom Cruise, Kevin Kline, Pierce Brosnan, Scott Bakula, Bruce Boxleitner and Sylvester Stallone, to name a few. Though I look *nothing* like most of these men—and Cruise is wicked short—I have always taken the compliments for what they are worth: a superficial ego boost.

That said, I do understand and greatly appreciate my decadeslong comparisons to John Ritter.

Enter KC Schulberg, a man whose career has included the evaluation of countless actors based on character and characters as well as their physical attributes. At the end of our interview, KC commented: "Randy, you know who you remind me of?" Naturally, I expected to hear yet another name from the tall brunette family of leading men, but I was wrong. "You remind me of Jonathan Winters."

I was dumbfounded. Though Jonathan Winter's comedic talent was legendary, my mental pictures of Winters are from his later years in life. I thought to myself: "Really? Jonathan Winters? Am I really that old?" Followed by: "Wow, I must be a lot fatter than I thought!"

Sensing my confusion yet understanding the incalculable depth of an actor's vanity, KC continued: "You do know there was a time when Jonathan

Winters was young and attractive. Right?" To which I laughed and playfully responded: "Oh, I remind you of the young, HOT Jonathan Winters!"

Thankfully, KC was kind enough to ignore my egomaniacal tendencies and explain: "Randy, you have the same twinkle in your eyes that Jonathan Winters had."

In a salute to my overt—and embarrassing—occasionally shallow nature, I had failed to look beyond the surface of KC's comment. I focused totally on the *outside* with no regards for the *inside*—of the comment *or* Mr. Winters.

To this day, I don't think I have *ever* been paid a more unexpected, generous or deeply meaningful compliment. It was MAGIC!

Now, Phil *and* Randy introduced Randy to Tyler....

Denise Wauters

TYLER MATHISEN

Considering Tyler Mathisen grew up just outside the nation's capital in Arlington, Virginia, he appears to be completely untouched by the more negative connotations often associated with politics and/or politicians. Although the politically correct Mathisen credits his success to the oft-quoted "right place, right time" myth, his appeal and intensely inquisitive nature reveal a different story.

Eric Schurenberg, editor-in-chief of *INC.* magazine, recalls, "When I met Tyler, I thought he was the most gentlemanly person I had ever met: gracious, polite, courteous. Today, he is the manifestation of what it means to be empathic—in person and to his television audience."

Tyler's achievements may actually be better described by spinning a popular saying about failure into the more apropos "the best *parlayed* plans." A graduate of the University of Virginia, he didn't simply rely on Lady Luck—each new résumé entry added precious new skills to his now impressive curriculum vitae.

For example, by deliberately continuing his education in the workplace, Tyler *parlayed* his college-improved editorial skills into an early position writing "how-to" books for Time-Life. The organization provided him an even more important *how to.* "I learned how to understand, explain and make complicated information easier to understand." A quality Tyler is now most admired for as a journalist.

Prior to joining CNBC in 1997, Tyler was a highly respected, award-winning writer, senior editor and top editor for *Money* magazine. However, once again, he *parlayed* his ongoing education and developing communication skills into a new role as money editor of *Good Morning America* (1991-1997), thus placing him behind the keyboard *and* in front of the camera.

To Phil Beuth, "Tyler projects amazing credibility—in double and triple doses." Schurenberg adds, "He is a master of directing energy."

As should be the goal of any journalist—but is the reality for a select few—Tyler advises: "Never believe you are the smartest man in the room; always be willing to learn something new."

Today, the much heralded Tyler Mathisen co-anchors CNBC's *Power Lunch* and *Nightly Business Report*, an award-winning evening business news program for U.S. public television.

SHOWMEJONES.COM

"Never believe you are the smartest man in the room; always be willing to learn something new."

—Tyler Mathisen

Before they married, Joanne LaMarca Mathisen worked alongside her future husband at CNBC. Her early impression: "Tyler was the first 'talent' I had worked with who didn't view himself as 'talent'—he was one among us. To Tyler, it's not about him, it's all about telling the story." Now a senior producer on NBC's TODAY, she adds: "These days, guys like Tyler are hard to find."

Take him off-camera and Tyler seems to display what can only be referred to as a "focused calm." Though you quickly appreciate his very human need to make the most of his time, his demeanor is never frenetic. He is thoughtful, confident and kind. What's more, Tyler is a thinker: you *literally* see the wheels turning in his eyes. But most of all, you know his mind is churning in a selfless yet heartfelt attempt to make the most of your time together.

Though there appears to be no uniformly accepted definition of what it means to be "a good man," just ask yourself how many times you have described someone using those three simple words. I suspect the answer will be a single-digit number.

Nevertheless, ask around about Tyler and terms like honest, respectful, caring, ethical and dependable are likely to be mentioned. As seen through the eyes of his wife, colleagues and countless strangers who faithfully watch him each week—good man Mathisen ticks all the boxes above. In fact, what could be more important *to any man* than to one day be described as "a good man"?

The answer: Nothing.

Have you figured out who is next in line?

Kevin Randall Jones

JOANNE LAMARCA MATHISEN

To discuss the highs and lows (lows, be gone), the ups and downs (up only, please) and the personality and morality of TODAY Senior Producer Joanne LaMarca Mathisen, it's Kathie Lee Gifford who first storms out of the gate: "There is no perkier cheerleader, more enthusiastic supporter or more hard-working producer than our Joanne. We all adore her!"

However, it's Gifford's on-air partner-in-wine, Hoda Kotb, who metaphorically pulls up a chair for an all-things-JLM chat fest: "What Joanne does—and what we try to do on the show—is bring joy. That's what Joanne produces: joy." Of course, this leads to the question: Is there a more important job description than "to produce joy"? What's more, do these three words have to appear on a daily to-do list for joy to prevail?

Note: *Gentlemen, please keep reading. Just as the ability to understand the women in your lives is essential, the art of producing joy is, by no means, gender specific.*

"When Joanne walks in the morning meeting, she is like a bright light," says Kotb. "You're already happy and you don't really know why. There are certain people who are so full of positivity that their cup runs over and fills up yours. She is one of those people who understands women because she is a friend to so many."

What better role for the upbeat SUNY Oneonta alum and one-time budding fashionista than to be the off-camera kingpin of TODAY'S Kathie Lee and Hoda segment, a.k.a. "The Happy Hour."

A young Joanne LaMarca would ultimately abandon her goal of a fashion career in favor of a more life-enriching path. To explain this youthful, career-altering cerebral light bulb, Joanne points to her clothing and asks: "Do we really need this vest in fourteen different colors?" She then pauses, smiles brightly and playfully adds: "I mean, Randy, does it matter that your shorts don't really match your shirt?" Tragically, they did not. (*Stupid, stupid man.*)

But that's another of Joanne's charmingly camouflaged skills: the ability to tell the truth in a way that bypasses tears in favor of cheers. To Hoda: "She feels like your best friend when you meet her—she produces the show in the same way."

Of course, it's a slippery slope to manage workplace friendships. Nonetheless, many of us have long-lasting relationships that began in the office yet flourished in the outside world.

Naturally, we appreciate it when others enjoy our company. Even so, it's infinitely more meaningful when one's true nature is exposed, when a mutual admiration society emerges that not only reflects one's sense of humor and disposition, but reveals something deeper: commitment, compassion, shared beliefs and a complementary work ethic. When this happens, the strengths of one friend all but dissolve the weaknesses in the other—e.g. Kathie Lee and Hoda.

Like so many of us, Joanne has a job that, when done properly, makes others look good. For the working masses, it's bosses, clients, shareholders and co-workers. For her, it's Kathie Lee, Hoda, and an ever-changing group of guests with a plethora of personalities, principles, attitudes and agendas.

In addition, her job is to look for life lessons in others, managed ever-so-effectively through an ironclad appreciation of her ability to learn something new every day. A scenario that exists for most of us, assuming we remain open to the possibilities. Some of Joanne's favorite educators include:

Suze Orman: "*She makes you realize exactly what matters and what doesn't.*"

E.L. James, author, *Fifty Shades of Grey*: "*She is proof that you don't have to be twenty-five years old to realize your dreams.*"

Cher: "*Being courageous enough to be yourself in a world where society dictates who you should be is amazingly brave to me.*"

To be sure, celebrity status is not a requirement for finding yourself on Joanne's admiration radar. "In 2011, Madonna Badger lost her three daughters and her parents in a fire in Connecticut," she recalls, "The fact that she can get up every day and face life astonishes and inspires me."

If it's true that a business' culture is driven from the top down, then Joanne LaMarca Mathisen comes close to achieving the status of (corporate) cultural icon. She is reflected in her televised product, and her product is reflected in her. The laughter. The joy. The insight. The refreshing honesty. "Very few people walk into a room and change it," Hoda observes. "You always know if Joanne was there. She changes the room, and she makes it better."

SHOWMEJONES.COM

"It's important to make people laugh every day. I have no patience for people who don't put life in perspective. You don't realize how blessed you are until you pick apart your life and look at others."

—Joanne LaMarca Mathisen

For her part, Joanne, herself, explains the success of the show and the power of camaraderie in very simple terms: "Women love to see other women get along."

And yes, for those who appreciate the value of embracing one's inner child, Hoda also suggests: "Joanne's been in the business a long time, but she still has that sense of wonderment." For Wonderment Woman Joanne: "It's important to make people laugh every day. I have no patience for people who don't put life in perspective. You don't realize how blessed you are until you pick apart your life and look at others."

Is there a reason I have quoted Hoda as much as Joanne herself? Yes. Joanne (talks about and) puts others first. A fact that also reveals the not-so-secret secret to making friendships work, workplace or otherwise.

Will Joanne LaMarca Mathisen be stunned to see my editorial lens focused on her in such a personal way? Yes, most likely. Are Hoda and I concerned? No, not really. As a society, we have no greater responsibility than to shine the light on those who selflessly work behind the scenes for the purpose of making us look good; for bringing out our best by putting us first; for producing our joy and designing our success.

Now, back to Hoda: "If you were to line up the people who consider Joanne a close friend, you would not be able to see the end of the line." For friend-magnet Joanne, and so many like her: "Feeding your soul is as important as feeding your family."

If you are one of the millions of viewers of the fourth hour of TODAY, Joanne LaMarca Mathisen is the best friend you never knew you had. For everybody else, invoke your inner JLM and try putting others first…

TODAY!

FRIENDSHIPS DON'T ALWAYS FOLLOW the nice, neat linear path outlined here. And there's certainly no requirement that our friends provide any sort of benefit, other than unconditional love and support.

However, did my celebrated conga line of friendly column subjects end with Joanne? No, in fact, that's where is seemed to have begun all over again—a fact leading me to exclaim: *Hoda phone, it Kotb true*, but look who sat down in Randy's *thought seat* next!

But as they say in the entertainment biz, stay tuned for more.

STAR SEARCH

In late spring of 1972, Mid-Missouri went Hollywood. A movie musical version of Mark Twain's classic, *Tom Sawyer*, was set to be filmed in Arrow Rock—just a hop, skip and a jump from my hometown of Columbia. I begged, pleaded and initiated self-induced hyperventilation until my parents agreed to take nine-year-old me to the open call for movie extras.

My persistence, hysteria and irregular breathing patterns eventually paid off as my mom and dad hauled me and thirteen-year-old sister, Paula Perfect, to the open call for *Tom Sawyer* at the local Ramada Inn. *Already sounds glamorous, don't it?*

After an excruciatingly long wait, made even more intolerable by intense Missouri heat and suffocating humidity, Paula surrendered and agreed to accept a new ukulele as opposed to fame and glory. However, as Paula always knew how to proffer a *perfect* deal, I have long suspected that ukulele acquisition was part of her master plan all along. As for my dad, a mere stringed instrument purchase must have seemed a small price to pay for access to the comfort of air conditioning.

I fiercely dug my heels in and insisted I stay, as this was my big chance to be discovered. And yes, my loyal mother stayed at my side. I am also quite sure the mere suggestion that we abandon the audition process altogether would have resulted in a public spectacle—a dramatic performance of grand proportions courtesy of me—in the Ramada parking lot.

When my number *finally* came up, so to speak, I walked into the casting room and dutifully stood on the line in front of the camera. Of the few weary men in the room, none seemed terribly interested in honoring Mark Twain's legacy *or* launching my career. Most appeared to be focused solely on getting the native hillbilly casting done quickly and without much fanfare.

My audition, which consisted of me stating my first name, last name and age, was briefly interrupted by a formidable scruffy man in a ball cap. Having noticed my oversized boy belly, Mr. Scruffy grunted sarcastically, "suck it in kid." This was followed by a series of intermittent chuckles from other members of the film's staff. Despite Mr. Scruffy's insinuating barb, I stood there defiantly, *sucking it in* and *sucking it up* while I completed my brief but epic audition.

Up next: the agonizingly long wait for the phone call that never came. A time period marked by foul language, crying jags and shrieks of a pending Armageddon—but this was simply my mother's way of dealing with *my* hyper-emotional state. Alas, *chubby* was apparently out of style in Mark Twain's Hannibal, Missouri, and I was shunned from the movie.

Despite my egregious omission, the show did go on with the balance of the *Tom Sawyer* cast and crew landing in Columbia, and nearby Arrow Rock, at the beginning of the summer of 1972. Having pushed my Mr. Scruffy-induced humiliation into the recesses of my mind, that summer was pure magic. After all, I had convinced myself that I would find a way to become a memorable part of the *Tom Sawyer* filmmaking process anyway.

The above sentence, my dear friends, is called "foreshadowing."

On several occasions, my family traveled to Arrow Rock to experience the magic of movie making in person. I was unabashedly star struck when I met Johnny Whitaker, who was cast in the title role of Tom. And Whitaker literally ran down the street to escape after our initial meeting. *I'm not kidding.*

However, my most vivid memory is from the day they filmed the scene introducing the characters of Whitaker's Tom Sawyer, to Becky Thatcher, played by pre-pubescent screen goddess Jodie Foster.

I could barely contain my excitement as Mom, Dad, Paula and I propped up our lawn chairs in the middle of the dirt streets of Arrow Rock to watch the action unfold in front of Becky Thatcher's house. I was about to breathe Jodie Foster AIR.

Among my mother's most admirable qualities is the fact that she has truly never met a stranger. So, at some point during the filming, she managed to bond with Jodie Foster's mom, Brandy.

Seated in my lawn chair, both hands clutching my now empty soda can in fervent anticipation, I watched as Johnny was hoisted into an upside-down position and left dangling from a tree. Dressed beautifully in a petticoat-lined yellow dress, Jodie appeared on the front porch and engaged in spirited dialogue with the then upside-down Johnny. A massive camera was mounted on what appeared to be a simulated train track, and huge microphones hovered above both Jodie's head and upside-down Johnny's butt.

Clearly, the exhilaration of the moment finally got to be too much for me, and my nervous energy centered itself on my only available outlet.

It was the "pop" heard round the world—or at least loud enough to ring out twenty miles east of Arrow Rock in Columbia.

You see, when one depressed the top of a '70s-era soda can and then suddenly released that pressure, it sometimes made a sound—*a very loud sound.*

Though I am certain this all happened very quickly, in my horrified, adolescent mind, slow motion prevailed as heads slowly began to turn in my direction. The director, the crew, the spectators, my parents, Paula Perfect,

JODIE!

Brandy Foster and, of course, Jodie and upside-down Johnny—all of them were staring at me—the chubby boy in the Husky shorty shorts fidgeting in the lawn chair clutching the smoking gun: a scene-annihilating, ear-splitting soda can.

My self-preservation instincts immediately kicked in and I too decided to turn around and conduct my own faux investigation as to the source of the disruptive noise. As my head was approaching the ninety-degree mark, my somewhat substantial stomach sank to my knees, for directly behind me was *a whole lot of nothing*—nary a hapless spectator to take the blame off my shoulders *or my can.*

My mother—the queen of spontaneity in regards to childhood crisis management—swiftly removed the offending soda can from my hands and, without missing a beat, resumed mom-chatting with Brandy Foster as if nothing had happened. Brandy, a mother herself, took the cue and responded in kind.

Thanks to an impressive display of dual-maternal instincts, all was once again right with the world. Heads returned to normal forward positioning and the film work continued. The upside was that I got to watch Johnny get reinserted into the tree so he and Jodie could film the scene all over again. However, this time, both mothers made sure I remained beverage-free.

After filming ended, things heated up again. With Brandy now an unofficial part of our entourage, we made our way to the sidewalk adjacent to the Thatcher House set as we headed off to the next location.

Then, without warning, Jodie bolted from the steps in front of the house and, in a spectacular show of athleticism, vaulted over the white picket fence to face her mother. As impressive as it was, Jodie's Olympic-style dismount stuck just inches from a very startled *me*. Mama Foster was *not* pleased. "Jodie, you're in a dress with a petticoat! You could have gotten caught on that fence and hurt yourself. And you may even have fallen on that poor boy (*that's me!*) and hurt both of you. Now you apologize."

> ## SHOWMEJONES.COM
>
> **"I am music.**
> **I am drama.**
> **I am speech.**
> **I am art.**
> **I *am* my arts education."**
>
> —Randall Kenneth Jones

Though I am sure Jodie was thinking, "Yuck—Soda Can Boy," the acrobatic actress wisely chose to obey her mother and quickly provided the requisite, if less-than-enthusiastic, apology, "Uh, sorry."

But at that moment, nothing else mattered. I just saw Jodie Foster get in trouble—in public, no less. Jodie Foster had to apologize to me. *Thank You, God!*

Despite the fact that an airborne Jodie Foster could have ended my very existence that day, what really killed me was the sudden realization that mega-child-star Jodie Foster was just as pathetic as I was. Both Jodie and I suffered titanic embarrassments that very same day and, from my vantage point, it was simply wonderful.

Jodie fostered a new sense of normalcy in my life. I wasn't just pitiful Soda Can Boy; I was the most ordinary child on the planet.

Shortly after that, I began acting and singing in earnest, and I occasionally tread the boards today. Nonetheless, as a marketer, writer and speaker, I make my living being *analytical* (music) and *creative* (drama). I make presentations to groups, both large and small (speech). What's more, I dream up imaginative concepts and work with a team to bring these visions to life (art).

I am music.
I am drama.
I am speech.
I am art.
I *am* my arts education.

EDDIE MEKKA

In the spring of 1978, I was cast in Rock Bridge High School's production of *Man of La Mancha* as one of the rough and tough band of "muleteers"—typecasting, of course.

On opening night, I assumed my pre-show position alongside the other "prisoners," crouched tightly underneath the newly constructed thrust platform stage, only to discover that the rear seam of my costume pants had completely ripped open as I crawled into position.

Teen Randy
(in a whisper)
Rodney. Rodney. My pants just ripped
open in the back. We don't leave the stage
for the first thirty minutes of the show.
What do I do?

Rodney Hill
(struggling to be helpful)
Uh…don't turn around?

From my now *literal* prison under the platform in front of the gymnatorium stage, I was unexpectedly redefining the entire concept of "opening night." I learned two extremely valuable lessons that evening: 1) no matter what, *cover your ass* and; 2) never allow your mother to repurpose a McCall's pajama-bottom pattern for a public event.

As young performers, we were also forced to *create*. We didn't have access to countless interpretations of our roles via YouTube. In fact, I had to make do with only *three* television networks. (The horror!) My parents had radio. My grandparents had books. And I guess if you go far enough up the Jones Family Tree you may find a subset of stone-age Joneses dancing around a fire and grunting—a.k.a. a *modern-day* Jones family reunion.

In my younger days, when it was said that *everyone* knew of a specific public figure—that actually meant *everyone*. Of course, that's assuming they had a pulse and/or a TV set.

Though his "product" is a character and his service is "entertainment," Eddie Mekka is a walking tribute to the notion: There's No *Business* like Show Business. From actors and crew to journalists and admirers, Mekka radiates self-confidence and warmth alongside his relentless desire to entertain. At our breakfast meeting, he practically put on a one-man show in an attempt to coax a smile out of our sullen waitress. We ultimately concluded she must not have any teeth.

Hired by the legendary Garry Marshall as a comedic actor, Mekka would step into the shoes of Carmine "The Big Ragoo" Ragusa for eight seasons on TV's *Laverne & Shirley*. However, in demonstrating a noteworthy management lesson, Marshall wisely showcased the many talents of Eddie Mekka. "He pulled me aside and said, 'Let's make a list of all the things you can do,'" Eddie recalls.

Imagine the power we would gain through a comprehensive understanding of, not just all of *our* personal skills, but the wide-ranging talents of those around us.

With a résumé that included singing, dancing, boxing and gymnastics, Mekka and Marshall transformed Carmine into a much more talent-diverse character, starting from the moment Eddie—as Carmine—literally danced into our living rooms in 1976.

In person, whether revealing humorous anecdotes about a whimsical anatomy lesson from Broadway-legend Gwen Verdon or sharing a bottle of Ouzo in a Ford Pinto with Chita Rivera, Eddie Mekka clearly loves his work—and his work loves him right back. Unlike other actors who shun their legendary characters, Eddie embraces Carmine's legacy but maintains equal passion for his current projects. He explains, "Carmine opened the door for people to know Eddie Mekka."

Having more recently traveled the country in numerous productions of, for example, *A Funny Thing Happened on the Way to the Forum* and *Fiddler on the Roof*, Eddie embraces the fresh creative energy that accompanies each new production. Rather than replicate the exact same product each time, he challenges himself with each new collaboration, "If you see another actor who has something new and exciting, jump on their wagon and be a part of it."

From a traditional business standpoint: why just *reproduce* when you can *revitalize*?

He is also steadfast in his belief of maintaining positive work relationships. "The people I have been nice to—it has paid off."

On acting, Eddie quotes the infamous theatrical proverb, "If you can't be honest, you have to learn how to act." Though, to an actor, "honest" refers to a truthful portrayal of a character, by using "honest" as a character *trait*, it resonates equally well off the stage. After all, no one wants to deal with a business professional who is acting the part.

THERE'S LITTLE DOUBT that the average worker is sometimes forced to metaphorically *tap dance* his way through various workplace minefields. However, after decades in the spotlight, Eddie Mekka's longevity, positive energy and people-first attitude prove the importance of *being comfortable in your own shoes*.

As a teen, I was an extremely loyal *Laverne & Shir*ley fan. Though I never

Drew and Karen Attanasio Photography

had the courage to try milk and Pepsi, most in my circle were a Lenny, a Squiggy or an even more ridiculous combination of both. Legions more wanted their own Boo Boo Kitty. However, I just wanted to be Eddie Mekka. I ached to have his theatrical training and talent, the likes of which were rarely seen on television, much less primetime TV.

Several decades later, as I was preparing to make my entrance on stage as crossdressing theatre director Roger DeBris in a Naples production of *The Producers*, it hit me. As a theatre kid, I never once thought to myself: "Wow, wouldn't it be great if Eddie Mekka could see *me* perform one day." Though I have always been a dreamer—the concept of singing and dancing *for* Eddie was simply too far afield. Yet it was about to happen: *The Big Ragoo was in the house.*

As I stood backstage in my Chrysler-Building-inspired gown and heel-destroying pumps, prepared to perform one of the greatest comedic roles ever written for musical theatre, Eddie's signature song began to play in my head. I realized, in ways too numerous to explain, that my editorial journey had quite literally taken me from *Rags to Riches*. Since that fateful day, I don't just *expect* the unexpected, I stack the deck *in favor of* the unexpected.

And that, ladies and gentlemen, is a very exciting way to live.

SHOWMEJONES.COM

"You can have a sense of humor only if you're confident in your strategy."

—Darrell Hammond

DARRELL HAMMOND

Chances are the average American worker is never going to be subject to a chorus of "boos" forcing him or her out of the conference room. Nonetheless, early in his career, *Saturday Night Live's* Darrell Hammond was occasionally the target of the aforementioned public disapproval for a job *not* well done. Yet he persevered.

Much has already been published about the intense competition between cast members of the iconic television sweatshop known as *SNL*. Though many of us work in businesses that provide a product or service to the public, Darrell Hammond's less tangible product was *laughter*. His considerable tools included the ability to impersonate some of the most powerful and recognized men in the world: President Bill Clinton, Vice Presidents Al Gore and Dick Cheney, Senator John McCain, Donald Trump and an Alex-Trebek-loathing Sean Connery.

With Hammond's laying claim to the longest tenure of any *SNL* performer (1995-2009), one might expect him to preach the gospel of maintaining a healthy sense of humor in the workplace, but Hammond ultimately sermonizes the value of hard work, determination and goal setting. In 2014, Hammond returned to *SNL* to replace legendary announcer, the late Don Pardo.

Crediting the work of W. Edwards Demming, an American statistician, professor and consultant best known for his work in post-World War II

Japan, a young Darrell adopted the practice of setting reasonable weekly goals. His expectation? By year's end he would achieve "exponential improvement" through fifty-two subtle-yet-discernible enhancements in his comedic skill set. This Demming-inspired process continued for twelve years and countless stages until, at the age of thirty-nine, he found his way to New York's fabled Rockefeller Center and *Saturday Night Live*.

The veteran comic's survival technique revolved around a goal of providing something for everyone—attempting to make both Republicans and Democrats laugh. His mantra: "Never get personal and don't play to half the house." In addition, Darrell's benchmark for joke selection was for each on-air remark to represent no more than the comedy equivalent of, in his words, "a locker room towel snap."

He also recognized the importance of understanding his audience. For example, if a person or topic warranted two or more consecutive mentions in the *New York Times*, Darrell intuitively knew additional study was in order. And though his well-honed craft would ultimately bring laughter to millions, Darrell maintains, "You can have a sense of humor only if you're confident in your strategy."

Though the Melbourne, Florida, native may chide himself for his University of Florida cumulative 2.1 GPA, the self-deprecating funnyman was certainly clever enough to successfully navigate turbulent political waters and ever-changing public attitudes—all while having the eyes of the world on him for many high-profile years on *SNL*.

As former President Bill Clinton once said to him, "I make the headlines; you turn them into gold."

The bottom line: Set goals, persevere, provide something for everyone, and, when appropriate, confidently snap the towel.

Denise Wauters

KASSIE DePAIVA

T hough the infamous office water cooler was originally intended to provide workday refreshment, it symbolizes much more. We meet, we drink, we chat and, like it or not, we gossip. Yes, office drama is a somewhat inescapable byproduct of human nature.

However, in today's workplace, the methods for sharing office tittle-tattle have actually diversified due to emails, texts and social media. Say what you will about office gossipmongers but, at least at the water cooler, your employees are talking directly to each other as opposed to haphazardly relying on emotionally-bereft technology.

Venerable daytime actress Kassie DePaiva understands the concept of *drama* more than most. It's her job. DePaiva, who made her television debut as Chelsea Reardon on *Guiding Light* in 1986, famously went on to portray daytime diva Blair Cramer for twenty years on *One Life to Live* from 1993 through the series finale in 2013.

I first met Kassie toward the end of *OLTL's* extraordinary run and before her Emmy-nominated turn as Eve Donavan on *Days of our Lives*. However, twenty years in the same role—*in any industry*—is a feat worth exploring and celebrating.

Specific to *OLTL*, she says, "There's never been a dull moment"—an enviable goal for anyone who has chosen to eschew job-hopping in favor of professional longevity. Though countless people struggle to define the boundaries between personal and business, Kassie celebrates her time on *OLTL*. "I have matured into a woman through Blair—both of us have evolved over the years."

Of course, Blair, who Kassie describes as "a bad girl who makes bad mistakes for good reasons," has a résumé that actually includes the pushing of an adversary out of a second-story window. Then again, who among us has not fanaticized about giving the big heave-ho to a co-worker who "makes bad mistakes for (supposed) good reasons"?

When it comes to work ethic, Kassie, Blair and Eve abruptly part company. Kassie describes her work style as "hyper-prepared" and "disciplined."

"I think most people reap the benefits of me being a multitasker," she says.

Kassie also skillfully debunks the inevitable association between *soap opera* and actual *human drama*: "If someone says to me that their office is like a soap opera, I say 'Great! You get to be creative, take chances and occasionally rock the boat. Plus, you get to do something new every day.'"

Naturally, the poser in me was not yet satisfied. When I requested a *live* demonstration of "daytime drama," Kassie wasted no time. With my business partner Denise Wauters poised and ready to capture every over-the-top moment, my soap-opera-themed photo shoot began.

Kassie effortlessly transitioned from one classic move to the next—with me, the soapy neophyte, reacting as best I could. In quick succession, she coaxed me to display a litany of emotional reactions: love, hate, anguish, fear, lust, shame and remorse. She fondled my hair—first, the hair on my head and, once provocatively exposed, the salt-and-pepper mass on my chest. She "slapped" me, ignored me and grew bored of me—she adored, explored and romantically floored me.

So adept is Kassie DePaiva at her craft that the photo shoot of my dreams lasted approximately one minute, twenty-three seconds. All this from a woman who, to this day, remains one of the most focused, astute, generous and *emotionally grounded* individuals I have ever come across.

But what about the often unnecessary hoopla that, at one time or other, we all have to endure? To *daytime drama queen* Kassie DePaiva: "There is nothing wrong with a little drama. If you pay attention and work through it, you have a chance to learn more about yourself and the people you work with."

Another option? The next time your co-worker's favorite vendor's boss' first cousin once removed gets pregnant by the pool boy, simply understand it's (literally) none of your business.

Kevin Randall Jones

PAUL PHILLIPS

L ots of folks have great stories about their time in the trenches. For Paul Phillips, whose career path led him to the fabled bright lights of Broadway, the anecdotes come with a bit more drama, a lot more laughs—and vastly elevated star power.

Born October 1, 1925, Paul was raised in a series of foster homes in New York. At age seventeen, he joined the Coast Guard during World War II. Two years later, he landed on the Great White Way, his heart set on a career as an actor. In relatively short order, the affable Phillips would develop an unexpected friendship with renowned actress Gertrude Lawrence, a relationship that would dramatically change his young life.

It was Lawrence who first suggested he make the career move from *on stage* to *backstage*. Paul also looked at the practicality behind his famous mentor's suggestion: "Stage managers worked more often," he recalls.

According to Paul's former colleague, Broadway veteran Michael Rupert: "A stage manager is responsible for protecting the integrity of the show once it has opened and the director has left. A good stage manager is worth his or her weight in gold." As a man with an appreciable heart of gold, Paul Phillips explains it a bit more simply: "I took care of the details."

In traditional business terms, a stage manager is one-part chief operating officer and one-part human resources administrator—responsible for product development, human capital and brand management on a grand scale. There are also those who say S.M. stands for "stress management," not "stage manager."

Like any effective leader, Paul also researched his "stars" in advance of each new project—this included their reported quirks, goals and work styles. His remarkable credits include the original Broadway productions of *Fiorello!, Sweet Charity, Mame, Pippin, Chicago* and *The Best Little Whorehouse in Texas*. Essentially, Paul Phillips spent his career protecting the integrity of some of the greatest American "products" of all time. It is also clear he did so, in part, through a series of selfless acts: by celebrating the considerable gifts of his illustrious colleagues.

To this day, when Paul discusses his celebrated leading ladies, he elevates the concept of "waxing poetic" to a reverential art form. "I never lived with my mother. My favorite memories are the times I spent with the great ladies of the stage," he said. In addition to Lawrence, he worked alongside Tallulah Bankhead, Angela Lansbury, Beatrice Lillie, Ann Miller, Chita Rivera and, his dear friend, confidant and "soul mate," Gwen Verdon. In a business whose lifeblood is the exploration of human emotion, Gwen and Paul unapologetically crashed through the invisible door traditionally separating "business" and "personal."

"Gwen and I saw each other—or talked to each other—every day for almost forty years." A blessing by anyone's standards, Gwen's photos and memorabilia define the spirit of Paul's quaint Naples condo.

It was also Gwen who encouraged Paul to accept the job as stage manager for 1967's legendary *Judy Garland: At Home at the Palace*. "Gwen said, 'Paul, don't believe everything you read. Do it and help her,'" Paul recalls. In a salute to the importance of perception vs. reality, Paul lovingly describes Garland in three passionate yet equally emphasized words: "She…was… wonderful."

When veteran Broadway actor Michael Rupert assumed the title role in *Pippin* in late 1974, he quickly began personally taking on his character's negative energy and almost left the show. "I remember telling Paul how lonely I was in my [private] dressing room, Rupert recalls. "He suggested I just move downstairs to the boy's dressing room—and I did. I finally became friends with all the guys. Paul's advice helped me get back on my feet."

And my next phone call? Broadway legend Chita Rivera, Phillips' *Chicago* colleague.

At the onset of our conversation I confessed my nervousness to Rivera. Though I was not previously a part of her life, she had been part of mine since I was fifteen years old and purchased the original Broadway cast recording of *Chicago*. Her response? "You think *you're* nervous, I just met the Pope!" Safe to say, the equally charming *and* disarming Chita won that round. My pulse returned to normal.

Papal issues aside, Rivera gushed: "Paul is a warm, sweet, gentle guy. He was put on this earth to help, to heal—to make other people feel their worth. By doing so, Paul's worth stood out. He's a quiet man, but that's what makes him a powerful man."

As for his enduring friendship with Gwen Verdon—Rivera adds: "I defy anyone to say Paul was not the best keeper and friend anyone could have. I believe Paul would have taken a bullet for Gwen."

Perhaps Paul Phillip's irrefutable legacy is also best stated by Rivera: "Paul provides proof that there are people in this world who are truly good people—that gentlemen still exist." Rupert adds: "Paul not only respected those he worked with, he treated us as if we had real value."

Yes, workplace boys and girls, that is why they call it the "Good Old Days"—emphasis on *Good*, not on *Old*.

Dawn Lebrecht Fornara

TOMMY TUNE

When discussing the attributes of native Texan Tommy Tune – one of our nation's most prolific song and dance men—it seems only fitting to look at the numbers:

- Ten Tony Awards
- Eight Drama Desk Awards
- Three Astaire Awards
- One National Medal of Arts
- One star on the Hollywood Walk of Fame
- Fifty-plus years on the American stage
- 78.5 total inches when measuring from the top of his head to the bottom of his feet

Widely admired for his kindness, generous spirit, attitude and yes, his altitude, Tommy suggests: "I never felt that I had to be oppressive with people. Part of that is the gift of height—speaking from a slightly higher position than most people gives you some sort of unspoken authority. You don't have to be as forceful—or so I have been told."

With his heart resting effortlessly on his sleeve, Tommy proceeds to applaud education, wisdom and traditional family values as proof of the popular notion: it's better to give than to receive.

"The tone of my life was set early," he recalls. "At 5 o'clock our business was to be in the kitchen with Mother and Dad. All of us made the meal— every night. I believe that the fraying of the American family is caused by not having that. When you dine with someone, there's something so right about it that serves you throughout the rest of your life.

"I would not have gone down a successful path if it had not been for my parents and my teachers; they formed me," Tommy says. "All teachers and mentors help you along the way because they each offer a different perspective."

For a man of his stature, the list of those he *looks up* to is delivered with great passion and unmatched reverence. Tommy quickly segues into an affectionate discussion of his early influencers, including dance teachers Emmamae Horn and Camille Long Hill, as well as his high school drama teacher, Ruth Denney.

He then pauses as if to place extra emphasis on the magnitude of his next line: "The greatest man I have ever met was Mike Nichols. He is the highest individual I have met in my lifetime. He was like family." Mike Nichols is best known simply for being "Mike Nichols"—a powerhouse director on Broadway and in film.

---SHOWMEJONES.COM---
"I like people who are highly intelligent and don't talk down to you because of that intelligence."
—Tommy Tune

"I like people who are highly intelligent and don't talk down to you because of that intelligence. Nichols was like that for me," Tommy recalls. "He was far more intelligent than me, but he never made me feel inadequate.

"He shared himself, his supreme intellect and huge talent—he just folded you into the conversation. You felt comfortable. You went away feeling better than you did when you came in—feeling higher than when you arrived."

Qualities worth emulating.

Next up: Tommy Tune on Broadway legend, director/choreographer Michael Bennett.

"He helped me to understand everything I can do. Sometimes we don't know what we are capable of until somebody tells us. Once Michael told me something, I believed it—and he told me to 'never fear.'" For all of us, fear impedes performance; it's the literal show stopper.

Yes, actor, director and choreographer Tommy Tune could have spent our time together speaking of his enviable accomplishments; however, he chose to focus on the gifts of others—those he credits with molding his character and shaping his career. In a sense, Tommy took his time in my editorial spotlight and generously gave it away.

However, Tommy's decision to look beyond himself actually makes perfect sense. The act of creative thinking is at the root of Tommy Tune's success. His brilliant career has been defined by the external expression of one creative notion after another. His accomplishments reflect his ability to embrace his vision—and talent—and sculpt them for the benefit of others.

As with many successful creative types, Tommy is professionally wired to *give* as opposed to *receive*. After all, an inspired thought that goes unspoken is of no use to anyone.

Tommy Tune, the ultimate showman, is a teacher and educator of the highest order. He has repeatedly shown audiences the true meaning of the joy of live theatre just as he has influenced countless professionals on the importance of not just reaching, but reimagining their potential. What has he taught us today? Those who have skillfully educated us should be held in the highest possible regard.

For example, I have enjoyed a lifelong relationship with my fifth grade teacher, Mrs. Patsy Watt of Columbia, Missouri. Even today, Mrs. Watt is among the first to applaud my successes. Nonetheless, if I fall short, she'll tactfully "grade" my work with the expectation that improvement will follow—and it does.

Twenty years after her passing, I wrote of my beloved high school drama teacher, Jackie Pettit White. For her family, the tribute was a gift as rich in nostalgia and emotion as it was in professional validation and undying respect. Even better: the incomparable Jackie Pettit White now shares *Show Me* space with the inimitable Tommy Tune.

There was a time when reaching out to a former teacher or mentor might have presented a challenge. However, with all the online resources available today, there's really no excuse. Tommy and I agree: each of us has the responsibility to seek out and acknowledge our cherished mentors and educators. By doing so, we don't just share our gratitude; we demonstrate the fruits of their erstwhile labor.

"Our teachers don't even know the tremendous energy and courage they give us," he explains. "If you have one great teacher in your life, you're really blessed. I have had so many. All teachers deserve to be honored."

In short, Tommy Tune is a gentleman and gentle man. And for him, success is measured by our enthusiasm to teach and mentor, as well as our collective willingness to actively learn from those who cross our paths.

Now I ask you: Have you thanked a teacher today?

SHOWMEJONES.COM

"No profit grows where is no pleasure ta'en."

—*The Taming of the Shrew*

WILLIAM SHAKESPEARE

The business community has produced its fair share of visionaries: Bill Gates and Steve Jobs have made an undeniable impact on commerce with earlier industry titans like Rockefeller, Morgan, Carnegie, Vanderbilt, Ford and Edison transformed power, construction, transportation and commerce in bold and formidable ways.

There was a business world prior to the industrial revolution and the internet.

A little more than 400 years ago, a visionary entrepreneur named William Shakespeare transformed the entertainment industry unlike anyone before or since. So adept was Shakespeare at exposing the human condition, his observations crossed all boundaries of love and loss, power and corruption, success and failure.

Though many claim an ability to channel the spirit of this great man from beyond the grave, no interview is necessary to explore his prophetic business acumen. All these years later, Shakespeare's words speak louder than his human voice ever could. With the help of my good friend—Shakespeare-addict John McKerrow—I took a more careful look at C-suite Shakespeare. Here is what I found:

On choosing your profession
"To business that we love we rise betime, And go to't with delight." —*Antony and Cleopatra*

On time management
"Tomorrow, and tomorrow, and tomorrow; creeps in this petty pace from day to day." —*Macbeth*

On negotiation
"Let every eye negotiate for itself And trust no agent; for beauty is a witch Against whose charms faith melteth in blood." —*Much Ado About Nothing*

On debt
"Neither a borrower nor a lender be, For loan oft loses both itself and friend, And borrowing dulls the edge of husbandry." —*Hamlet*

On success vs. failure
"Screw your courage to the sticking place, And we'll not fail." —*Macbeth*

On corporate image
"The purest treasure mortal times afford Is spotless reputation—that away, Men are but gilded loam, or painted clay." —*Richard II*

On integrity
"This above all: to thine ownself be true, And it must follow, as the night the day, Thou canst not then be false to any man." —*Hamlet*

On work/life balance
"No profit grows where is no pleasure ta'en." —*The Taming of the Shrew*

True, Shakespeare's undeniable business lessons were often set against a backdrop of greed and deception; however, the fathers of the industrial revolution were known to figuratively have blood on their hands as well.

William Shakespeare's enduring lessons of right and wrong—of sacrifice vs. success—must continue to be heard. In a modern world of extended work weeks, texts replacing conversation, unanswered email, jammed Outlook calendars and bottom lines overshadowing blood lines, the Bard's insight has never been more relevant.

And what would William Shakespeare say if he were around today?

"I toldeth you so."

Bewitched

Before I began writing my column, my new Southwest Florida home had already presented me opportunities to rub elbows with some extraordinary talent. The day I met jewelry designer David Yurman, I appeared to be completely void of bling. That was before I dug into my shirt collar to retrieve a Yurman-designed necklace. "I hate wearing jewelry—*except yours.*" Naturally, there's no such thing as a brand manager who doesn't like to come face-to-face with a self-appointed brand ambassador.

And as I like to fancy myself a budding literary star, imagine my elation at coming face-to-face with my "colleagues," Augusten Burroughs and Nicholas Sparks. To be clear, I was a legitimate guest at Sparks' and Burroughs' events; I was not hiding in the bushes outside their hotels.

Having read every one of his published works including *Running with Scissors*, I essentially genuflected before a bemused Burroughs to express my admiration. Though this is probably not the first time Augusten has brought a gentleman to his knees, my very public—albeit nonsexual—approach seemed to come as a surprise.

And Sparks, who's *The Notebook* remains one of my favorite books and films, found himself in an impromptu men's room conversation with me, his ebullient fan. *No, I did not see "it" and you people need to stop asking.* But every self-respecting man must wash his hands before leaving a restroom. Why do it alone?

Growing up in the '60s, '70s and '80s, especially in small-town America, most of us couldn't fathom the concept of fame. We all thought we wanted celebrity status, but we didn't really know what it meant. And we certainly didn't have many opportunities to cross paths with a member of the rich and famous.

The irony is that I would eventually be part of a college vocal jazz group with Sheryl Crow. What's more, I did not cast future ABC News darling, Elizabeth Vargas, in the first play I directed in college. As my shortsightedness obviously *ruined* her shot at a professional stage career—therefore plunging her into the bowels of network news—*in my mind,* she's been out to get me ever since. *Paranoid much, Randy?*

Kate Capshaw (a.k.a. Mrs. Stephen Spielberg) was a teacher at my high school, and country music's Sara Evans is forever stuck calling me "cousin" because of her mother's decision to marry into my extended family. But there was a time when they were all nobodys like me.

Let's hear it for obscurity!

Whether we achieve fame or not is one thing, but our collective obsession *with* fame—and those who have secured their spot in the public eye—appears to be limitless. Clearly, I am no exception.

In 1979, a petite powerhouse vocalist from Lindenhurst, New York, burst onto the national music scene. Her debut album, In the *Heat of the Night,* soared on the Billboard Chart largely based on the strength of her breakthrough hit, "Heartbreaker." Patricia Andrzejewski Benatar had arrived and I, for one, was bewitched.

When it was announced that the incomparable Ms. Benatar was scheduled to perform in my Missouri hometown in 1982, I immediately knew she and I were going to love each other—the only question was *when?*

Flash forward thirty-three years…

Erin Rew

PAT BENATAR & NEIL GIRALDO

The ampersand deserves more respect. As punctuation's definitive celebration of collaboration & mutual benefit, the "&" has grammatically represented the concept of "separate but equal" for eons. Where would peanut butter be without jelly? Aren't night & day inherently dependent upon each other? And Ben & Jerry's? Flawless.

Though many appreciate the relationship between fire & ice, music fans are more likely to recall an enduring '80s rock anthem as opposed to a pair of scientific adversaries. As elements, fire & ice can destroy each other, but Pat Benatar & Neil Giraldo's "Fire and Ice" is just one example of the pair's irrefutable synergy. As a means to showcase compatibility—and exhibit recognition—the ampersand rocks. As do Pat & Neil.

A multiple Grammy winner, Pat Benatar has had two multi-platinum albums, five platinum albums, three gold albums and nineteen Top 40 singles, including the Top 10 hits, "Hit Me With Your Best Shot," "Love Is a Battlefield," "We Belong" and "Invincible."

Neil "Spyder" Giraldo has been a professional musician, producer, arranger and songwriter for more than four decades. In fact, Pat credits Neil's innovative vision with creating the signature Benatar sound.

I met with Benatar & Giraldo—Pat & Spyder—backstage at Artis—Naples.

All Fired Up

"This was a collaboration from the start," Pat explains. "He and I met. That was it. It was insanity. We hired everyone else. We started from day one—he and I, me and him. A duo." To Spyder: "We respected each other—we were on an equal playing field. We are still equals."

Despite this alleged equality, the name up in lights was always "Pat Benatar." Yet, to her: "He was everything I wasn't. I was a classically trained musician. I had no idea how I was going to make this transition from what I was to what I wanted to be. He was the catalyst; he helped me find my way."

The question is: Don't we all need a Spyder?

In truth, the public largely misinterpreted Spyder's role in the launch of the Benatar brand: "I didn't come in as a 'guitar player'; I came in as a creator. Guitar was only a means to an end."

Though Pat claims the pair tried to maintain a strictly professional relationship, they failed. They married in 1982 and have served as each other's muse ever since. Despite their shared success, Pat was always bothered by the lack of credit afforded her influential husband. So, in an ego-free move, one unheard of in an industry drowning in endless self-regard, she spearheaded a campaign to rebrand the pair as "Pat Benatar & Neil Giraldo."

Now, who among us can think of another example of a successful person—*in any industry*—who has made the conscious decision to share his or her individual limelight in such a high-profile manner? "I started switching it [to Pat Benatar & Neil Giraldo] in 1997. It was a fight. Promoters wouldn't put it on the marquees. It would be in the contract and they would take it down right before we got there."

Spyder was denied his share of the credit because their record company's agenda was at odds with Pat's perspective. "I wanted to tell the real story." And she did.

We Belong

Ironically, today's marquee positioning of Benatar (left-of-ampersand) & Giraldo (right-of-ampersand) also reflects their individual penchant for left-brain/analytical and right-brain/creative thinking. To Pat: "Spyder's like a mad scientist. When you're a crazy, visionary person, you have to have an advocate—and that's me. I reel him in. He's so 'out there.'" She laughs and adds: "My job is to translate so that 'humans' will understand him."

But the pair's much celebrated yin and yang symbolize inestimable mutual benefit: "I'm a person who likes roller coasters because they give the illusion of being dangerous, but I want to be strapped in. That's who I am," Pat suggests. "He is a skydiving, crazy person. He doesn't want to be strapped in—ever. He would jump without a chute. I love that. I would never do that. He pushes me so that I can enjoy that vicariously through him."

Precious Time
Benatar & Giraldo eventually abandoned the oppressive record company system in favor of a family business approach—one that enabled their daughters, as well as trusted friends and colleagues, to (sometimes quite literally) come out and play. Daughter Haley Giraldo runs the pair's blog while daughter Hana Giraldo contributes artwork.

"As much as Spyder loves being the mad scientist, I really love business," Pat says. "Singing is the thing I do the least. Running this boat is what I do all day." As many already know, when your focus is on *family*, your personal values must take center stage.

SHOWMEJONES.COM

"Don't let people get inside your head, because they can destroy a really good thought. They can take the steam out of a really positive attitude. They can destroy dreams."

—Neil "Spyder" Giraldo

When asked to share the best piece of advice he has given his daughters, Spyder passionately responded: "Don't let people get inside your head, because they can destroy a really good thought. They can take the steam out of a really positive attitude. They can destroy dreams."

Pat's suggestion for the rest of us: "You have a choice—every day—to try and do the right thing. You have to try and have the balance of doing the right thing for others and doing the right thing for you." She is not willing to sacrifice the needs of those around her for personal gain: "I won't do it. There's no reason that everyone can't benefit."

Why does she carry such a heavy burden of responsibility? "Because I believe that the gift is divine; you have to be a good steward. It's your only obligation," she states candidly. "And it's not because I'm so 'good.' It's not that I'm taking the high road. I'm wired that way. There is no choice. This is my DNA. Spyder's the same way—we were raised like this."

Non-Giraldos, take note.

Hit Me With Your Best Shot

In my younger days, I didn't know I had an entrepreneurial spirit. That changed the day Pat Benatar brought her *Get Nervous* Tour to town. As Pat's visit corresponded to my college days as a singing telegram messenger, I concocted a scheme whereby the City of Columbia would ostensibly send a telegram as a warm and welcoming display of Benatar love. Naturally, I would personally deliver said musical message. *And it worked.*

On November 9, 1982, boss Vikki, groupie Rick and I arrived at the stage door at the agreed-upon time. I nervously knocked on the huge metal door only to be greeted by a less-than-jovial face peering out from behind—an *Oz-Emerald-City* déjà vu moment on a grand scale. The talking-head even informed us that we would *not* be granted admission. And here I was, sans dead-witch broom and having left my ruby slippers at home.

> ## ShowMeJones.com
>
> "You have a choice—every day—to try and do the right thing. You have to try and have the balance of doing the right thing for others and doing the right thing for you."
>
> —Pat Benatar

While I may not have been aware of having any sort of entrepreneurial spirit, I was well aware I was Nell Jones' *spirited* son and one simply did not say "no" to me or my mom—especially after one had already said "yes." Despite being dressed for my telegram delivery as Prince Charming, in light of these new unpleasant circumstances, I was forced to assume the role of a not-even-remotely-Cowardly Lion while my balloon-handling "Tin Man" and "Scarecrow" colleagues stood awkwardly silent.

In other words, I pitched a fit.

Just as Pat Benatar musically maintained that *Hell is for Children*, on that evening in 1982, *hell* was reserved for the door-guarding moron who evidently thought Vikki and I blew up seventy-two helium balloons for no reason. To this day, it is best to never deny me access to anything even *remotely* Benatar-related.

Finally, and without explanation, the door opened and we were in. (*Wow! The squeaky wheel really does get the grease.*)

As opening act, Saga, delivered *On The Loose*, I was on the way to creating a brand new saga of my own. My heart pounded in tandem with the Saga drums as we traversed two more hallways. Then, without warning, our escort pulled back a curtain to reveal the great and powerful Wizard of Applause herself, Pat Benatar. *Oz metaphors be damned—Pat Benatar is literally the woman behind the curtain!*

But I was "on" and there was no looking back. For approximately five minutes, with new husband Neil Giraldo politely standing by, Pat Benatar was all mine! Even a falling house wasn't going to stop me.

When Pat expressed concern that she might hurt me if she took the bended-knee seat I offered, I exclaimed: "Oh my God, Pat, you weigh three pounds—just sit." *She did.*

Dressed as "Prince Charming" and assisted by the wow factor of six dozen balloons, I gave my musical heart and soul to Mrs. Giraldo—as well as a personally penned adaptation of her song: "Hit Me With Your Best Shot."

Once I suggested she sing along on the final chorus, Pat enthusiastically complied as I bounced her up and down on the aforementioned knee. *Still nothing broke—including petite Pat.*

When we finally finished *firing away*, I politely asked Pat to autograph an extra printed copy of the telegram. She agreed under the condition that I sign *her* copy first. (Yowza!) And after subtly begging for my confiscated camera to be returned—"Without a photo, no one in Prince Charming's kingdom will believe Prince Charming was here"—the apparatus magically reappeared and the requested photo op was completed before my triumphant exit.

For the next six months, *nothing* could get me down:

- Cliffs Notes for *King Lear* **sold out the day before Intro to Shakespeare exam**—*fine.*
- **Watching MTV with Nina Blackwood though I prefer Martha Quinn**—*okey dokey.*
- **U.S. President Ronald Reagan calls for an international ban on chemical weapons**—*whatever.*

Pat Benatar's kindness—and generosity of spirit—changed my life that day. I left the venue feeling as if I could accomplish anything. In fact, I felt *invincible*. Without knowing it, Pat taught me that I could take my own creative notions and—through perseverance, hard work and patience—forge a new reality outside of Columbia's city limits.

Thirty-three years later, I *finally* got to say "thank you" to Pat Benatar. Having spent more than three decades wondering *when and if* a reunion would take place, her comment, "I don't just remember the telegram, I remember *you*," made my *will-this-ever-happen* heart go all Grinch: it grew three sizes that day.

"Thank you": two syllables created by eight simple characters requiring only nine keystrokes to complete.

Two brief sounds that flow effortlessly off even the most discriminating tongue.

A verb and a pronoun that, when placed side-by-side, grow exponentially in stature, importance and value.

More than that, a "thank you" is timeless & recognition matters.

VANESSA WILLIAMS

When Derek and I first got together in 1996, I lightheartedly stated my position on our long-term potential: "The day Vanessa Williams knocks on our front door and says, 'Sorry, Derek, it's time to go. Randy is mine now,' you must agree to bow out gracefully." And now, with a 0.25 mg dosage of Xanax coursing through my veins to settle my nerves, despite being a front-door no show, Vanessa Williams was *on the phone.*

In truth, Vanessa didn't seem all that interested in discussing her—albeit, fascinating—past. Though, according to her, she has "no problem expressing my feelings," she also understands that we all have differing opinions about people, places and past events. As is often said: It's all relative. Vanessa was crowned the first black Miss America in 1984—a high-profile event followed by much Sturm und Drang—and eventually public redemption. However, to evaluate her or *anyone* based on a single event from more than thirty years ago is a disservice to them, as well as an obstacle to our collective ability to learn *from* them.

Without question, Vanessa Williams has proven to be unstoppable. She has sold 25 million records worldwide and achieved success on Broadway and in film. She has also become a television mainstay with, for example, high-profile roles on *Ugly Betty* and *Desperate Housewives.* Some would say there is nothing Vanessa can't do.

Nonetheless, she doesn't seem to find it terribly exhilarating to talk about herself. Instead, her enthusiasm shines when discussing the joy of being surrounded by creativity and talent. "She feeds off of it," suggests Carmen Ruby Floyd, Vanessa's bandmate. To Vanessa: "I am lucky to have had such a level of excellence come to me—the material and the teams."

That said, when she is discussing the irrefutable support of her family, Vanessa Williams glows. Born in 1963 and raised in Millwood, New York, she and her brother Chris were products of a very special form of higher education. Simply put, their parents—music teachers Milton and Helen Williams—held their children to *higher* standards.

For most of us, childhood education is defined by the three R's: reading, writing and arithmetic. In the highly musical Williams' home, several more non-negotiable "R's" were added to the scholarly mix: responsibility, reliability, resourcefulness, resilience and respect. Skills that complement any number of life's lessons.

Ask almost any parent and they will likely share the hope to be a positive role model for their children. With the 2012 publication of her bestselling autobiography, *You Have No Idea,* Vanessa became the celebrity standard of unconditional parental support.

How? She used her substantial star power to shine the spotlight on her hero. She shared authorship—and the limelight—with her indefatigable mother, Helen Williams.

Once again, yet in a very literal way, for Vanessa Williams, it was all relative. "We were firm, but fair—at home and in the classroom," says Helen Williams. And Vanessa agrees: "Our house ran like clockwork. I got my work ethic from my parents. I love discipline. People know I will be on time and I will be prepared."

Young Vanessa also added an additional "R" word, one that Helen Williams claims is not a direct result of life in the Williams household: risk-taking. "Vanessa is much more adventurous than my husband and I," laughs Helen. For her part, Vanessa defiantly credits her success to "always taking chances in my career and my life."

In fact, Vanessa is overjoyed when those risks pay off and someone says to her, "'I had no idea you could do that.'" Despite her multi-platform success, she admits: "I feel the most alive when I'm on stage."

Of course, what is live theatre if not one of the most powerful experiential connections possible between product and consumer? From a business standpoint, what could be more "alive" or enviable?

Though Helen Williams credits her daughter with carving out her own success, when I happened to note: "You sound like Vanessa," she cleverly corrected me: "No, Vanessa sounds like me."

Vanessa's considerable body of work has grown exponentially over three decades. Whether part of an original master plan, she has also graciously embraced her immutable, parent-inspired role as an educator, a responsibility that naturally accompanies that of "role model." After all, Vanessa Williams is nothing if not the product of "education" and all its sometimes unexpected yet glorious underpinnings.

I DID GET TO MEET VANESSA IN PERSON after her local concert. For the first-time *ever*, I was rendered almost speechless. My ability to produce sounds seemed to suffer from a leading "uh" prerequisite and a six-words-per-sentence limit: "*Uh*, this is Derek." "*Uh*, I talked to your mom." "*Uh* yes, I loved the concert." "*Uhhv* course, let's take a picture." And to shake things up a bit: "Thank you, *uh*, thank you."

Can Vanessa's success be summarized in a single melody? No. Nor would she want it to be. However, her influence is scattered throughout her extensive résumé. Just look at Stephen Schwartz's lyrics from the 1996 Academy Award-winning song, "Colors of the Wind" from *Pocahontas*—words she famously brought to life.

> *You think the only people who are people*
> *Are the people who look and think like you*
> *But if you walk the footsteps of a stranger*
> *You'll learn things you never knew you never knew.*

When it comes to art imitating life—or better yet, art *stimulating* life—these words epitomize why I wrote this book.

Lastly, for those who feel at odds with Father Time—either personally or professionally—just remember it was Vanessa Williams who musically taught us to "Save the Best for Last."

Sound advice. I am also quite sure Helen Williams would agree.

CYNTHIA RHODES

C ynthia Rhodes really doesn't want to do an "interview." In fact, she hasn't sat down with a member of the press in more than twenty years. A Nashville native, Rhodes appeared in a series of wildly popular films including *Flashdance* and *Staying Alive* in 1983. However, her most iconic role is dance instructor Penny Johnson in 1987's enduring *Dirty Dancing*.

Though more projects came her way after bringing pregnant Penny's cautionary tale to life, in the public's mind, by the early '90s, the actress had all but disappeared. Why? Cynthia Rhodes had a baby. It was a simple choice: motherhood was more important—and she never looked back.

I was introduced to Cynthia during one of her visits to Southwest Florida. There I was, face to face with one of my heroes from my days studying theatre and dance in college. A woman whose portfolio continues to epitomize the value of education and training to scores of wannabe dancers, singers and actors. Regardless of your desired career path, there's no shortcut to success. Simply take a tip from dancer Cynthia Rhodes and—sometimes quite literally—*work your butt off.*

Just as *Dirty Dancing* taught us that "Baby" was corner averse—at a minimum, we learned we shouldn't put her there—my typical journalistic process had essentially taken Baby's undesirable spot at the ninety-degree convergence of two brick walls. What? No interview?

In truth, I fell victim to one of the most damaging practices today: "But I always do it this way"—seven words that destroy innovation and creative thought. Though Cynthia respected my role as a journalist, she simply wanted to spend time with Randy the new friend, not Randy the interrogator. So, did I "interview" her? No. Was I allowed to write about the "experience" of spending time with one of my idols? Yes. "I would be honored," she said.

Cynthia likely understood what I had forgotten: in the end, it's all about our experiences—not our salaries, titles, résumés, bank accounts or even our precious interview processes. Regardless of your business, it's ultimately about the experience your customers have with your products and services. In life, it's about the experiences we have working together, learning together, growing together—of people looking each other in the eye and communicating in real time.

SHOWMEJONES.COM

"Kill 'em with kindness."

—Cynthia Rhodes

For her, life after Hollywood has been about the unparalleled experience of being a mother to her three sons. And what began as my Type-A-inspired horror at having my interview process upended became an encounter I will never forget. One of my personal heroes got to "experience" my work firsthand.

Time with Cynthia added more proof to the theories of "listen," don't just "hear," and "observe," don't just "see." Goals worthy of consideration for anyone willing to unplug and reboot their thought process. But most important, Cynthia helped me create a new memory.

I shared a quote I unearthed from Sylvester Stallone, Cynthia's *Staying Alive* director. Stallone had put forward the notion that she "would sooner quit the business before doing anything to embarrass her parents." Though the comment was made more than thirty years ago, Cynthia had never heard it before. Nonetheless, she smiled warmly and agreed. Cynthia is most assuredly the product of her parents' belief system and their enviable sixty-five-plus-year "love affair." Because yes, you can take Cynthia Rhodes out of the south, but you can't take the "southern girl" out of the Rhodes.

The lesson? When deliberating on how to react to a challenging situation, ask yourself this: "What would my parents want me to do?" Though many of us ignored this concept in our teens, it's certainly worth another looksee as we grow older.

Despite my editorial platform—one that celebrates the benefits of honesty and positive communication—I've certainly fallen victim, at times, to those who find it more interesting to disrespect and deceive than to be transparent and truthful. Cynthia's advice: "Kill 'em with kindness."

When I cited a specific example, she replied: "You're focusing on the negative. The question is: what did you get out of the process that was positive?" Naturally, Cynthia was right on both counts. Southern charm wins again.

Cynthia Rhodes is a refreshing anomaly—a woman whose ego-free persona has not diminished her confidence, her highly principled and spiritually aligned life, or her steadfast support of the people and causes she loves. She does not need to tell you how great she is to feel good about herself. Furthermore, she doesn't need you to pat her on the back either—she much prefers to do the patting.

She is also proof of the ongoing power each of us has to inspire others through our work—regardless of our area of expertise. "Her performances confirmed everything my dance-teacher mother, Mickey Lebrecht, taught me," said Dawn Lebrecht Fornara, resident choreographer at The Naples Players. "Cynthia had style and technique. She was a triple threat. She danced with such joy and freedom. As a young dancer, I longed to *be* her."

Cynthia also changed the life of a (then) ten-year-old Ryan Khatcheressian of Leesburg, Virginia. "My epiphany occurred when Cynthia performed the song *Finding Out the Hard Way* in *Staying Alive*. I remember being so moved at the emotion in her voice and the way she found the meaning in every single word. It was in that moment I knew I wanted to perform."

And the long-term impact? Khatcheressian, a high school business teacher and seasoned entertainer, puts his Rhodes-inspired passion to use every time he stands on stage or, more important, addresses a group of students.

Drew and Karen Attanasio Photography

One evening during her visit, as "Actor Randy" stood backstage overwhelmed with the knowledge that Cynthia Rhodes was in the audience, I couldn't help but think about the hours I had spent obsessing over her talent. However, I never once considered the possibility that she would personally experience mine. To the extent possible, with six-inch platform shoes adorning my now monstrously clunky feet, I had a little extra spring in my step as I tap danced my way through "Puttin' on the Ritz" in *Young Frankenstein* that night.

Though much has been written about the value of teachers and education, less has been printed about each individual's everlasting ability to inspire others. Why? Most of us, including Cynthia, have no idea we're doing it. The point? Live each day as if every choice you make will inspire someone to write about you in 2046.

Ah! Sweet mystery of life, at last I found you.

Best of all, Cynthia Rhodes lives and works in a no-regrets world. The opportunities are endless, overtime is welcomed, and the benefits package can't be beat.

> ## SʜᴏᴡMᴇJᴏɴᴇs.ᴄᴏᴍ
>
> "I'm the 'happy' writer. If you read my books and don't feel like kicking the cat or yelling at the kids, then I've done my job."
>
> —Janet Evanovich

JANET EVANOVICH

Has the term "working mother" been bounced around so long that we no longer think about what it really means? Ask a mother her thoughts and the responses are sometimes whimsical yet always passionate—everything from "'Working Mother' is redundant" to "I don't have time to talk about this." Sure, all mothers are celebrated on one day every May. In other words, we set aside 1/365th of the year to work at honoring moms.

New York Times bestselling author Janet Evanovich is, in her own words, "a mother first." Throughout her impressive literary career, the assiduous Evanovich has already written approximately the same number of books as appear in the Bible. And she isn't done yet. With staggering career sales in the millions, Evanovich quips that her books have been translated into "everything but Farsi and Klingon." Her twenty-plus volume "Stephanie Plum" series is responsible for more than 40 million books sold.

When asked the secret of her success, Janet cites "respect for the consumer" and "family support" before finally being pressed to credit herself with: "some talent." Just what you'd expect coming from a mom: others come first. However, to Janet: "If it's all about you, you're never going to be a success. Your concern should be for your audience—and proving you are a part of their group." Advice that should resonate regardless of your occupation.

Essentially, Janet was a "committed mother"—no pun intended—long before she became "Bestselling Author Janet Evanovich." Prior to selling her first book at age forty-eight, she test drove any number of jobs before eventually creating the car-maiming Stephanie Plum. From the telemarketing room to the mail room—from being a customer service rep for a colonoscopy bag manufacturer to a half-day career selling used cars, Janet Evanovich has most certainly *lived* in the real world.

Of course, to author Janet, "I produce a product for me and others like me. I'm a 'working girl', not a 'lady who lunches.'" Moreover, with her *mom* hat firmly in place, Janet pulled off an enviable magic hat trick: transitioning from "working mother" to "mother working."

Today, her maternal sensibilities are vividly displayed in her flawed yet relatable characters, her wicked sense of humor, her fifteen-hour work days, her almost superhuman ability to multitask, her celebration of her blue collar roots and, above all, the importance she places on family.

"We all have an agenda as creative people," Janet says. "My books reflect families, communities and values. If I thought I would never do my own laundry or go to the supermarket again, I would lose an important connection to my audience—I'd lose Stephanie Plum."

For her core reader—including countless mothers, sisters, daughters and grandmothers—Janet is proud to place herself on the same side of their table. "I'm the 'happy' writer. If you read my books and don't feel like kicking the cat or yelling at the kids, then I've done my job."

JUST A FEW MONTHS AFTER THIS COLUMN was published, Janet graciously agreed to sign books for me, Derek and the kids to give as holiday gifts. As my dad was never much of a reader, I asked if he wanted one and I was surprised when he said, "Yes."

Early that January my father called and said: "You can tell that Janet that was the funniest book I ever read." Yes, he had read the entire book—in less than *two weeks*. But that was just the beginning of my father's love affair with Janet Evanovich. Two weeks later Dad reported the completion of two more books in the Stephanie Plum series—No. 4 and No. 7. Three weeks after that he had added numbers 16, 9, 12 and 19 to his list of devoured Evanonovels.

Now, my list-making Virgo side was horrified he was reading them *out of sequential order*, but my sisters and I knew what had to be done. Janice and Paula started scampering around Mid-Missouri—going to garage sales, book stores, libraries and even the occasional dimly lit back alley—

Steven Brent Brown

hoping to score some more *Plum* to assuage our father's increasing Janet Evanovich addiction.

By July of that year, my father, the former one-book-a-year reader, had completed the entire twenty-plus volume Stephanie Plum series. Not long after, with my poor father plumb out of Plum, I exclaimed: "Dad, I can't ask Janet to write *faster* just so you have something to do."

For those times when new Plum wasn't available, Dad went rogue and agreed to read anything as long as it was penned by Janet.

Janet's final interview comment stayed top of mind during this entire keep-Dad-reading process: "I'm the 'happy' writer. If you read my books and don't feel like kicking the cat or yelling at the kids, then I've done my job."

My father's *job*—a job he chooses to do without protest—is to take care of my mother, who suffers from Alzheimer's. Though there are good days and bad days, as my caretaker father watches his wife of sixty-plus years slowly fade, he learned to trust "happy writer" Janet Evanovich for his daily dose of guaranteed joy.

By faithfully sticking to her defined mission, writer Janet Evanovich—a "working mom" turned "mother working"—touched my family like no other.

There. Are. No. Words.

GET SMART

In the 1960s and '70s, my father lived the perfect Ward-Cleaver life-style—but the day ten-year-old me brought home a condom purchased from the bathroom at the neighborhood gas station, there was no place private enough for Ken Jones to hide. He almost chose to move out of the house.

You see, after a fun-filled day of neighborhood bike riding and public-re-stroom shopping, my friend Jeff and I returned to my house. Immediately upon our arrival we filled our newly purchased gas station condoms with water—as alternatives to traditional *water-balloon* weaponry—only to dis-cover that they resembled boobs when filled and paired together.

As we made our way through the house with our water-logged flying breasts, we passed my mother in the kitchen. Assuming we had nothing to hide, her innocent inquiry of…

MOM
What do you two have in your hands?

…resulted in two bulbous waterrubbers being held up to her face.

My mother almost dropped a meatloaf on her foot. She subsequently in-formed my dad that *he* was going to field this awkward what-is-a-condom issue—alone and *unprotected*, so to speak.

Later that afternoon, my poor father was clearly in over his head. And just like Mr. C. in my elementary school sex education class, he nervously jingled the loose change in his pocket as he attempted to explain the appropriate use of condoms on an adult-sized penis. However, I was fascinated!

TWEEN RANDY
Wow, Dad, I didn't know that…so how
does a rubber really work?
How do you wear it?
When do you wear it?
Can I keep it and try it on later?

To this day I will never know why *one*—much less *two*—adult men would associate a discussion on sex with pocket change.

Now, flash-forward to the late '90s when it was my turn to be put in the sex-education hot seat.

The day I educated my children about sex, all by myself, was on the *same day* and at the *same time* as per their mutual DEMAND. To begin, I was forced to use my extremely limited artistic skills to draw pictures of the male and female anatomy. I also found myself wishing I could wallop each child with a waterboob, if only to distract them long enough to run screaming from the house.

Knowing the theme of the discussion that was taking place, Derek *vanished*. "Sex talk?" Poof, GONE!

But I held my ground as it shifted wildly below my feet.

DAD RANDY
(subtly pleading)
Maribeth, wouldn't you rather wait and
discuss this with Mommy?

TWEEN MARIBETH
(forcefully)
"NO! TELL ME NOW!"

Like it or not, the sex talk is a parent's job and I was stuck—all by my lonesome—without the advantage of Maribeth's mother to lead the unavoidable discussion on the various uses and misuses of a woman's "vajayjay." So there we were at the kitchen table—trembling father alongside curious preteen son and daughter. I was armed with a piece of paper, a Bic pen, a quickened pulse rate and somewhat vague memories of seventh grade biology *and* of the vagina.

My son Kevin accepted the "male" information with relative ease.

TWEEN KEVIN
Okay. Thanks. I'm going back to my Play-
Station now.

And he was gone. But my daughter provided the payback for my condom-themed reign-of-terror on my father some twenty-five years earlier. Already armed with a playgrounder's arsenal of half-truths, Maribeth hit hard:

TWEEN MARIBETH
So, is it really water that breaks?

And…

TWEEN MARIBETH
Will my boobs be bigger than Aunt Paula's?

Hell, MY boobs are bigger than Aunt Paula's.

TWEEN MARIBETH
When will I get to see a penis for real?

Wait. It gets worse. The ultimate attack on my nervous system?

TWEEN MARIBETH
How long does it take for the penis to finish?

In hindsight, I am surprised I did not die.

Nonetheless, my next thought: DO NOT SCARE THE CHILDREN ABOUT SEX. Yet, on some subconscious level I likely wanted to shock the shit out of them. The penis-to-body size ratio on my poorly executed male illustration showed an alarmingly huge appendage guaranteed to fit absolutely *nowhere* I can think of. And my drawing of the female reproductive system resulted in Maribeth's keen eleven-year-old observation:

TWEEN MARIBETH
Daddy, your female reproductive system
looks like a moose head.

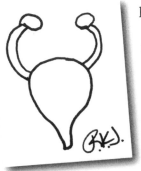

I looked more closely and she was correct. It looked *exactly* like a moose head.

Yes, I had done my parental duty and boldly faced my precocious daughter in what ultimately became a battle of wits—a fight I would *never* win.

But learning is *exactly* what we all must do: Get smart, pay attention, be inquisitive and *push past the boundaries that limit us*. Whether the tutorial comes from our children's antics, a precarious meatloaf, an ill-conceived illustration, or the creativity found in the invention of the world's first sexually-transmitted-disease-defying flying waterboob, there's a lesson to be learned in practically *everything* we do.

ShowMeJones.com

"Be positive. People want to deal with positive people. Positivity is contagious."

—Joe Abruzzese

JOE ABRUZZESE

Whether or not our job titles contain the word "sales," we are all doing it. All companies and organizations sell *something*: products, services, concepts and/or emotions. However, each of us will forever be responsible for selling the most emotionally charged product of all: ourselves. Don't think you're in "sales"? Think again.

Joe Abruzzese, president of advertising sales for Discovery Communications, oversees all sales efforts for Discovery's U.S. networks as well as Discovery Digital Media. He also played a critical role in leading the launch sales strategy for the transition of Discovery Health Channel to OWN: Oprah Winfrey Network.

Prior to joining Discovery Communications in 2002, Abruzzese held the top sales post at CBS for eleven years and spearheaded the acquisition of the corporate sponsorships necessary to launch the *Survivor* television series in 2000. He was inducted into the Broadcasting & Cable's Hall of Fame in 2011.

Based on his abundant success in his field, it's easy to conclude that Joe has elevated his sales skills to an art form. However—and perhaps more important—he instinctively knows how to sell *himself*. For Joe, putting his best foot forward seems as effortless as a walk in the proverbial park. He's confident, conversant and comfortable with himself. As a result, Joe immediately puts you at ease.

What's more, his "best foot" will undoubtedly be encased in a very professional pair of shoes. Why? Other than an affable and approachable manner, there's nothing *business casual* about him. Joe Abruzzese is a suit and tie guy. He has fashioned a belief in the power of the first impression—in the importance of eliciting his desired client/prospect reaction: "'They are successful. How can they make me successful?'"

As seen above, his answers to questions often come forth in his client voice, not his own. Why again? Joe Abruzzese consistently puts himself in his client's shoes. His key opening questions: "What are YOU trying to accomplish? How can I help YOU? How can I use my product to help YOU?"

"There's no agenda outside of making them successful. That's not 'selling,' that's being on their side," he suggests. "You have two ears and one mouth—that should be the proportion of listening to speaking."

Today, there are more than two billion reasons that speak to Joe's sales success and personal finesse; *more than two billion* is also the total dollar volume Joe and his team book annually in advertising sales across all Discovery platforms. Now, get this: this same $2-plus billion is secured without the *benefit* of a formal contract. In fact, he never uses one. Notes Abruzzese: "I once outlined a $120 million deal between CBS and Budweiser on a napkin."

Joe operates by three highly traditional yet refreshing philosophies.

First: *"Trust—you have to prove you can be trusted. Taking responsibility leads to trust. If you break that trust, it's over."*

Second: (in Joe's voice): *"I will never, ever renege on a deal."* (Once again, Joe goes back to the client voice): *"'Joe's word is his bond.'"* Clearly, the aforementioned bond is infinitely more potent than a document full of potentially mind-numbing legalese.

Third: *"Be positive. People want to deal with positive people. Positivity is contagious."*

Sadly, in today's somewhat litigation-impaired and honest-communication-bereft world, the notions of "trust" and "your word is your bond" may actually feel like brand new concepts to some. Likewise, if positivity is truly contagious, few would argue our collective need to somehow engender a positively powerful positivity epidemic on a global scale.

Many of us hold the belief that anyone who accepts money from employers—or clients—has a responsibility to be a champion for their brands. One's commitment certainly should not end in the parking lot each day. Even those organizations that take advantage of our volunteer manpower are equally deserving of our unabashed enthusiasm—our willingness to promote brand awareness to all who cross our paths. Okay, so not everyone in line at Target wants to hear about my relationship with the *Naples Daily News*, but given the chance, I will certainly tell them.

Joe Abruzzese is not just a staunch brand ambassador for Discovery Communications, Joe Abruzzese *is* his brand. He represents the very essence of Discovery and the definition of *discovery*. "What I do is who I am," he says. "You look at our shows and they pretty much all have a positive message."

Though he maintains his brand "solves curiosity in a very entertaining way," the same could easily be said of Joe himself. After all, what is successful selling if not the process of turning initial curiosity into enjoyable commercial reciprocity? Then again, he represents entities whose names include words that inspire—such as "discovery," "learning" and "investigation." Terms that also reflect the very core of Joe's naturally upbeat personality.

Don't we all essentially wish for a career that revolves around "discovery?" Don't we ache for a professional journey underscored by exploration, insight, knowledge and innovation? Plus, assuming we all must sell ourselves, doesn't an enlightened version of self ultimately provide substantially more value?

Even Joe's enthusiastic response to my initial email request spoke volumes: "I would love to talk." How often do any of us hear that these days?

There's that word: love. It is one thing for us editorial altruists to continue to hype the concept of "loving" what you do; however, it's infinitely more persuasive when gentlemen like Joe Abruzzese lead by "loving" example.

Besides, shouldn't *discovery* be a way of life?

TOP SECRET

Ladies and gentlemen, the time has come for the big reveal—*Show Me's* hopefully-not-too-hidden agenda. This book is not intended to promote big-name brands, Ivy League educations, massive bank accounts, showy titles or even disreputable bunny rabbits.

Though many who have chosen to read *Show Me* likely did so in hopes of having an inside peek at someone they admire from afar, the truth is, *Show Me* is intended to showcase people and principles, not prominence and profits.

The ability to expand our horizons is omnipresent: in person, on the phone, in meetings and on elevators and, yes, in *carefully selected* social media postings. The simple question is: are you truly paying attention to the educational opportunities situated right in front of your face?

That said, when fame is absent:

> *"We continuously have to remind people of who we are."*
> —Jason Odell Williams, playwright, novelist, producer, Renaissance man

I personally love "talent." I will go to great lengths to surround myself with talented people. (And yes, that includes conducting more than 100 interviews and writing a book!) Though I am clearly an advocate for courtesy and respect, I have been known to be more forgiving when the ill-behaved person in front of me is a *talented yet well-intentioned* ill-behaved person—anything to feed my addiction for creativity, ingenuity, knack and know-how.

SHOWMEJONES.COM

"We continuously have to remind people of who we are."

—Jason Odell Williams

Plus, the more we absorb the talent and knowledge around us, the better prepared we are to influence the opinions of those who try to define us.

Notice the Little Things

"How are you today?" This question is an essential opening to many outbound business calls—the ultimate test to determine how the conversation is going to go. For those on the receiving end, many issues impact the response—such as workload, priorities and the caller's perceived value—to whatever extent they have already *bought* what the caller is *selling*.

Anyone who has experienced the awkward wait time between "How are you today?" and the reply should take heart at Richard Broome, executive vice president, public affairs and communications at Caesars Entertainment Corp. Note his response to my prearranged call: "I'm fine, thank you. So what are we talking about today?"

In roughly four seconds, Broome's attentiveness, focus and positive attitude spoke much louder than his words: *Thank you for calling on time. Please remind me of your objectives. Yes, you have my undivided attention. However, as I have a full schedule, can we please focus on the topic at hand? And finally—I'm sorry, but I don't have time to chat about the weather today.*

My reaction? Fair enough. *Let's go!*

Get *all up* in his or her business

For most, our education and character are a combination of our parents' influence as well as our upbringing, education, experience and the influence of various characters who have come in and out of our lives. And where do we meet these individuals? At work, in line at the grocery store, at our chosen house of worship, at civic functions, at public school events—anywhere people with fired-up brain cells gather. *Don't dismiss the neighborhood grocery store example; everyone eats.*

The concept of listening and learning is by no means restricted to *A-List* mentors. Your group of influencers can easily be culled from *a list* of folks who reside in your local community. Business owners and/or operators can be found in every county in the country. Though their company shares may not be traded on Wall Street, they often bring a *Main Street* sensibility to both personal and professional development.

These four "Business Class" subjects may have achieved extraordinary success, but none of them moved directly into the C-suite. They all got there by working hard and choosing their mentors wisely. Although their professional coming of age happened in various communities throughout the country, their advice today is universal.

> *"It's not just about boss and employee; having an understanding of peer relationships is equally important. The more you know about what drives someone's behavior, the better you can empathize—and communicate—with them."*
> —Dolph von Arx, former chairman, president
> and CEO of Planters Lifesavers Co.

> *"It's so important to focus on one or two critical issues at a time. Don't be like the guy in the circus who has a lot of spinning plates on top of sticks. It's hard to keep the balance. Focus on one or two."*
> —David Hall, former CEO of the Vision
> and Dental Business Units of United Healthcare

> *"I never believed in the concept of a 'consensus,' because, to me, a 'consensus' is nothing more than 'decision averaging.' I preferred to focus on establishing an alignment of beliefs and strategy within my teams."*
> —Mike Hanson, former president
> and general manager of Eli Lilly Japan KK

> *"In negotiations, I want my opponent to be at their best and experience the best 'game' they've ever had. If I win, then it means more."*
> —Craig Bouchard, *New York Times* bestselling author, *The Caterpillar Way*

Breaking News

Perhaps your list of advisers could include members of your local media. You never know when *and if* their star will rise, potentially leaving you to bask in their increased intellectual glory.

Before Karna Small Bodman became deputy press secretary to Jim Brady and (later) senior director and spokesman for the National Security Council, she was a broadcast journalist in San Francisco. However, Bodman went on to become an active participant in the political process, a role that necessitated the need for almost daily meetings with President Reagan from 1980 to 1986.

In fact, even Karna turned to an outside source to advise *me* on writing:

> *"'The best way to get your point across is to entertain.'"*
> —George Bernard Shaw, author/playwright, via Karna Small Bodman,
> journalist, political insider and novelist

Politically Correct

Though I understand why those who occupy—or wish to occupy—our nation's highest offices receive the vast majority of the mainstream press, the pillars of the American political system are found much closer to home. Countless unsung heroes inhabit local, regional and state government— veritable fixtures in our various hometowns who, without fanfare, serve as the backbone of our government.

I dare say, our local leaders have much to teach us. Well, we *elected* them, so we should certainly hope that's the case. By her own admission, Donna Fiala is just one of many public servants whose commitment is to people first and politics second.

> *"I don't need this job—I want this job."*
> —Donna Fiala, Collier County, Florida,
> District 1 Commissioner

Which raises the question: whether your bread and butter come from the business community or the political arena, how many of us are truly ruled by those who *want* their job?

Considering our success in business is often inextricably linked to our ability to manage company politics, exercise diplomacy and gain the trust of colleagues and/or the public, Fiala and those who selflessly serve without the aforementioned fanfare ultimately become an inspiration to us all. Whether or not you agree with Donna Fiala's *politics*, it's difficult to argue with her *process,* one worth adopting as our own: "You have to go where the people are."

Love Thy Neighbor

For many years, I have turned to my former neighbor, Pat Boos, for *advice* and, in a sense, *consent*—i.e. her approval that my latest hot idea won't leave me standing in the cold. Boos, the former senior vice president of marketing for Time Life, and a gifted listener, was a conveniently located ear for many years. What's more, my readers discovered that her *voice* demanded attention as well.

For instance, when I asked Pat for her guidance on successfully climbing the corporate ladder, she offered: "Perform at a level higher than your current level." Meaning: if you are a manager, perform as a senior manager; if you are a director, display the traits of a vice president.

In addition to her professional mantra—"Show Up, Dress Up, Be Up"—Pat's best advice actually targets a sizeable audience:

> *"Don't act like a woman in business;*
> *be a good business woman."*
> —Pat Boos, former Senior Vice President of Marketing, Time Life

Though this comment may appear to be gender specific, it is not. Pat Boos' lesson is one that every professional *male* should learn, support and respect, too.

Don't believe me? Ask your mother, sister or daughter what *she* thinks.

Out of the Mouths of Babes

True, those of us of *a certain age* are not always kind when discussing the (alleged lack of) character of those whose age begins with a one, two or three. Assuming that *a certain age* is defined as age fifty or above, many of us must also take responsibility for raising the aforementioned ones, twos and threes. If we're unhappy, a look in the mirror will likely disclose a source of blame.

Just as our parents may have been horrified by, for example, the lyrics to Billy Joel's "Captain Jack," we may find ourselves shocked by today's rap music—a.k.a. Really Annoying Prattle. *In the '70s, my sister Janice's incessant playing of Joel's* Captain Jack *almost caused my poor mother to have a brain hemorrhage.*

In our youth-obsessed culture, many of us ache for a reunion with the youthful energy of our past—especially when we recognize it in the eyes of the Gens: both X and Y, and/or the millennials.

The Artist

Millennial Neapolitan Lazaro Arbos came face to face with a very new reality in a rather spectacular way—on Season twelve of *American Idol*.

Though *Idol* touted itself as a singing competition, heart-string-tugging Arbos, who placed sixth, is perhaps equally known for his speech. With a prominent stutter that completely disappears when he sings, Lazaro elicited an emotional response on *Idol* that made him the unofficial spokesperson for a very deserving group whose challenges are rarely given a national voice—the stuttering community.

But if you think about it, what workplace neophyte hasn't searched, sometimes in vain, to find the right words to illustrate his or her skills, goals, opinions and ideas? In so many ways, Lazaro is like countless other young people seeking to find their voice and make their mark on the world. It's just that his exceptional journey was broadcast for all to see.

> *"Don't give up—no matter who gives up on you."*
> —Lazaro Arbos, former *American Idol* contestant

The Author

Another shining example of today's millennial generation can be found in author and educator Julia Cooke. An advocate for understanding and respecting diverse cultures, Cooke, an adjunct professor at The New School in New York City, recognizes that her work is a careful balance of curiosity and discipline based on her ability to "listen with a generosity of spirit."

Her first book, *The Other Side of Paradise: Life in the New Cuba,* intertwines profiles of seven young Cubans—the last generation raised under Fidel Castro—with her experiences as a journalist living in Havana.

Why do cultural differences—divergent beliefs, customs, practices and social behavior—create so much ignorance and so many headlines? Borrowing Julia's words: *failure* "to listen with a generosity of spirit."

Even in business, a *corporate culture* is defined by a company's values, practices and traditions and/or the atmosphere reflected in people's dress, behavior, interaction and communication styles. Culturally speaking, who among us doesn't want to circumvent office politics and *fit in* at work?

In Julia's view, no culture, Cuban or otherwise, can be understood without an appreciation of its population. In business, failing to understand people—your employees and customers—will result in corporate culture chaos.

It's simple, really. Taking the time to understand different belief systems and ways of life—whether defined by geography, profession, lifestyle or age—will enhance our experiences at home, in the workplace and beyond. And leave it to author, adventurer, educator and millennial superstar Julia Cooke to also suggest timeless advice for all culture-conscious collaborators. If you wish to assimilate, contribute, produce and profit:

"Don't be a tourist; be one of the locals."
—Julia Cooke, author, *The Other Side of Paradise:*
Life in the New Cuba

The Doctor

Like the dedicated Olympic athletes he so passionately admires, Dr. Cade Copeland and his wife Kristen embodied both a competitive and entrepreneurial spirit when, at age twenty-five, they opened their chiropractic and functional medicine practice in 2010.

Spend a few minutes in Copeland's company and his infectious, youthful enthusiasm—as well as an appealing degree of authenticity and compassion—quickly becomes evident. Moreover, his office's *open floor plan* promotes his goal of patient kinship—each receiving support from his care but also finding strength, encouragement and insight from the relationships formed with their peers.

Though Corporate America's walls may be somewhat more figurative in nature, few would argue the benefits of breaking down obstacles and encouraging collaborative and productive environments.

In short, BRING DOWN THE WALLS.

"Everybody's definition of a champion is different, but each person can live to their absolute fullest potential. Most important: we all have the ability to champion—and be champions for—the lives of others. Be open."
—Dr. Cade Copeland, Founder, LIFEstrength Health Center

Yes, it is easy to fall under Arbos, Cooke and Copeland's spells—their passion, vision, energy and intellectual fountain of youth. The trio's natural, evocative charm can easily become like a drug for the aging soul. And just as our parents were perpetually perplexed by us, we may not always identify with the youth of today. But we can't get enough of them either.

No, Pat Benatar may never personally hit *you* with her best shot; however, an academic shot in the arm likely awaits you: down the hall, across the street or around the corner.

Simply seek and ye shall find.

Robert Green Jr.

Kevin

ROBERT GREEN JR.

Jennifer Marlowe, portrayed by actress Loni Anderson, served as the receptionist at the fictitious AM radio station known to '70s-era television viewers as *WKRP in Cincinnati*. Anderson's Marlowe was legendary for many things: among them, greeting WKRP's assortment of misfit guests, answering phones—and generally looking good while doing so.

Keenly aware of her impact on the business, this alleged member of the "Sisterhood of Blond Receptionists" also famously remarked, "If you saw our minimum salary, you'd have a heart attack and die." Understandably, Jennifer Marlowe was the highest paid staff member at WKRP.

Hair color aside, people who serve as receptionists, hosts, cashiers, security, and information booth personnel are Corporate America's proof of the old adage "you never get a second chance to make a first impression." Or do you?

Though my daughter Maribeth demonstrated exceptional performance as a Florida Gulf Coast University student, at FGCU, *exceptional performance* begins *before* one has officially landed on campus. Just take a slight right toward the Information Booth off the main entrance and Robert Green Jr. will quickly demonstrate the true meaning of those two words. It is impossible to leave Green's post without a smile on your face.

As Maribeth was studying social work, I logically chose to take her to my Ryan Ferguson interview. As my son Kevin received a degree in film, he was a natural choice to attend and photograph several "Business Class" interviews. However, the *only* time I invited both of my children to accompany me was the day I met with Robert Green Jr.—his outlook, personal history, personality and performance are *that* special.

I have yet to figure out if it's a positive sign or a tragic embarrassment that, as a man in my fifties, I had *never* had a conversation with an African American who was raised in the South *during* segregation. On the plus side, I was lucky to have escaped environments laced with overt racial tension. My children are color blind—their generation, at least those in their immediate social circles, have proven to be delightfully open-minded. However, without this firsthand exposure, our collective understanding of racial bias is a compilation of hearsay, television programs, news reports and history books. In other words, it's not *personal*.

SHOWMEJONES.COM

"You always get a second chance to make a first impression."

—Robert Green Jr.

Continually upbeat and consistently charming, Robert himself quips, "Even my grandmother told me I came out smiling the day I was born." A product of segregated Shreveport, Louisiana, an undaunted Robert Green Jr. still recalls his enthusiastic waves on his way to school to the white children and adults on the other side of the street. Pass by his post today at FGCU and he's still waving.

As a youngster, Robert made a very conscious decision: "I don't want to be a victim." Moreover, those lucky enough to be on the receiving end of his signature catchphrase—"you know you are my friend"—may be surprised to learn that a young Robert first uttered this expression to defuse a spat between two friends with their sights on the same girl.

In the years that have followed, Robert has lifted the spirits of countless friends, family, co-workers and guests with these very same words. With an educational background that includes studies in business, religion and theology, he shares potentially life-altering advice: "If we learn to understand each other, we will have a more definitive appreciation for life itself."

Somehow, coming from someone with Robert's affability and rich perspective, a quote that could seem commonplace gains much more impact.

When asked to define his job at FGCU, he simply states, "I've had the same job all my life—waving 'hi' and making people happy." When challenged to share his view on the power of first impressions, Robert is quick to point out: "You always get a second chance to make a first impression."

And a third, and a fourth...

Like so many others on our businesses' front lines, Robert Green Jr. is worth his weight—and waves—in gold.

ONE DAY AT A TIME

With the knowledge that some of my work in the marketing field revolved around managing the four-color printing process, for reasons known only to her, my mother once called me with the following warning: "Don't let anyone talk you into printing any money."

Seriously? Printing money? My mother thinks I want to add counterfeiting to my list of skills? "Dad, when did Mom get addicted to prescription drugs?" Nope, she had not.

Alas, as I have learned to accept that the genetics leading to my personal brand of creative thinking start in her gene pool, there must be a reason for this somewhat shocking display of deductive reasoning. After all, what has my mother taught me every day of her life? **Taking any comment at face value is downright boring.**

There are times when certain words or phrases become so widely used and recognizable that we no longer consider the full scope of their meaning. On a subconscious level, our minds immediately accept some definitions as "understood" even though, if asked, most of us would struggle with verbalizing their personal impact.

Consider this: the concept of "a sense of purpose" was likely implanted in your head some time ago. However, when was the last time you thought about its actual role in your life?

What is your sense of purpose? How do you define it? What's more, if it's missing, how do you find it? And finally, when was the last time you *printed the money?*

As a young man, I would have defined a sense of purpose as something that led to a compliment:

"Good work"
"Attaboy."
"You should be proud."

And the most exciting, yet potentially the most misleading of all: *"You won!"*

In fact, a series of actions and/or activities leading to "better luck next time" teaches us so much more.

I'm the first to admit, I talk way too much. As my brain constantly signals to my vocal chords to get to work, the process of learning to listen was, at times, painful. Ah, the classic narcissist mantra: Enough about me—what do you think of me?

Thankfully, I came to realize that a sense of purpose is not related to a compliment, but comes from our ability to complement the lives of others.

Once I contained my motor mouth and dialed up the power of my Ken-Jones-hereditarily-enhanced Dumbo-sized ears, though the compliments increased, my desire to actively complement the gifts of others grew at an exponentially faster pace.

A *compliment* is a regular, run-of-the-mill noun.
To *complement* comes from—and leads to—emotion.
A *compliment* comes and goes quickly.
To *complement* can—quite literally—last a lifetime.

Show Me showed me my sense of purpose. Though I'm a huge supporter of finding common ground, every time my words complemented the goals and/or inspired the actions of someone else, the borders confining my mental and emotional state were vastly redrawn.

If your sense of purpose doesn't make you, and others, feel something special—with a tip of the hat to my seafaring community of Naples, Florida—you, my friend, are missing the boat.

No, Mother, I do not—nor have I ever—printed money. But be proud, dear, sweet, perpetually unpredictable Nellie Pearl Jones: with any luck, I've imprinted a little bit of value on the lives of others.

I'm sure that's what you wanted all along.

Kevin Randall Jones

RANDY WAYNE WHITE
THINK LIKE A WRITER

Mystery, mayhem, malfeasance, marauding bandits and the occasional murder: words that describe *New York Times* bestselling author Randy Wayne White's home, the sensational Sanibel Island, Florida. Despite White's extraordinary imagination, the crime rate on sleepy little Sanibel is actually considerably less than the national average.

Since 1990, Randy Wayne White has created a series of wildly popular novels featuring adventurous marine biologist Doc Ford. Almost all of his novels begin in Southwest Florida.

In a scene reminiscent of Hooterville's less-than-convenient phone service in the '60s television show, *Green Acres*, Randy—a young, resourceful telephone-service installer—"borrowed" long-distance phone lines from atop Ma Bell's telephone poles to call around the country seeking new opportunities. As a result, he was hired in 1972 to work on the copy desk at the *Fort Myers* (FL) *News-Press*.

Later, Randy mixed various writing projects with his other passion: working as a light-tackle fishing guide at Tarpon Bay Marina on Sanibel Island. As for any similarities between fly fishing and fiction writing, he suggests: "Both are very hard work. As with writing, there is an articulateness to fly fishing. Both are very procedural."

Though a writer often works alone, interruptions and distractions are often his or her greatest foes. In response, Randy advises: "Turn off the internet!" He has even been known to seek the peace and quiet afforded him by the privacy of Amtrak's sleeper coaches. Randy Wayne White has not owned a television set since his sons were young.

Randy's celebrated literary success has placed significant demands on his time. Though "yes" may be the preferred answer when attempting to open doors, its arch rival—"no"—often becomes a necessary evil once you find yourself on the other side trying to get your work done. Randy agrees: "The tough thing about writing is you go into a room alone, you close the door and you do your work."

SHOWMEJONES.COM

"I spend very little time hoping for praise. I prefer to listen to people than talk. You can't learn anything with your mouth open."

—Randy Wayne White

For a man who can turn a phrase with such incredible finesse, when questioned about the secret to success, Randy wastes no time in providing straightforward, commonsensical responses: "Be on time, show up slightly early, do a little more than the other person, and associate with good people." He pauses briefly and continues: "Do your work. Don't complain. Don't make excuses."

Apparently, he also has a creative well that is unlikely to run dry. "I never run out of ideas. I have too many, actually. If I'm not careful, I can end up writing two or three books," he explains. In fact, his yardstick for a feasible creative vision is to proactively "summarize my novel in one sentence."

Regardless of the project in question, yes, you can—and should—try this at home.

Writers teach us through their words, but we teach the writer through our collective actions. Though Randy claims, "I have met very few 'stupid' people," he is clearly more accepting than most insofar as the unpredictability of human nature. He also puts forward the notion that what may be considered irrational to some is typically quite rational in the mind of the beholder.

Even if writing is not your professional calling, imagine the benefits of *thinking* as a writer:

- An uncompromising focus on the story and/or project at hand;
- Enhanced listening skills and wordplay;
- An uptick in intuitive thinking as well as a heightened understanding of—and appreciation for—the differences that exist between us.

Essentially, a writer seeks to find what is interesting and/or unique about people, places and events. Sometimes, taking life at face value provides no value.

It's no mystery that thoughtfully sequenced words are the backbone of our collective beliefs and values. As the skill of writing has increasingly found itself reduced to a series of hashtags, abbreviations and sound bites, the heart of the writing profession and a substantial part of the reader's response have become compromised.

We owe a debt of gratitude to Randy Wayne White and all his similarly skilled scribes. With his clever juxtapositions of nouns, adjectives, action verbs and imagination, he has continued to excite our minds across a vast backdrop of stimulating scenarios and delectable language.

According to Randy: "I spend very little time hoping for praise. I prefer to listen to people than talk. You can't learn anything with your mouth open."

All this said, there's one thing you will likely never see this laptop-laden outdoorsman and water-worshipping wordsmith do: fish for compliments. He doesn't have to. The compliments leap right into his boat.

SHOWMEJONES.COM

"It's knowing that your door is always open and your path is free to walk."

—from "Gentle on My Mind,"
music and lyrics by John Hartford

KIM CAMPBELL
BE CARING

E ventually, each of us is going to have two jobs: caregiver and care-taker. The first focuses on the physical care of a loved one; the latter carries an emphasis on shepherding their legacy. That is, if we're loved—and lucky to live long enough.

True, the hours are long and the work is tough. No, the pay can't be measured in dollars and cents, but the rewards are steeped in value. In the final analysis, isn't one's demonstrated *value and sense* more important than *dollars and cents?*

For Kim Campbell, the wife of legendary country/pop singer Glen Campbell, value is found in hugs, smiles, laughs and making memories. However, Kim's personal worth is best demonstrated in her faith, compassion, commitment, advocacy and, ultimately, in bravely finding peace and acceptance. You can't put a price on that.

> *"It's knowing that your door is always open*
> *and your path is free to walk."*
> —from "Gentle on My Mind," Music and lyrics by John Hartford

Glen Campbell: Twenty-one Top 40 hits with two hitting No. 1. Six Top 20 albums plus twenty-seven country Top 10 singles and nine country No. 1 albums. Add multiple Grammys and industry awards on top of Campbell's television legacy, and his enduring star status is impossible to deny.

Kim Campbell: Majored in dance at East Carolina University before traveling to New York City to perform at Radio City Music Hall. She married Glen in 1982 and is the mother of three of his eight children.

It's not that Kim Campbell consciously emerged from the shadow of her famous husband. Glen Campbell's 2011 Alzheimer's diagnosis, has, little by little, removed that shadow to reveal a (perhaps) reluctant yet increasingly powerful advocate—a modern-day professional caretaker and caregiver, emphasis on "care."

This increase in visibility is most evident in Glen and Kim Campbell's decision to publicly share his battle with Alzheimer's by documenting Glen's 151-show Goodbye Tour. The result is the powerful and compelling documentary, *Glen Campbell: I'll Be Me.*

"Glen wanted to make the documentary—it was his passion," says Kim. "He was well aware of what he was doing. He wanted to let people know what it was like to live with Alzheimer's." After all, most of us don't parade our dementia patients around town. As a result, positive role models, especially for those families dealing with the early stages of the disease, are hard to find.

By greenlighting the film, the Campbells brought forth the musical parade and the educational fanfare. Most important, they provided a message of God's love and a family's indestructible bond juxtaposed against the music of an icon.

"There's the upside of risk and there's the downside of risk," says Kim, "When we went out on the road, we tried to minimize the risk as much as possible. To give Glen the support he needed to do what he loved to do." Is there more potent advice for finding professional fulfillment than to do what you love to do? Or, to understand how the concept of "risk vs. reward" either inspires or impedes that path? Or, for that matter, to care?

Again, for Kim: "One of the greatest gifts of the film is that people dealing with Alzheimer's and dementia will know they are not alone."

For those of us in this situation, two unpretentious yet powerful-when-paired words come to mind: "thank" and "you."

"Try a little kindness. Show a little kindness."
—from "Try a Little Kindness,"
Music and lyrics by Curt Sapaugh and Bobby Austin

"I'm passionate about being an advocate—helping remove the stigma of people getting—and families living with—that diagnosis," Kim says. "Also, there's a stigma attached to long-term care that needs to be removed." Of equal importance is protecting her husband's legacy. For her, it's not just his music; it's the human side of Glen as a caring, loving, generous, funny person.

Want more explanation? Look to his final recording as evidence:

"I'm Not Gonna Miss You"
Music and lyrics by Glen Campbell and Julian Raymond
I'm never gonna know what you go through
All the things I say or do
All the hurt and all the pain
One thing selfishly remains
I'm not gonna miss you
I'm not gonna miss you

Kim adds: "As Glen kept saying: 'Don't worry about me. I'm going to be okay. You're going to carry the pain.'" And she has, quite gracefully—but not by herself.

"Someone who has dementia needs an incredible support team," she shares. "But the primary caregivers can't survive without a support team *for them*. If you are doing it 24/7 without a break, it will break you. It will consume you."

Then again, where would any of us be without our support teams?

"I needed help to continue to be who I am. I know Glen would want that." The result? With her newfound public voice and emphasis on advocacy and education, it seems that "I'll Be Me" has become a metaphor equally powerful in describing the glory that is Glen *and* Kim Campbell.

"And I need you more than want you and I want you for all time."
—from "Wichita Lineman," Music and lyrics by Jimmy Webb

So what is Kim Campbell's "business?"

Simple: to care. After all, she has spent her married years "being a mom, taking care of Glen, taking care of my family."

In other words, Kim Campbell is a proud member of the most dedicated workforce in our country—a profession that boasts more skill at scheduling, budgeting, multitasking and problem-solving than one can see in a sea of CEOs. A group responsible for influencing massive consumer spending and raising the next generation of C-suite executives, country music entertainers, social workers, filmmakers, teachers—and yes, caregivers and caretakers: WORKING mothers, those who truly define what it means "to care."

"I can't share the past with Glen," she says. "I can't share planning a future with Glen. But I can share each moment with Glen. He is teaching me to live in the moment."

Lesson learned.

Finally, is there a single word that best describes Kim Campbell's life as a wife, mother, advocate and takin'-care-of-business woman?

Yes, there is: Memorable.

> "I understand what 'no' means. I think the bigger thing is knowing when 'no' doesn't have to mean 'no'—when there are other alternatives and possibilities."
>
> —Mitchell Gold

MITCHELL GOLD
PROVIDE COMFORT

Mitchell Gold, co-founder and "chair-man" of home furnishings company Mitchell Gold + Bob Williams (MG + BW), wants to make people comfortable—in every sense of the word.

comfortable · [kuhm-fer-tuh-buhl] · *adjective*
1. Providing physical comfort: a comfortable chair.
2. Free from stress or anxiety: comfortable in one's surroundings.
3. Producing feelings of ease or security: a comfortable person; a comfortable evening at home.
4. Sufficient to provide financial security: comfortable earnings.
5. Happy, content.

In the late 1980s, with a résumé that included Bloomingdale's and The Lane Co., Mitchell Gold felt comfortable enough to combine creative forces with partner Bob Williams and go out on his own. In doing so, the pair swiftly took ownership, literally and emblematically: "A brand has to be super authentic and honest. That's why we named the company using my name and Bob's name," says Gold. "It's not a 'Barrel'; it's not a 'Barn.'"

As a nation, we place a premium on comfort and convenience. This is seen in how we live, what we buy, and in our ever-expanding waistlines—a situation many attribute to a national comfort food obsession.

It's also not shocking to suggest that some define comfort based on a first-person view of the world—i.e. me, me, me, me and finally, me. Mitchell Gold is all about finding comfort in—and providing comfort to—the universal "we." One likely reason? As a young gay man, he wasn't always made to feel—well—comfortable.

To understand Mitchell's ongoing—yet sometimes uncomfortable—quest for comprehensive comfort, let's break it down, one definition at a time.

Providing physical comfort

Mitchell points to an early *Oprah* segment on home decorating as inspiration. "What came out was that it was a very anxiety-ridden experience for people," he recalls. "That led us down the road—how do we make people more comfortable?"

The duo also took a much broader view of the meaning of "comfort." For Mitchell: "It was not only the way a sofa or chair sat, how it felt to your tush, but also that every aspect of a sofa would be comfortable." He also insisted their products be comfortable to the eyes and on the pocketbook. More than twenty-five comfortable years later, MG + BW has grown to $150 million in annual sales.

Mitchell Gold + Bob Williams, which started with dining chairs (hence Gold's imaginative title: "chair-man"), now provides upholstery, case goods, lighting, accessories, rugs, bed linens and artwork. The company participated in the redecoration of the Obama White House, and its products have appeared on the sets of several movies and TV shows.

"One of the conventional wisdoms of the industry is, if you have something exclusive and special, you can get extra margin on it," Mitchell says. "I wanted to sell it at a great price and sell a ton of it—and we did."

Free from stress or anxiety

Anxiety crushes comfort.

Mitchell is the proud editor of *CRISIS: 40 Stories Revealing the Personal, Social and Religious Pain and Trauma of Growing Up Gay in America.*

"We wanted to be participants in creating a world that was comfortable for kids who are coming of age and realizing their sexual orientation or identity," he says. "Whatever is natural for a person should be comfortable."

Published in 2008 and featuring coming-of-age stories from noteworthy members of the LGBT community, the timeless book has literally been hand-delivered to many of our nation's leaders in politics, religion and education. It was Gold's remarkably inspiring book that planted the seed in my mind to write a book based upon a series of interviews. The result? You're reading it.

Mitchell Gold is also co-founder of Faith in America, a non-profit dedicated to educating people about the harm religion-based bigotry causes LGBT Americans. In his view: "I don't want any kid to go through what I went through in high school."

As for Mitchell's definition of pride? "It's not about feeling proud and better than anyone else—being arrogant or pompous—it's more about not feeling *less* than anyone else." To Mitchell Gold, less is NOT always more.

Producing feelings of ease or security

In 1989, same-sex couple Mitchell Gold and Bob Williams based their manufacturing in "the buckle of the Bible Belt," rural North Carolina. It remains there today, an essential part of the local business community. Proud of their ongoing focus on family, Mitchell shares: "When we wanted to open a daycare center in 1999, our insurance company said 'that's a lot of liability; you don't want to do that.'"

So, does Mitchell Gold do "no"? "I understand what 'no' means. I think the bigger thing is knowing when 'no' doesn't have to mean 'no'—when there are other alternatives and possibilities."

Sufficient to provide financial security

"My parents always lived beyond their income," he says. "No matter how much you make, live within your means and then you aren't under pressure to do crazy things."

Happy, content

"When Bob and I started, we were together as a couple. Unfortunately, after fifteen years, we decided to live apart," Mitchell says. "But we love and respect each other—the business is our child."

When all is said and done, Mitchell Gold's passion surfaces most when the comfort of a human being's way of life is compromised. Yes, he still sings the praises of Bob, his employees and their shared creations, but he ultimately seems comfortable that the quality of the product speaks for itself.

"This is what I want on my tombstone: Mitchell Gold: He edited *CRISIS*, a game changer for a lot of people. He wanted a daycare center—and he got it."

Another option? Mitchell Gold: comforting, indeed.

"I really hate that computers try to guess what we're saying all the time, and because people rarely proofread what we've written, we end up sending messages that aren't clear, or that we don't even mean."

—Susan C. Bennett

SUSAN C. BENNETT
USE YOUR VOICE

Helen of Troy may have been the face that launched a thousand ships, but Susan of Atlanta is the voice that launched a million road trips. Susan C. Bennett is the original voice of Apple's groundbreaking "Siri," the seemingly magical "intelligent assistant" that enables users of Apple iPhone 4S and later—as well as newer iPad and iPod Touch devices—to speak natural language voice commands to operate the mobile device and its apps.

As a popular voiceover artist and singer, Susan has appeared on hundreds of radio and TV commercials for such clients as McDonald's, Macy's, Goodyear, Papa John's, Fisher Price and more. She is also the voice of Delta Airlines gates worldwide as well as numerous GPS and phone systems.

Alas, even the very human Susan C. Bennett has been subjected to technologies' fickle nature—but more on that later.

Apple's Siri, launched in 2011, is the result of voice concatenation and masterful programming. Concatenated speech is described as recorded words that are spliced together by a software program to provide a spoken response to a human user.

Susan explains: "Apple bought my voice from a company called Nuance. All of the original Siris worldwide were paid our regular hourly voiceover rate, but weren't compensated for usage." When she recorded in 2005, Susan thought she was just doing messaging for phones. "To this day, I have no idea who at Apple chose my voice for Siri."

Six years later, Susan's life profoundly changed. "To all of a sudden be one of the world's most heard voices required an adjustment," she says. "However, when that voice became a *persona*, people developed a relationship with it. The original Siri did have a bit of my personality. I do have a dry sense of humor."

For those who have tested Siri's tolerance for bad taste, her ability to take a witty yet whimsical high road is legendary. Like Siri, Susan excels at clever riposte—and her friends and acquaintances have put her through countless, occasionally stupefying, Siri-themed interrogations:

Question: "Susan, why did Siri give me the wrong directions last week?"
Susan: "She does that on purpose. She's a real jokester. She'll send you to the wrong place just for fun."
Lesson: When it comes to the use of technology, a sense of humor must prevail.

Question: "Susan, how do you know all those answers?"
Susan: "I'm really smart."
Lesson: Sometimes, self-confidence is the only solution.

My attempt at a never-been-asked question: "Is Rosie the Maid from *The Jetsons* your hero?"
Susan: (laughs) No, I have to say that my hero is HAL from *2001: A Space Odyssey*.
Lesson: The newest technology always wins.

Perhaps most popular: "Susan, do you talk to Siri?"
Susan: "No, I talk to myself enough as it is."
Lesson: The sound of one's own voice is not all it's cracked up to be.

In case you are still wondering, Susan C. Bennett has never accepted live questions from actual iPhone users out in the field.

Of course, Siri's undeniable mistakes are almost never credited to a user's accent or inarticulate nature. Why? We live in a world where the end-user is always right—on so many fronts. Yes, many have had difficulty communicating with Siri; conversely, chatting with Susan is refreshingly effortless.

Although she is responsible for originally intoning the ultimate high-tech know-it-all, Susan is less tolerant of those who claim to *know it all*: "I tend to avoid them," she admits. "However, I try to give people the benefit of the doubt. Everybody has an opinion, of course. That's why I think silence is underrated and under-appreciated."

When Susan-the-voiceover-actor speaks, there's a paycheck involved. On the other hand, we all know people who place an innate value on everything they say. Like it or not, those who love to hear the sound of their own VOICE OVER everyone else will likely never be too far out of earshot. They are everywhere.

There are essentially three ways to define "the voice." First, the actual sounds we produce. Second, a means to express thoughts, articulate opinions and inspire change. Third, a popular TV show on NBC.

When it comes to the topic of vocal expression, Susan is not at a loss for words: "The voice is as personal and unique as our face and our fingerprints. It reflects our perceptions of the world. A great deal of what we're trying to say can be heard in the voice—beyond what the words are saying. The pitch, the pacing—it relates very much to emotion."

Irony alert! Susan also assumes a position that is at odds with Siri's basic job description: "I have a problem with the changes in the English language caused by technology. Because everything is so abbreviated now with texting and social networking, I don't know that we're expressing ourselves as clearly as we could if we used some of the great and beautiful vocabulary of our language.

"Also, I really hate that computers try to guess what we're saying all the time, and because people rarely proofread what we've written, we end up sending messages that aren't clear, or that we don't even mean."

Technology sometimes seems poised to supplant anyone and anything. Even Susan C. Bennett's original Siri has been replaced by a new sound-alike (ish) voice—one likely concealed by mountains of non-disclosure agreements.

Nonetheless, we always remember our first love, car, job, and dare I suggest, our first concatenated voice crush. Look at it this way: Dick York was replaced by Dick Sargent as Darrin Stephens on *Bewitched* in 1969, but don't many of us still identify most with Darrin No. 1? Susan's trailblazing vocals set the standard by which all other Siri-ous concatenators must follow.

But hold the iPhone, there's more. Susan wryly confesses: "The original voice of Siri is a complete 'non-techy.' If there's a wrong button to push, I will find it!" Yep, a Siri-less Susan C. Bennett would rather sit down and share a laugh and cup of coffee than text, tweet, post or email. Come to think of it—talk is gloriously cheap, but technology isn't.

So the next time Siri appears to be sending you to Timbuktu as opposed to your local IHOP, don't blame Susan C. Bennett or Apple or Siri. Just stop the car and politely ask for directions.

Actually *talking to someone* may do you a world of good.

HODA KOTB
APPRECIATE THOSE AROUND YOU

" *Is it too late to do that thing that made me so happy when I was young? Could what matters most to me finally be the center of my life? Can I really trust this yearning voice in my head and longing in my heart? Do I feel like I'm where I belong?*"

Though Hoda Kotb's *Where We Belong* was published this year, the above passage describes how I felt in 2012 before I launched my "Business Class" column.

Geographically, Naples, Florida, is an extraordinary place to live, but moving to a new community cannot heal all that ails you if—due to your intellectual wear and tear—you somehow lost yourself en route. The process of writing my column, and connecting with the bighcarted people who gave it life, "literarily" gave *my life* brand new meaning.

The irony, though "Business Class" featured interviews with a number of well-known personalities—movers and shakers of all shapes, sizes, industries and idiosyncrasies—as I've indicated before, it's never been about *celebrity*.

To begin, most won't have access to the likes of Erin Brockovich, Barbara Corcoran, Jack Hanna, Sonny Jurgensen, Suze Orman or Willard Scott. It's true, I'm outrageously lucky. In the twenty-five years I lived in the Washington, DC, suburbs, my most memorable brush with fame happened the day I gassed up next to the Oscar Mayer Wienermobile at a Lansdowne, Virginia, Shell station.

Nonetheless, everyone should carry the expectation that he or she can have the inspirational access necessary to learn to be the best they can be. Success isn't measured by our ability to trend on Social Media. It's more important to follow the trends established by those who have proven they know how to succeed *and be happy*—household-name-status notwithstanding.

At its core, "Business Class" and, subsequently, *Show Me* have been an exercise at looking for the intersection of "business" and "class." And there is perhaps no better example of the marriage of these enviable qualities than National Broadcast Co. favorite, Hoda Kotb.

Since joining NBC in 1998, Hoda has served as a correspondent for *Dateline NBC*. She has covered a variety of domestic and international news stories, as well as human-interest stories and features across all NBC News platforms. In the process, she has won three Gracie Awards, a Peabody Award, and an Edward R. Murrow Award.

A *New York Times* bestselling author, since 2008 Kotb has also had the opportunity to wine, dine and unwind with co-host Kathie Lee Gifford on the fourth hour of NBC's TODAY.

In reality, one's "celebrity" does not necessarily impact Hoda's interest *or* her curiosity. "Whether I am interviewing a celeb or Betty Bowling Alley, I like people who *tell the truth*," she explains. "The best life lessons I have ever learned are from people who are honest."

She then reeled off a litany of inspiring Joe and Josephine Averages who have recently crossed her path. Her point? "Every single person you meet knows something you don't know." But no matter who is involved, motivating another human being is never an *average* act; it's always *extraordinary*.

When asked to describe her talent, Hoda paused and responded: "I'm a good listener. I'm more concerned with being *interested* than *interesting*. When you talk, you're not learning; when you are listening, you are."

Despite the entrée her high-profile job affords her, Hoda Kotb does not have the market cornered on personal or professional development, nor would she want to. Like many of us, she's always *in the market* for added information and self-awareness.

For example, let's say you live in the heartland and the most prosperous business in town is a farm. Hoda and I would naturally suggest you set up a sit-down with that highly efficacious farmer. In many other communities, the most successful business owner may operate a restaurant. Given the chance, he or she may be able to cause your thirsty-for-knowledge cup to runneth over. So just ask.

For anyone who has seen Hoda's work, most report a rapport, a kinship with the digitized image that has been magically zapped into their living rooms. And *friendship* is a topic she embraces with zest and zeal: "They say you are the sum total of the five friends you spend the most time with. You become who you are with them. If you don't know who you are, look at your circle. If it doesn't feel right, make it better."

Interestingly enough, Hoda didn't define her personal top five influencers as either personal or work-related, but that's no real surprise. Hoda Kotb cares most about caring and character, not someone's social or professional circles.

SHOWMEJONES.COM

"Every single person you meet knows something you don't know."

—Hoda Kotb

As for the boundless creative energy existing in those around us, Hoda is clear: "I think everybody has certain things they do well. The rest of us just have to seek it out."

True, it took me six months to pin down the always-on-the-go Ms. Kotb. During this time, my NBC BFF became her assistant, Kathy Ryan.

According to Hoda, "Kathy Ryan is a treasure. I think I chose Kathy and she chose me." Kathy, who has been working with Hoda since 2007, could also be described as the organizational wind beneath Hoda's impressive professional wingspan. Kathy makes the flight reservations and Hoda soars.

When asked to describe their relationship, Kathy says: "We are professional when needed, but good friends when not. She's more a friend, but there are many times we just have to get down to business." Anyone else thinking: best-case scenario?

Can enough truly be done to celebrate those who support us? Hoda explains: "Everyone has someone who counts on them; who makes them laugh; who has insight." And when it comes to extolling the virtues of the supportive Kathy Ryan, my guess is Hoda Kotb could write a book. Plus, let us not forget the support Hoda's televised presence consistently provides the viewing public.

Besides, who among us would not prefer to work with—and learn from—a friend? Of course, Hoda Kotb is everybody's friend. "Hoda never met a stranger," says Kathy. "She makes everyone feel as if she has known them for years."

When asked to share Hoda's single best quality, Kathy Ryan, a woman who doesn't seem very interested in spewing out unnecessary words, answered quickly and succinctly: "Generosity." Though I considered asking her to expand upon her one-word answer, I didn't. Less *is* more and "generosity" requires no qualifiers. Generosity truly is its own reward.

And Hoda's final piece of real-world advice: "You have to just be happy in your life and realize you get to go home at night."

Whether she is at home, at work, on the air and/or in the hearts of those she knows and all those she'd *like* to know, Hoda Kotb is exactly where she belongs—and as a result, the rest of us are that much better off.

THOUGH THE HODA INTERVIEW TOOK PLACE on the phone, with the knowledge that Derek and I planned to be in New York two weeks later, Hoda graciously invited us to be her guests at the live broadcast of TODAY's Kathie Lee Gifford and Hoda segment.

A bastion of television news and entertainment, TODAY has been around so long it seems inconceivable that anyone could live under a rock so substantial as to be unfamiliar with the broadcast; however, now in New York, the rock Derek and I were headed to see was none other than New York's fabled Rockefeller Center and The Today Show's broadcast studio.

Naturally, my NBC BFF Kathy Ryan was on-hand to symbolically roll out the red carpet and usher us to the studio in time for the 10 a.m. broadcast, whereupon the lovely Ms. Kotb greeted us, quite literally, with open arms.

Still, it quickly seemed more interesting to view the experience through Derek's eyes. Just a few days prior to this event, he had innocently inquired: "What ever happened to Paris Hilton?" PRESTO! Here was Paris talking to KLG and Hoda.

Derek also has a fondness for biographies and BOOM, there's filmmaker/ biographer Oliver Stone in the flesh. Had TODAY Senior Producer Joanne LaMarca Mathisen made a surreptitious effort to produce a Derek-themed show? Better yet, was karma attempting to make this day as memorable as possible for Derek?

Yes, karma was and karma is, in fact, a bitch.

Kathy Ryan, an ace at all-things organizational, including people moving, spent the next fifty-eight minutes navigating us safely through the brilliantly choreographed maze of television cameras, portable set pieces and gargantuan power cords. Although we were given a heads-up that Hoda may include us in the broadcast, as we weren't exactly "Oliver Stone" or even "Paris Hilton," we assumed our participation would require very little effort. Derek and I certainly didn't think we'd be called upon to, for example, pinch hit at a live cooking demonstration. Truth be told, there has been very little media demand for my expertise at cereal-bowl filling.

As the show entered its last commercial break, a flurry of activity ensued in preparation for the final "goodbye" segment, including the placement of a curved bench—a single set piece made possible by the merger of three independent units.

Our new friends from Philly, a quartet who had won a trip to visit KLG and Hoda through a fundraising auction, had already been moved into place on either side of the already centered Hoda and KLG. When I happened to glance in Hoda's direction, she appeared to be gesturing for Derek and me to join them on set. I paused briefly to make sure I had read the signals correctly, and Hoda nodded and signaled again.

And then came the most infamous words of warning in the English language: "Ten, nine, eight…"—the countdown had begun to, once again, go live.

My single thought? THERE IS A CAMERA UP THERE CALLING MY NAME! HODA BABY, I'M COMING!

True, as an actor, I'm no stranger to having to rush into position right before the lights come up on stage, but this was my first time doing so on national television. As I arrived at my spot on the bench, I swiftly turned, propelled my bum toward the bench and made contact…

AND THE BENCH BEGAN GOING AND GOING AND GOING…

The set piece was on wheels! As I careened toward the back wall of the studio, Derek, who had dutifully followed me, turned to sit and sit he did: DIRECTLY ON THE FLOOR. Derek go boom.

AND WE WERE LIVE.

So yes, we are now on the air. KLG and Hoda are all smiles. I'm somewhat tucked away in the rear of the shot. Derek is clearly visible, having fallen squarely on his tush. One of the Philadelphians was saved by her resolute right butt cheek, the one miraculously still residing on the secure center unit of the three-part sectional as my nomadic piece flew out from underneath her.

But seriously, how was I to anticipate that the combination of my brisk speed, momentum and, yes, my somewhat significant butt size was poised to potentially destroy The Today Show set? Before a staggering number of television viewers, no less?

Then again, perhaps Derek missed his professional calling altogether. In my mind, I immediately began to plan my public explanation strategy: "Derek is training to be a stunt man."

Ah, but let's once again look at this scenario through Derek's eyes. Here was the man I had spent more than twenty years of my life with—flat on his bum on national television—and what did we do? We did what Derek always does: We laughed. We laughed hard and we laughed long. I mean, what else is there to do at that point?

Though the television audience was treated to a whimsical "Man Down!" from both Hoda and KLG, after confirming the absence of broken bones and/or blood loss, the pair continued as if nothing had happened. (Ah, professionalism!) Thankfully, the camera cut away from our televised apocalypse to allow Derek's bottom to re-surface.

But it was Hoda's final on-air words that will forever make me snort with glee. "'Wipe Out!' Are you alright?"

WIPE OUT—the nickname I will be calling Derek for the remainder of our time on earth—and assuming I have my way—for quite some time thereafter!

However, in Derek's eyes, it was just a blip. Yes, I know he would have preferred it had been my butt on the line, so to speak. I'm also aware his preference would have been for the television audience to see the FULL STORY, including the bull-in-a-china-shop part where my instinctual lust for the limelight, coupled with my ass, inadvertently caused his disaster. But he didn't crawl under a rock. He was utterly unfazed.

The elusive full story is simply not always on display, no matter what we do. Sometimes, the only option is to accept what we know to be true and just move on.

His later quip? "It's not like I'm Steve Harvey and I announced the wrong winner of Miss Universe."

But Derek's real secret? Despite life's ever-distracting hurdles, Derek, who had just become talk show road kill, has never lost sight of his goal that LIFE should be lived with the same passion and excitement as LIVE TV. To him, when you fall down, getting back up is the only option—literally and figuratively.

And in the spirit of "expect the unexpected," I'm now convinced that karma, Derek and Kathie Lee are in cahoots, working on some sort of clever comeuppance in retaliation for the day I almost killed TODAY.

To which I say: BRING IT! Kathy Ryan will protect me. And Hoda will cheer her on.

Bernadette La Paglia

Sue Monk Kidd
Embrace the Power of Language

Twenty-six.

That's the number of letters in the alphabet.

All told, they represent twenty-six inimitable tools to create an endless number of words, phrases, paragraphs and messages.

Words incite action, reaction, vim, vigor, yin, yang, emotion, promotion and devotion.

Words define rhyme and season reason.

Words start wars and end them.

But for all of us, words advance careers and, of greater importance, words define them.

Though we have often heard: "choose your words wisely," how many of us fail to heed this oft heralded and potentially life-altering warning? Who among us are remiss in handling our written language with—shall I say—"Kidd" gloves?

To *New York Times* bestselling author Sue Monk Kidd, words matter: "I think that writing can be a spiritual practice. To write is also to pray—without the classical way we think of praying. It's about having a conversation with our soul. It takes us out of loneliness and into solitude. To be alone with ourselves in the best sense of the word."

A self-described product of a pre-feminist world, Sue places more emphasis on the authenticity of the writer than on the words themselves. She explains: "I've worked very hard on my craft, but I have tried, most of all, to write truthfully from my own voice and not someone else's voice."

Her truth is, quite ironically, reflected in her name—a trifecta of organic descriptors:

Sue: a first name as unpretentious and humble as is its owner.

Monk: a maiden-name nod to her contemplative and spiritual nature.

Kidd: a surname reminder of the importance of maintaining one's youthful curiosity and boundless imagination.

"We are all creative people no matter what kind of work we are doing," she says. "We need to give room to let our imagination play. We have to give it space to let it browse around."

And what is the enemy of our collective playground of the mind? Our perception of time as offering *limited*—as opposed to *limitless*—potential. Sue's collection of thought-provoking work challenges us to rethink the very meaning of "time well spent."

For Sue Monk Kidd, noteworthy notions necessitate wordplay: "When something is compelling to me, I start playing with it."

Unlike most writers who tend to find a home in one genre, Sue has fearlessly followed her literary muse.

Religion and Spirituality: *When the Heart Waits* (1990), *The Dance of the Dissident Daughter* (1996), *Firstlight: The Early Inspirational Writings* (2006).

Non-fiction: *Traveling with Pomegranates: A Mother-Daughter Story*—a 2009 memoir co-authored by Sue and daughter, Ann Kidd Taylor.

Fiction: *The Secret Life of Bees* (2002) sold more than six million copies in the U.S. and eight million copies worldwide. *The Mermaid Chair* (2005) reached No. 1 on the *New York Times* bestseller list and remained on the hardcover and paperback lists for nine months. *The Invention of Wings* debuted on the *New York Times* bestseller list at No. 1 in 2014 and was subsequently chosen for Oprah's Book Club 2.0.

Yes, words are Sue Monk Kidd's business, but isn't that actually true of most of us? The written word? The spoken word? To Sue: "Our words matter, our language matters—an email, a text or if we're in conversation with each other." It's safe to say that the *careless word* benefits no one.

One might ask: is writing about winsome word player Sue Monk Kidd a daunting task? Yes. How did I find it in myself to do it? Trust. Sue, herself, describes writing as "a radical act of trust."

I *trusted* in the palpable warmth and philosophical inspiration that naturally accompanies Sue's written and spoken words. After all, time spent with Sue Monk Kidd feels more like an intellectual journey than an interview. Just as a bee is forever linked to honey, one cannot deny the sweetness, the natural fluidity of her well-crafted verse and luxurious language. Sue Monk Kidd inspires soul searching in its most primal and truest form. She invites you into her cerebral home. Once there, you wish to stay forever.

Though *The Invention of Wings* is an exploration of the many faces of freedom, as a wordsmith, Sue seems to represent those of us who feel most free when immersed in thought—when confidently submerged in the introspective process that leads to meaningful written or verbal expression.

SHOWMEJONES.COM

"I have come to the conclusion that language is going to endure—something innate in us needs to be uplifted by language."

—Sue Monk Kidd

Her skill as a writer is perhaps best seen in her ability—no, her unyielding *need*—to live inside her story. To allow the characters to speak through her as she assumes the dual role of storyteller and guardian of their truth.

Daughter Ann Kidd Taylor adds: "She is honoring the deepest impulses of her heart. This is what makes her happy, what brings her alive. It's important to her to honor that voice inside of her." As should the rest of us. After all, many think our attention-span-deprived culture is erasing the skill of composition, one YouTube video at a time.

Sue Monk Kidd remains optimistic: "I have come to the conclusion that language is going to endure—something innate in us needs to be uplifted by language."

In truth, we all have access to the power of the pen. Yes, vocabulary, syntax and structure play critical roles in showcasing the technical skill of a writer, but Sue Monk Kidd ultimately proves: to trust in one's heart is to always win the day.

She also dares us to think, embrace and celebrate—to listen to our authentic inner voices. To embrace the mystery within. To celebrate—not just the potential power of words—but the responsibility that accompanies the use of all language.

Not one to dance around complex issues, Sue shares: "I have a very sensitive response to injustice. I feel some obligation—almost redemptive—to write about it." She consequently challenges us to explore the concepts of passion and compassion—and above all—to discuss it.

But most important, Sue Monk Kidd and I certainly agree on one critical issue. Despite our shared love of language, in the end, neither one of us wants to be responsible for:

The last word.

THIS IS YOUR LIFE

Allyson Klavens-Theis

Me

Taryn Winter Brill

From our earliest days, we are coached to pursue our dreams. However, when it comes to the advice we receive from speakers, scribes, celebrities and C-suiters, said advice often emanates from those who have already achieved notoriety and/or rampant success.

However, *I'm one of you.*

I risked my financial future to complete this project—a literal labor of love. Suze Orman would have a meltdown if she knew the details. And I am wise enough to *never* lie to Suze Orman.

I was recently asked why I continued to pursue this project in the first place. The only answer I could provide was "I had no choice." These interviews—and the successive intellectual stimulation and lifestyle education—assumed ownership of my soul. Though I often comment, "I have not been this poor since I was twenty-five years old," as cliché as it sounds, I always add: "But I have never been this rich either."

And all of this happened simply by tapping into the brainpower connected to one relatively small city in Florida.

The majority of us won't achieve our dreams exactly as planned. Who teaches *us* how to evolve without complete-goal realization? Someone must collect our garbage, yet I dare say that very few children dream of a life of trash and refuse. How do we reach a balance between never giving up (important) and embracing our reality (equally important)?

The answer is found by understanding and tapping into our individual, ever-evolving definitions of success. By publishing *Show Me*, I have now achieved a dream I never knew I had. And how do I keep it all in perspective? I listen to my husband's hilarious yet practical voice ringing in my ears: "Randy, just remember, you're Darrin Stephens, *not* William Shakespeare."

For those of you keeping score, some variation of the word *listen* appears fifty-one times in *Show Me*. Actually, its fifty-three times if you count my urging you to listen to your inner voice as much as you listen to the voices of those around you.

I have always found comfort being a member of the general public. As a descendant of farmers, shopkeepers, laborers, truck drivers and stay-at-home mothers, I was raised to *appreciate* more and *desire* less. Then again, who speaks for us alleged *nobodys* of the world? After all, no one achieves fame and/or fortune without our direct or indirect consent.

No sooner had I accepted my status as an *ancestor of normal* than everything changed. I learned that my maternal great-great-great-great grandfather, Richard Sappington, fought under Nathaniel Greene in the Battle of Brandywine on September 11, 1777. He also served alongside General George Washington at Valley Forge in 1778. As a bodyguard to General Washington, Richard was also present at the surrender of Cornwallis at Yorktown October 10, 1781.

Hmm. Perhaps some of Pappy Richard's fighting spirit took up residence in my DNA profile after all. My fearless mother certainly never walked away from a good fight.

And for those who ask where I got my sense of humor, when I recently told my father I was on the cusp of qualifying for a senior citizen discount, his swift, unedited, utterly brilliant response: "I'll take fifty-four again and pay extra."

I'M WORRIED. THEN AGAIN, I'M PRETTY much always stressing over something. My self-tormenting nature is also probably one of the main reasons that a man from Missouri, with a somewhat simple upbringing, managed to become a modest success. But for years, I feared I wouldn't pass along something—*anything*—to my children that guaranteed long-term value.

On the other hand, I worry just enough to make things happen, too.

When I was packing to move a few years ago, I found all these wonderful old family pictures buried alongside my high school yearbooks, programs from my stage productions, and samples of creative work from various client relationships. I participated in the shows so I recognized each program. And I *did* the work, so I remembered the portfolio items, too.

As for the family photos, I knew most of the people but didn't necessarily recall all the occasions represented. In my family, I have shown the most interest in our kinfolk—grandparents, aunts, uncles, cousins. Hence the reason a lot of my family's nostalgia may have ended up in boxes in my garage.

The truth is, when someone dies, they take a lifetime of knowledge, experience, wisdom and advice with them. *That's a tragedy.* What is the point of living a life, raising children, overcoming obstacles and learning to navigate a variety of situations and then selfishly taking it all to the grave?

When I didn't recognize someone's face, my creative side kicked in and I looked for stories in the pictures. What I didn't *know*, I could make up. Hell, discovering and telling stories is my raison d'être.

After flipping over a folder of old newspaper clippings, I discovered several timeworn photos of an absolutely stunning young woman named Georga. I knew her name because some old-timer had wisely labeled the pictures. *But who was Georga?* I don't recall anyone by that name. Based on the age of the photo and her clothing, my best guess was that Georga lived sometime around the turn of the century—1900, not 2000.

Then I found another picture of *Georga and Fred.* Now we're getting somewhere. *No…wait…I don't know of any prehistoric Freds either.*

But there she was, my beautiful Georga, dillydallying on a porch with a chap I began to refer to as Farmer Fred. Georga met someone! She was in love—I could tell. I was oddly happy for Georga and yet, other than the story I was creating in my mind, I still couldn't identify her.

Who was Georga?
Did she find true love?
Did she have children?
Was she successful?
Did she have a happy life?
What happened to her?

Looking at Georga and Fred it was suddenly another box, many years from now, that I feared.

Who was Randy?
Did he find true love?
Did he have children?
Was he successful?
Did he have a happy life?
What happened to him?

I don't want my children, or grandchildren, or great-grandchildren to search for *my stories* in a box of old photos. I want them to know *me*—to understand what was important to me and *why*. I want them to meet—and learn from—the most influential people in my life. *And wow, do I have a distinguished list of influencers!*

But more than that, I refuse to take my life lessons to the grave.

The day after the Georga/Fred photo discovery, I began composing my stories—fence-vaulting Jodie, the less-than-cogent preteen umpire, the pet chicken dinner, the hemorrhoid-befuddled child doctor, the attack bunny. *Six years later*, in an effort to up my ante, I began writing the "Business Class" series.

But Georga and Fred also needed me. *Let the obsessive-compulsive search begin...*

Georga S. Yates was born on April 22, 1888, in Howard County, Missouri, to fifty-seven-year-old Thomas B. Yates and his wife, forty-five-year-old Mildred Yates. She joined a family that consisted of two older sisters: seven-year-old Victoria and eleven-year-old Mary, *my great-grandmother.*

Georga was my great-great aunt.

Mary, Victoria and Georga Yates were beautiful young women. My great-grandmother Mary was the oldest sibling. I recall attending her 100th birthday celebration shortly before her death in 1977. Next came Victoria, or Aunt (pronounced *ain't*) Vickie, who shared a room with her sister at New Franklin, Missouri's, Golden Hour Retirement Home. And surprisingly, despite all the time I spent visiting Georga's two older sisters, *I don't recall ever hearing her name.*

Georga's name was, in fact, spelled *Georga* and not *Georgia*. My guess is that my great-great grandparents, Thomas and Mildred, must have considered the extra "i" to be superfluous. Then again, they *were* a tad mature to be adding a new baby to the mix. Perhaps Granny and PawPaw Yates were simply too exhausted to consider all the extra "eye" *dotting* that would be required in the years to come.

Charles "Fred" Doles was born on May 12, 1886, in St. Joseph, Buchanan County, Missouri. His travels eventually brought him to Howard County and to Georga. They were married by the Reverend R.M. Hinze in Boonville, Missouri, on January 26, 1910.

By 1920, Mr. and Mrs. Doles were living in the Big Apple. Fred sold real estate in Manhattan and Georga worked as a saleswoman in a department store.

Once I learned of Georga's *retail sales* career, my imagination went into overdrive. Despite rumors that the character of Auntie Mame was based on actress Gertrude Lawrence, maybe Georga *knew* the real Auntie Mame, or even better, perhaps Georga was the secret inspiration for Patrick Dennis' outrageous Auntie Mame character. Was southern-boy Fred retooled as Mame's love interest, Beauregard Jackson Pickett Burnside? The idea was just too delicious to dismiss.

The West Coast eventually beckoned and the Doleses left New York City for California. In 1950, Georga and Fred were managing an apartment building at 533 S. Westmoreland Avenue in Los Angeles—just a short walk from the motion picture mecca of the world, Hollywood.

How did they live? What did they see? Whom did they meet?

Did Georga and Fred sit in the bleachers and watch the red carpet extravaganza at the 1950 Oscars? Did they witness, firsthand, *All About Eve's* Bette Davis and *Sunset Boulevard's* Gloria Swanson dolled up in old-Hollywood glamour? Better still, what if budding screen legends Marlon Brando and Jack Lemmon *lived in* their building on Westmoreland Avenue? Did Brando get loaded one night and jokingly yelp *Georgahhhhh* instead of *Stellahhhhh*—and the famous inflection stuck?

Fred Doles died on April 2, 1952, in Los Angeles. Mr. and Mrs. Doles were married for forty-two years and, *though childless*, if their life in pictures is any proof, their love stood the test of time.

Georga passed away on October 2, 1980, in Los Angeles—twenty-eight years after losing Fred, and the same year I graduated from Rock Bridge High School. And it was Braemoron Carrie Cramer ("Danny Partridge with boobs") who ultimately located Georga's gravesite at Forest Lawn Memorial Park in the Hollywood Hills.

I shared this earth for eighteen years with Georga Yates Doles, yet I never knew she existed.

Perhaps most alarming, with no heirs, Georga and Fred Doles—their lives, their work, their love—were just one generation away from being totally forgotten. Like Lerner and Loewe's mythical village of *Brigadoon*, Georga and Fred had already begun to vanish into the mist.

As their great-great nephew, I am honored and humbled to assume the responsibility for keeping Mr. and Mrs. Doles' mostly-imagination-fueled-legacy alive.

Then again, in addition to inspiring this permanent collection of wisdom and memories, Georga and Fred ultimately *showed me* so much more.

So who was Randy?
This writer guy who liked to talk to people.

Did he find true love?
Yes, he most certainly did.

Did he have children?
Yes, Kevin Randall Jones and Mary Elizabeth Jones—the latter really liked cheese.

Was he successful?
All that really matters is that he thinks he was.

Did he have a happy life?
Yes and he never stopped trying to make it better.

What happened to him?
Your guess is as good as mine, but if he was one-half the man his father was, he did just fine.

ACKNOWLEDGMENTS

S how Me is a WE book, not a ME book.

This project never would have happened without the talent, support and inspiration received from so many extraordinary people. Please allow me to show *you* my boundless appreciation and respect for your remarkable contributions.

To Carole J Greene: My dear friend. My longtime editor. My mentor. My muse. You have my love, admiration and never-ending appreciation for standing beside me and so thoughtfully teaching me how to be a better writer. In so many ways, *Show Me* is ours.

To Erin Brockovich and Peggy Post: You are two of my life's greatest—and most unexpected—gifts. I hope that one day I learn to accept that I'm worthy of your love, support and respect—you certainly have mine, *and then some.* My gratitude is endless.

To Cynthia Rhodes: Based on our ages, you are better suited to play the role of *sister* or even *wife*. But when I think of the *magic* and the spiritual energy you brought to my life, only one job title will do: Fairy Godmother.

To Judy Berman: Though *Show Me* is intended to coach others through an assortment of potential struggles, you, my dear Judy, are the greatest business coach of all. Love you like crazy!

Derek

Me

Charlie McDonald Photography

To my husband, Derek Call Wakefield: You deserve more credit than most realize. More than two decades ago you got me to step out of my theatrical comfort zone and discover a captivating world beyond the footlights. Though I still don't quite understand your fascination with Rasputin, *you* are the most fascinating man I have ever known.

To Nancy Scott and Bobbi Kittner: I would never have advanced past writing sales letters and ad copy had you not convinced me I was a *real* writer. I am forever in your debt.

To Julia Ann Poore Hilgenberg: Thank you for your mid-1980s explanation that the word "that" does not need to appear in every sentence that I write. That and the fact that sentences read better once you taught me that the use of punctuation isn't really all that optional. #ThatHappens

To Jim Chambers, Kathy Edson, Jordan Schuman, Beth Wilhelm and my cousin, Jimmy Hudson: Each of you truly lit up every room you entered. Though you died far too young, your spirit, optimism and talent will forever be a part of so many lives. And now, with your appearance in *Show Me*, it's a part of countless more.

To Becki Forsee Jones: No one could ever ask for a more spectacular first love. But more than anything, your boundless love for our children puts you in a class by yourself.

To my maternal grandmother, Gladys Sappington Kyger Hudson Crane Crane: I just wish more people knew you were the funniest human being on the planet. And if that humor was reserved for just me, I'm a very lucky guy. #DoIHaveAGoat

To my paternal grandmother, Mary Lou Boggs Jones: No one ever loved me quite as unconditionally as you. Despite the Henny Penny chicken-dinner debacle—which I now believe must have been the result of a minor stroke or some other undiagnosed health crisis—*thank you* for always making me feel as though *being me* was enough. I miss you every day.

To my sisters, Janice Lynn Jones Nelson and Paula Gail Jones Brown: You. Are. Everything. That said, I really don't appreciate you forcing me to watch the flying monkey sequence of *The Wizard of Oz* when I was a child. That was kinda mean.

To my mother, Nellie Pearl Kyger Jones: Your ability to be uniquely *you* will forever inspire *me*. No matter what happens, I love you just the way you are.

To my father, Kenneth Paul Jones: I want to be *just like you* when I grow up.

To my children, Kevin Randall Jones and Mary Elizabeth Jones: *This is all for you.* This is my legacy and now it is a part of yours. I love you more than *mere words* can express. However, hashtags work great! #TheCheeseIncident #SaveFabio #StrawberrylessShortcake #PaperTowelsGoHere

Peter Berec

The Family
Paula Gail Jones Brown
Steven Brent Brown
Wade Barrett Brown
Whitney Nicole Brown
Gladys Sappington Crane
Owen T. Crane
Adam Jacob Crutchfield
Blake Kenneth Crutchfield
Darcy Grace Crutchfield
Delaney Lynn Crutchfield
Holly Ann Crutchfield
Max Lewis Crutchfield
Katherine Lewis Crutchfield
Victoria Yates Davenport
Charles Fred Doles
Georga Yates Doles
Becki Forsee Jones
Kenneth Paul Jones
Kevin Randall Jones
Mary Elizabeth Jones
Mary Lou Boggs Jones
Mary Yates Jones
Nellie Pearl Kyger Jones
Paul L. Jones
Randall Kenneth Jones
Cindy Hudson Klippel
Clayton P. Kyger
Janice Lynn Jones Nelson
Harris Evener Nelson II
Richard Sappington
Derek Call Wakefield
Kurt Wakefield
Margaret Jean Wakefield
Nathan Wakefield
Tabitha Wakefield
Tony Wakefield-Jones
Mildred Yates
Thomas B. Yates

The Mentors
Tony Ambrosiano
Ruth Baker
Judy Berman
Phil Beuth
Erin Brockovich
Elaine W. Cook
Michael Feuer
Joseph B. Forsee
Oleta Wren Forsee
Jeffrey Gitomer
Carole J Greene
Jeffrey Hayzlett
Larry L. King
Dr. Richard Klepac
Suzanne Leonard
Rich McElaney
Carol Odor
Bob Orr
Peggy Post
Karen Richards
Gary Rosen
Michael Rupert
Rhona Saunders
Robert Schmitt
Nancy Scott
Peter Thomas
Patsy Watt
Jackie Pettit White

The Support Group
Karen Frizzell Anglin
Dot Auchmoody
Susan C. Bennett
Karen Kayser Benson
Dr. Rob Bogosian
Pat Boos
Barb Brandon
Vikki Morgan Burton
Christopher Butterfield
Kylie Campbell
Virginia Canard

Claudia Cook
Ellen Cooper
John S. Cox
Hyla Crane
Soni Dimond
Kay Walker Frier
Sarah Ann Froese
LaDonna Wymer Gazaway
Reverend Dave Gipson
Karyn Hartman
Kelly Hill
David Hurst
Jane Johnson
Jeff Macasevich
Karen Gentry Manning
Robynann Martin
Lauren McAuley
Alexander McDonald
Charlie McDonald
Benson Morgan
Laura Needle
Charles Pascalar
Melissa Cunningham Phillips
Cindy Pierce
Sarah Remesch
Laura Spell
Tammy Wyatt Roberts
Gates Rodenfels
Ronna Rothenberger
Christopher Schelling
Mike Sheffield
Marci Seamples
Val Simon
John Sorey III
Laura Spell
Linda Spellman
Angelina Spencer-Crisp
Lori Staley
Margo Strawderman
Mary Beth Toomey
Mary Beth Nutter Tourbin
Kathy Travis

Debra Sapp Yarwood
Sue van der Linden
Marti Van Veen
Kay Waggoner
Bonnie Warner
Denise Wauters
Ron Yates

THE PHOTOGRAPHERS
Drew and Karen Attanasio
Peter Berec
Judy Berman
Steven Brent Brown
Keith Isaac
Kevin Randall Jones
Randall Kenneth Jones
Margo Jurgensen
Allyson Klavens-Theis
Bernadette La Paglia
Charlie McDonald
Peggy Post
Erin Rew
Derek Call Wakefield
Jo Ann Ward
Denise Wauters

NAPLES DAILY NEWS
David Albers
Bill Barker
Allen Bartlett
Jeffrey C. Bruce
Penny Fisher
Manny Garcia
Robin Lankton
Phil Lewis
Jeff Lytle
Dave Neill
Darren Nielsen
Dave Osborn
Harry Walker

SMART BUSINESS
Adam Burroughs
April Grasso
Dustin S. Klein
Fred Koury
Jim Mericsko

BUSINESS CLASS, *Subjects*
Joe Abruzzese
Tanya Acker
Randy Antik
Lazaro Arbos
Jay Baker
Larry Bakman
G.W. Bailey
Pat Benatar
Susan C. Bennett
Phil Beuth
Karna Small Bodman
Brian Boitano
Pat Boos
Craig Bouchard
Erin Brockovich
Richard Broome
Clyde Butcher
Kim Campbell
Mary Carillo
James Carville
Santa Claus
Neal Conan
Julia Cooke
Dr. Cade Copeland
Barbara Corcoran
Kassie DePaiva
Judge Patricia DiMango
Bill Donius
Carl Edwards
Bob Emfield
Janet Evanovich
Alana Feld
Nicole Feld
Ryan Ferguson

Michael Feuer
Donna Fiala
Bruce Fields
Carly Fiorina
Neil Giraldo
Mitchell Gold
Robert Green Jr.
Mimi Chapin Gregory
Kathy Griffin
Vicki Gunvalson
David Hall
Darrell Hammond
Jack Hanna
Sean Hannity
Mike Hanson
Jeffrey Hayzlett
Heloise
Beth Holloway
Kenneth P. Jones
Shirley Jones
Sonny Jurgensen
Sue Monk Kidd
Hoda Kotb
Rob Marciano
Mary Matalin
Joanne LaMarca Mathisen
Tyler Mathisen
General Barry McCaffrey
Jack McKinney
Eddie Mekka
Colin Mochrie
Gary Newsome
Candice Olson
Suze Orman
Bob Orr
Dr. David Perlmutter
Paul Phillips
Peggy Post
Robin Hauser Reynolds
Cynthia Rhodes
Gary Rosen
Brad Rutter

KC Schulberg
Willard Scott
Lynn Travis Stender
Peter Thomas
Stella Thomas
Tommy Tune
Dolph von Arx
Suzi Weinert
Randy Wayne White
Jason Odell Williams
Vanessa Williams

BUSINESS CLASS, *Special Contributors*
Jonathan Axelrod
Patty Baker
Karen Kayser Benson
Paula Jones Brown
Peter DeLuise
Paula Faris
Danielle Feinberg
Carmen Ruby Floyd
Dawn Lebrecht Fornara
Kathie Lee Gifford
Dan Harris
Magic Johnson
Ryan Khatcheressian

Kevin Kenneally
Billie Jean King
Hoda Kotb
Fred Koury
Robyn Kyger
Karen Gentry Manning
Jerald Mason
Dr. Phil McGraw
John McKerrow
Erin Moriarty
Janice Jones Nelson
Carol Nissenson
Regis Philbin
Chita Rivera
Tammy Wyatt Roberts
Ronna Rothenberger
Michael Rupert
Kathy Ryan
Eric Schurenberg
Jessica Stark
Ann Kidd Taylor
Brett Thompson
Kathy Travis
Martha Traxler
Bill Walton
Helen Williams

To Oprah Winfrey: No one will ever make a more significant contribution to humanity—to the greater good—than you. Your unrelenting commitment to personal empowerment has become a part of our collective DNA. This book would never have happened had you not shown me it was possible.

To Dustin S. Klein and April Grasso: I could not possibly find more passionate, collaborative, upbeat and supportive publishing partners. You both exemplify my platform in everything you do. You are *Show Me.*

To my beloved Fairview Elementary, West Junior High School, Rock Bridge High School, University of Missouri-Columbia, Virginia, Maryland, Washington, DC, Florida and Show Me State friends:
Thank you **for being there with me—and** *for* **me.**
Take a bow.